87046

Learning Resources Center
Collin County Community College District
SPRING CREEK CAMPUS
Plano, Texas 75074

WITHDRAWN

A Comprehensive Guide to Sports Skills Tests and Measurement

2nd Edition

D. Ray Collins
Patrick B. Hodges

The Scarecrow Press, Inc.
A Scarecrow Education Book
Lanham, Maryland, and London
2001

SCARECROW PRESS, INC.
A Scarecrow Education Book

Published in the United States of America
by Scarecrow Press, Inc.
4720 Boston Way, Lanham, Maryland 20706
www.scarecroweducation.com

4 Pleydell Gardens, Folkestone
Kent CT20 2DN, England

British Library Cataloguing in Publication Information Available

Library of Congress Cataloging-in-Publication Data

Collins, D. Ray.
   A comprehensive guide to sports skills tests and measurement / by D. RayCollins and Patrick
  B. Hodges.—2nd ed.
     p. cm.
  Includes bibliographical references.
  ISBN 0-8108-3884-2 (paper : alk. paper)
  1. Athletic ability—Testing. I. Title: Sports skills tests and measurement. II. Hodges, Patrick B.
  III. Title.
GV436 .C58 2001
796'.07—dc21
                                                    00-061945

CONTENTS

PREFACE

Published over 20 years ago, the first edition of this text was the first resource in physical education literature to feature a comprehensive compilation of scientifically authenticated sports skills tests. This second edition updates the test compilation and presents a user-friendly format that promotes its intent as a ready reference source.

Skills tests for 28 sports and a total of 86 tests appear in the book, ranging in application from junior high school level through college. The tests for each sport are presented in chronological order.

With today's emphasis on teacher accountability and student assessment, this text makes a timely entry into professional literature. Sports skills tests are valuable instruments for measuring student achievement.

An instructor's professional development is also served by this text. There are limitless opportunities for the enterprising physical educator to either revise existing skills tests or develop new ones based on the scholarship and detailed procedures, figures and tables presented herein.

Each chapter's bibliographical listing transcends the number of actual tests presented there. Our objective was to include references for all sports skills tests ever constructed, both authenticated and unauthenticated. To the best of our knowledge, this is the most complete reference listing available on sports skills tests and measurement.

ACKNOWLEDGMENTS

The first edition of this text acknowledged several persons at J. Sargeant Reynolds Community College: Dr. Joseph Lisowski, English professor, for his constructive criticism of the writing style; Sandra Preston and John Edwards for illustration work; and Pearline Harmon for library reference work. Continued acknowledgment is in order, for it was the quality of the first edition that enabled the development of this second edition. We are also grateful to the authors of the many sources from which the tests were derived and to the authors and publishers who permitted tables and illustrations to be reproduced.

In addition to the above, we further acknowledge the contributions of the following individuals: J. M. Nelson, Professor of Learning Resources and Technology Services, St. Cloud State University, for encouraging us to design the second edition of this book for the user rather than the publisher and for coordinating the mechanics of publishing this second edition; Debbie Josephson for her computer skills in converting the drawings and tables from the first edition into an electronic format; Ivan Maramis for creating some of the new illustrations; and Patricia Brothen for integrating the numerous text, tabular and graphic files into a coherent, legible, well-designed whole.

Finally, we sincerely thank the many fine staff members of Scarecrow Press who exhibited a high standard of professionalism through every step along the way toward this book's publication. Their encouragement and support are much appreciated.

Chapter 1

INTRODUCTION

HISTORICAL OVERVIEW

Although referred to as general motor ability tests, the Athletic Badge Tests of 1913 are generally recognized as the first sports skills tests ever devised. Developed by the Playground and Recreation Association of America, the tests included items from baseball, basketball, tennis and volleyball (Bovard, Cozens & Hagman, 1949). Shortly thereafter, a succession of similar tests were constructed. Reilly's (Reilly, 1916) test consisted of baseball, basketball, golf and tennis items. In 1918, Hetherington developed a decathlon of athletic events (Bovard, Cozens & Hagman, 1949).

Construction of sports skills tests accelerated after 1920 during a time when physical education was shifting toward a greater emphasis in that phase of instruction. Brace's (Brace, 1924) basketball test is credited as the initial sports skills test battery for the field of physical education. Other notable examples of skills tests that were completed in the 1920s include two for the sport of tennis. An experimental study by Beall (Beall, 1925) was conducted to determine a suitable test battery for the sport, and another battery was introduced by Anderson one year later (Anderson, 1926).

Sports skills testing became more sophisticated in the 1930s with the advent of tests developed by scientific procedures. Numerous quality tests have been constructed in the last 60 years; many of them are presented in this textbook.

Recognition of the need to standardize skills tests on a national level prompted the Research Council of the former American Association for Health, Physical Education and Recreation to initiate in 1959 what was called the Sports Skills Test Project, under the chairmanship of Frank D. Sills (Morris, 1977). Since that time, test manuals have been developed for football (1965), basketball (1966, 1984), softball (1966, 1991), archery (1967) and volleyball (1969). The original goal was to construct manuals for at least fifteen sports activities.

Promotion of the national sports skills standards could have influenced independent investigators because the 1960s and 1970s are the most prolific decades for test development in the better than eighty-year history of skills tests investigation.

APPLICATION OF SPORTS SKILLS TESTS

There are at least nine reasons for utilizing the many excellent sports skills tests in existence today. A discussion of each follows.

Measurement of Achievement. The primary purpose of skills tests is to measure student progress or level of achievement. Assessment of a course's content and methodology is largely dependent upon test results.

Grading or Marking. Students may be evaluated on the basis of their skills tests performance. A portion of the student's course grade is usually the result of the level of progress or achievement he/she demonstrates on skills tests.

Classification. Administering skills tests early in a class allows the instructor to immediately divide the students into ability groups, thus promoting individualized instruction. Intramural teams could also be equated this way.

Motivation. A number of students respond positively to a challenge. They often try harder to excel on a skills test than performing against their peers in class. Used properly, skills tests can serve as excellent motivators for student improvement.

Practice. Relating to the motivation purpose, some students practice test items in order to improve test scores. Monitoring of individual progress through self-testing is often the single greatest contributor to success in sports skills achievement. Coaches may require players to practice an item or items in a particular test, especially those that clearly reflect the skills required in game conditions.

Diagnosis. Psychomotor skill development is one of the basic foundations of physical education. Therefore, the ability to diagnose the performance level of students is paramount as a qualification for teaching physical education. Skills tests can assist the instructor in detecting weaknesses in student performance.

Instructor and Program Evaluation. Periodic use of skills tests may reveal areas of instruction needing increased emphasis.

Interpretive Tool. One of the ways the physical education program is interpreted to the administration, parents and the public is through the use of skills tests. When test administration is properly aligned with course objectives, a program's academic respectability is enhanced.

Competition. Since the competitive element is inherent in the structure of skills tests, they can be successful intramural and rainy day activities (Johnson & Nelson, 1986).

TEST FEASIBILITY

Several criteria must be met for a sports skills test to exhibit utility value. It should be easy to administer and score, plus lend itself to administration in a reasonable amount of time. Test preparation time should be minimal, and the necessary equipment and supplies should be standard for the particular sport or reasonably accessible. More importantly, a test should be valid, reliable and objective. Further elaboration on the latter three criteria follows.

Validity. Each test purports to measure a subject's degree of proficiency in one or more skills. When a test actually measures the skill or skills for which it is designed, it is a valid one.

Validation of sports skills tests is commonly achieved by determining the relationship between a test and an established criterion that equates well with the quality being measured by the test. This is called criterion validity. Most common of the test criteria in sports skills measurement are subjective ratings of experts and tournament rankings (known as criterion measure). Consequently, a student's test performance is supposed to relate well to the experts' rating of his/her ability or his/her standing in tournament competition.

Face or logical validity is sometimes claimed for sports skills tests. An example of this kind of validity is when a test requirement is the same as a particular skill required in a certain sport. It is not uncommon to see face validity claimed for test items that only approximate required game skills. In these cases, the face validity claim becomes much less defensible. Pure face validity is difficult to attain because the test environment and the game setting seldom resemble, and certain extraneous factors present under game conditions cannot be duplicated in a testing situation.

A less common criterion measure in sports skills measurement is the use of an established test which allegedly measures essentially the same quality for which a new test is designed. A weakness of this criterion is that the test validation fails to reveal which of the tests is the most valid measure of the quality each proposes to measure.

Statistical procedures commonly utilized in test validation include the Pearson Product-Moment coefficient of correlation *(r)*, multiple correlation (R) and rank-order correlation *(Rho)*. Each is discussed later in the chapter along with other measurement terms.

In determining which tests demonstrated sufficient validity value for inclusion in this text, the authors followed the correlation coefficient standards espoused by Garrett (Garrett, 1966) which are presented below.

> .00 to .20 denotes indifferent or negligible relationship
> .20 to .40 denotes low correlation, present but slight
> .40 to .70 denotes substantial or marked relationship
> .70 to 1.00 denotes high to very high relationship

Reliability. A reliable test is expected to produce similar or identical results when administered a second time to the same subjects under the same test conditions. The tester should be aware that a reliable test is not necessarily a valid one because measurement of a quality other than the one the test is intended to measure may produce consistent results from test subjects. On the other hand, a valid test administered by a competent tester invariably shows a high level of reliability.

In sports skills measurement, reliability coefficients are typically obtained by the test-retest, split-half and odd-even methods. The test-retest method is preferable for determining test reliability as the same test is given twice in its entirety with the results compared to determine their degree of relationship.

In the split-half procedure, results of one half of a test are compared with the other. The weakness of this procedure is that one half of the test may include different content or exhibit a higher degree of difficulty than the other. The odd-even approach, reflecting the degree of consistency in performance between odd- and even-numbered items, is superior to the split-half procedure because it assures coverage of similar content and better equates the degree of difficulty in the two halves of the test.

The authors followed the guidelines used in the aforementioned Sports Skills Test Project of the American Alliance for Health, Physical Education, Recreation and Dance when selecting the minimum reliability coefficient that a test must have demonstrated for inclusion in this text. In the project, the minimum reliability coefficient for test items scored on the basis of distance was .80, while a minimum coefficient of .70 was recommended for skills scored on the basis of accuracy and form.

Objectivity. How objective a test is depends upon the degree of consistency that two or more testers demonstrate in scoring the test. Tests of high objectivity invariably show high reliability because a tester quite naturally administers and scores the same test twice with greater uniformity than two different individuals. Clarke (Clarke, 1976) states that a highly reliable test may fail to contain an acceptable objectivity value in cases whereby two testers vary in interpretation of test procedures.

Generally accepted objectivity standards are presented as follows (Clarke, 1976).

.95-.99 very high; found among best tests
.90-.94 high; acceptable
.80-.89 fairly adequate for individual measurement
.70-.79 adequate for group measurement, but not satisfactory for
         individual measurement
.60-.69 useful for group averages and school surveys,
         but entirely inadequate for individual measurement

Few sports skills tests have been investigated for objectivity determination. This is particularly significant when instructors compare their students' test results with those of local peers or national norms. Comparisons of individual results or sets of results are more valid when based on data gathered by the same instructor. Test reliability is easier to achieve than test objectivity.

MEASUREMENT AND EVALUATION TERMS

In addition to the measurement and evaluation terms defined earlier in this chapter, others commonly used in this textbook and in education today deserve elaboration.

Formative Assessment. Continuous monitoring of student achievement throughout a unit or term, providing ongoing feedback concerning student progress and teacher effectiveness. To illustrate, an instructor may group his/her students in pairs for the purpose of scoring each other's performance during practice of some sports skill that lends itself to easy and objective measurement.

Summative Assessment. Data intended to verify a broad evaluation of student learning; used to assign grades at the end of a learning experience. Administration of a 5-item skills test battery at the end of a unit is an example.

Pearson Product-Moment Coefficient of Correlation *(r)*. Commonly used to determine validity and reliability estimates of sports skills tests, this statistical procedure measures the relationship between two variables. For example, the degree to which ability in controlling a wall volley in tennis measures playing ability in that sport can be estimated with this procedure. The degree of relationship is based on a positive or negative 1.0 maximum. Of the scientifically documented tests found in this text, the vast majority were done so by use of the Pearson Product-Moment procedure. Reference is sometimes made to correlation coefficients without identifying the statistical procedure. In those cases, the Pearson *r* was the correlation procedure utilized.

Rank-Order Correlation Coefficient *(Rho).* Like the Pearson *r* procedure, the rank-order method for determining correlation coefficients measures the amount of relationship between two elements. However, the *Rho* method is less exact than the product-moment method because only rank of scores is considered as opposed to the variance within the scores. Therefore, *Rho* is a cruder measure and less desirable correlation procedure than the Pearson *r.* It is particularly applicable in situations where the number of cases is 30 or less.

Multiple Correlation *(R).* Frequently in the development of sports skills test batteries, this procedure is used. Multiple factors are related to only one which determines how much a single item in a test battery relates to the others in combination.

Standard Deviation (s). In educational measurement, a common measure of variability in test scores is known as a standard deviation. Once the mean or average is determined for a set of scores, the tester needs to know how much each score deviates from the mean for evaluation purposes. The standard deviation represents segments of a particular distribution of scores. Six standard deviations are found in a normal distribution with three above the mean and three below. The middle two standard deviations contain approximately 68 percent of the scores.

T-Scale. Used to develop norms and make raw scores for a group more conducive to meaningful comparison, the T-scale converts those scores to normalized standard scores or T-scores. A T-score reflects the distance a raw score lies above or below the mean. With a mean of 50 and a standard deviation of 10, the T-scale extends five deviations to each side of the mean. Scores seldom range from more than a maximum of 85 and minimum of 15.

Percentiles. Also used to present test score norms, this standard score provides to the student a meaningful interpretation of his/her score position among peers completing a test. For example, a percentile rank of 70 indicates that 70 percent of individuals completing the particular test scored less than that amount and 30 percent scored better. The percentile method of determining variability cannot handle extreme scores as well as the T-scale and is based on the false assumption that distance between scores is uniform.

Spearman-Brown Prophecy Formula. In utilizing the split-half and odd-even methods for determining test reliability, the resulting coefficient pertains to only half of the test. Using the data collected this way, this statistical procedure allows an investigator to estimate the reliability value of the entire test.

Computation details for the various statistical procedures that are used in sports skills measurement extend beyond the scope of this text. For a fuller understanding of the above terms and others of less frequent mention in the book, the reader is referred to any basic statistics or measurement and evaluation text.

References

Anderson, L.E. (1926). *Tennis for women*. New York: A.S. Barnes.

Barrow, H.M., McGee, R., & Tritschler, K.A. (1989). *Practical measurement in physical education and sport*. Philadelphia: Lea and Febiger.

Baumgartner, T.A., & Jackson, A.S. (1982). *Measurement for evaluation in physical eucation*. (2nd ed.). Dubuque, Iowa: Brown.

Beall, E. (1925). *Essential qualities in certain aspects of physical education with ways of measuring and developing the same*. Unpublished master's thesis, University of California, Berkeley.

Bosco, J.V., & Gustafson, W.F. (1983). *Measurement and evaluation in physical education, fitness and sports*. Englewood Cliffs, New Jersey: Prentice Hall.

Bovard, J.F., Cozens, F.W., & Hagman, E.P. (1949). *Tests and measurements in physical education*. (3rd ed.). Philadelphia: Saunders.

Brace, D.K. (1924). Testing basketball technique. *American Physical Education Review*. 29: 159-165.

Clarke, H.H. (1976). *Application of measurement to health and physical education*. (5th ed.). Englewood Cliffs, New Jersey: Prentice Hall.

Clarke, H.H., & Clarke, D. (1987). *Application of measurement to physical education*. Englewood Cliffs, New Jersey: Prentice Hall.

Downie, N.M., & Heath, R.W. (1965). *Basic statistical methods*. (2nd ed.). New York: Harper & Row.

Eckert, H.M. (1974). *Practical measurement of physical performance*. Philadelphia: Lea & Febiger.

Franks, B.D., & Deutsch, H. (1973). *Evaluating performance in physical education*. New York: Academic Press.

Garrett, H.E. (1966). *Statistics in psychology and education*. (6th ed.). New York: McKay.

Haskins, M.J. (1971). *Evaluation in physical education*. Dubuque, Iowa: Brown.

Jensen, C.R., & Hirst, C.C. (1980). *Measurement in physical education and athletics*. New York: Mayfield.

Johnson, B.L., & Nelson, J.K. (1986) *Practical measurements for evaluation in physical education*. (4th ed.). Edina, Minnesota: Burgess.

Kirkendall, E., Gruber, J., & Johnson, R. (1987). *Measurement and evaluation for physical education*. Champaign, Illinois: Human Kinetics.

Mathews, D.K. (1973). *Measurement in physical education*. (4th ed.). Philadelphia: Saunders.

Meyers, C.R. (1974). *Measurement in physical education*. (2nd ed.). New York: Ronald.

Miller, D.A. (1988). *Measurement by the physical educator*. Indianapolis: Benchmark Press.

Morris, H.H. (1977). A critique of the AAHPER Skill Test Series. Paper presented at the American Alliance for Health, Physical Education and Recreation National Convention, Seattle.

Neilson, N.P., & Jensen, C.R. (1972). *Measurement and statistics in physical education*. Belmont, California: Wadsworth.

Phillips, D.A., & Hornak, J.E. (1979). *Measurement and evaluation in physical education*. New York: Wiley.

Reilly, F.J. (1916). *New rational athletics for boys and girls*. Boston: Heath.

Safrit, M.J. (1990). *Introduction to measurement in physical education and exercise science*. St. Louis: Times Mirror/Mosby.

Scott, M.G., & French, E. (1959). *Measurement and evaluation in physical education*. Dubuque, Iowa: Brown.

Stroup, F. (1957). *Measurement in physical education*. New York: Ronald.

Weber, J.C., & Lamb, D.R. (1970). *Statistics and research in physical education*. St. Louis: Mosby.

West, C. (1977). Paper presented at the American Alliance for Health, Physical Education and Recreation National Convention, Seattle.

Chapter 2

ARCHERY

INTRODUCTION

Although conducive to objective measurement, archery is not without problems in the evaluation of achievement. Test validity and reliability can be affected by certain factors which influence student achievement. This is especially a problem when the factors are uncontrollable. For example, natural elements such as extreme temperature and wind conditions may greatly affect one's performance. Inconsistency in the quality of equipment utilized may present a problem when scores are compared to national norms. Also, the amount and nature of practice prior to testing should be standardized whenever possible. These factors illustrate some of the shortcomings of using national norms or achievement scales but give emphasis to the need for test standardization at the local level.

HYDE ARCHERY TEST
(Hyde, 1937)

Purpose:

To evaluate achievement in archery by college women, utilizing the Columbia Round at distances of 50, 40 and 30 yards.

Educational Application:

College women.

Time:

A student should complete at least one distance (four ends of six arrows) per session. Three 60-minute class periods should allow ample time to administer the test to an archery class of 10 to 20 students.

Personnel:

An experienced instructor to administer and supervise the test. Students may serve as scorers.

Equipment and Supplies:

Standard 48-inch target faces (one per target), standard bows (one for every two students), matched arrows (six per student) and targets (at least four per class). Arm guards, gloves, finger tabs, quivers and field marking and record keeping materials are also necessary.

Facilities and Space:

A level or near level area of sufficient size to allow a minimum of 10 students to assume a shooting stance at each of three lines at distances of 50, 40 and 30 yards from the targets. The center of the gold in each target should be located four feet from the ground.

Directions:

It is recommended that a student shoot a minimum of 120 arrows at each of the three distances prior to taking the test. This recommendation does not include the recommended practice immediately prior to test administration. Only one practice end per distance is permitted at that time.

A total of 72 arrows are shot in ends of six arrows each. One practice end is permitted, and 24 arrows are shot at each of the three distances. The student is not required to complete the whole test in one class period but must finish at least one of the distance requirements (24 arrows) in each session.

Scoring Method and Norms:

The values used in standard target archery scoring are: gold, 9; red, 7; blue, 5; black, 3; white, 1; outside the white or missing the target, 0. An arrow striking two colors is assigned the score of higher value. If an arrow passes completely through the target face or bounces off the target, five points are given. Although seven points are commonly given in the above two instances, the five-point value is retained in the Hyde Test because the rule change to seven points was made after its development.

Scales were constructed by utilizing the data accumulated from over 1,400 student scores in 27 colleges in 16 states (Table 2.1). One scale may be used to evaluate the first round score of students having a limited amount of practice (maximum of 120 arrows at each distance), and another shows the best round score after more extensive shooting experience is attained. This scale is recommended for use at the end of an archery class to assess student achievement. Another scale is based on scores made at distances of 30, 40 and 50 yards. This scale may be used at any time during the practice period, but caution is given to the user to expect beginners to fall relatively low on the scale since it was based on final round scores. Table 2.1 shows total scores with corresponding scale values. A scale score of 50 reflects an average performance on the test. The scale values are helpful in the comparison of local norms to those collected on a national level.

Willgoose (Willgoose, 1961) suggested that the following scale score ranges estimate the quality of performance in the Hyde Test: Scale score 0-20, very poor; 21-40, poor; 41-60, fair or average; 61-80, good; and 81-100, excellent.

Validity and Reliability:

Using the composite score of three distances as the criterion measure, validity coefficients obtained were .82 for beginners and .96 for advanced archers at the 50-yard distance; .91 for beginners and .95 for advanced archers at 40 yards; and .89 and .93 for the respective ability levels while shooting at 30 yards. The group designated as advanced archers were 35 women who participated in the 1931 National Archery Tournament. The beginners were 75 college freshmen and sophomore women.

The literature review failed to reveal any studies which presented reliability coefficients for the Hyde Test.

Table 2.1
HYDE ACHIEVEMENT SCALES IN ARCHERY FOR COLLEGE WOMEN*

Scale Score	First Columbia Total Score	Total Score	Final Columbia Round (Target Score) 50 Yards	40 Yards	30 Yards
100	436	466	150	176	194
99	430	460	148	174	192
98	424	455	146	171	190
97	418	449	143	169	187
96	412	443	141	167	185
95	406	438	139	164	183
94	400	432	137	162	181
93	394	426	135	160	179
92	388	420	132	157	176
91	382	415	130	155	174
90	376	409	128	153	172
89	370	403	126	150	170
88	364	398	124	148	168
87	358	392	121	146	165
86	352	386	119	143	163
85	346	381	117	141	161
84	340	375	115	139	159
83	334	369	113	136	157
82	328	363	110	134	154
81	322	358	108	132	152
80	316	352	106	129	150
79	310	346	104	127	148
78	304	341	102	125	146
77	298	335	99	122	143
76	292	329	97	120	141
75	286	324	95	118	139
74	280	318	93	115	137
73	274	312	91	113	135
72	268	306	88	111	132
71	262	301	86	108	130
70	256	295	84	106	128
69	250	289	82	104	126
68	244	284	80	101	124
67	238	278	77	99	121
66	232	272	75	97	119

Continued on next page

	Table 2.1 (continued)				
	HYDE ACHIEVEMENT SCALES IN ARCHERY FOR COLLEGE WOMEN*				
Scale Score	First Columbia Total Score	Total Score	Final Columbia Round (Target Score)		
			50 Yards	40 Yards	30 Yards
65	226	267	73	94	117
64	220	261	71	92	115
63	214	255	69	90	113
62	208	249	66	87	110
61	202	244	64	85	108
60	196	238	62	83	106
59	190	232	60	80	104
58	184	227	58	78	102
57	178	221	55	76	99
56	172	215	53	73	97
55	166	210	51	71	95
54	160	204	49	69	93
53	154	198	47	66	91
52	148	192	44	64	88
51	142	187	42	62	86
50	136	181	40	59	84
49	133	178	39	58	82
48	131	174		57	80
47	128	171	38	56	79
46	125	167	37	55	77
45	122	164	36	53	75
44	120	160	35	52	74
43	117	157		51	72
42	114	153	34	50	70
41	111	150	33	49	69
40	109	146	32	47	67
39	106	143	31	46	65
38	103	139		45	64
37	100	136	30	44	62
36	98	132	29	43	60
35	95	129	28	42	59
34	92	125	27	40	57
33	89	122		39	55
32	87	118	26	38	54
31	84	115	25	37	52

Continued on next page

Table 2.1 (continued)

HYDE ACHIEVEMENT SCALES IN ARCHERY FOR COLLEGE WOMEN*

Scale Score	First Columbia Total Score	Total Score	Final Columbia Round (Target Score)		
			50 Yards	40 Yards	30 Yards
30	81	111	24	36	50
29	78	108	23	34	49
28	76	104		33	47
27	73	101	22	32	45
26	70	97	21	31	44
25	67	94	20	30	42
24	65	90	19	28	40
23	62	87		27	39
22	59	83	18	26	37
21	56	80	17	25	35
20	54	76	16	24	34
19	51	73	15	23	32
18	48	69		21	30
17	45	66	14	20	29
16	43	62	13	19	27
15	40	59	12	18	25
14	37	55	11	17	24
13	34	52		15	22
12	32	48	10	14	20
11	29	45	9	13	19
10	26	41	8	12	17
9	23	38	7	11	15
8	21	34		9	14
7	18	31	6	8	12
6	15	27	5	7	10
5	12	24	4	6	9
4	10	20	3	5	7
3	7	17		4	5
2	4	13	2	2	4
1	1	10	1	1	2

*Based on scores of over 1400 college students.
Scales arranged by Frederick W. Cozens.

From: Hyde, E.I. (1937). An achievement scale in archery. *Research Quarterly* 8: 108-116. Reprinted with permission from AAHPERD.

AAHPER ARCHERY TEST
(AAHPER, 1967)

Purpose:

To measure achievement in archery and to serve as a practice test for improvement of skill.

Educational Application:

Junior high and senior high school boys and girls (12 to 18 years of age).

Time:

Archery classes of 15 to 20 students should easily complete the shooting required at one distance in one class session. No more than two class periods are required for girls and a maximum of three for boys.

Personnel:

One instructor to administer and supervise while the students serve as scorers.

Equipment and Supplies:

Standard 48-inch target faces; bows ranging from 15 to 40 pounds in pull according to age and ability of student; matched arrows (eight to 10 per person), 24 to 28 inches in length with particular length fitted to bow and archer; accessories include arm guards, finger tabs, gloves, quivers and field marking and scorekeeping materials.

Facilities and Space:

A level or near level target range of sufficient size to test ten to fifteen archers simultaneously at a distance of 10, 20 and 30 yards. For testing indoors, a standard-sized gymnasium with appropriate backstops should suffice.

Directions:

Four practice arrows are permitted at each distance.

No more than four archers should shoot at any one target. Twelve arrows consisting of two ends of six arrows each are shot at distances of 10, 20 and 30 yards for boys, with the 30-yard distance eliminated for girls. The 10-yard distance must be completed before moving to the 20-yard distance, etc. Any students not scoring at least 10 points at one distance may not advance to the next distance mark.

Scoring Method and Norms:

The standard target archery scoring values are used: gold, 9; red, 7; blue, 5; black, 3; white, 1; outside the white or missing the target, 0. An arrow striking two colors is assigned the score of higher value. Seven points are scored for an arrow passing completely through or rebounding off the target.

The student's official score is derived by adding the totals made at each distance. The best possible score at each distance is 108 points; therefore, the maximum test score is 216 points for girls and 324 for boys.

		Table 2.2 PERCENTILE SCORES FOR AAHPER ARCHERY TEST (BOYS)*																		

		BOYS																		
	Age	12 - 13				14				15				16				17 - 18			
	Yards	10	20	30	Tot.	10	20	30	Tot.	10	20	30	Tot,	10	20	30	Tot.	10	20	30	Tot.
	100	91	70	45	195	96	75	50	210	100	90	81	270	100	100	95	270	100	95	85	270
	95	83	53	28	156	88	61	34	179	97	77	50	215	99	78	56	220	98	78	64	222
	90	78	44	24	138	80	48	28	160	94	70	41	195	97	71	47	205	96	72	53	206
	85	73	38	22	128	78	45	24	150	90	66	35	187	96	67	43	197	93	67	47	197
	80	70	34	18	122	75	41	21	146	88	63	31	177	91	63	40	189	90	63	42	190
	75	67	31	16	112	72	38	18	143	84	58	28	167	90	59	36	181	88	59	39	184
Percentile Scores	70	64	28	14	103	70	36	16	139	80	54	25	158	88	56	32	173	86	55	37	176
	65	61	26	12	98	68	33	15	136	78	51	22	149	86	54	30	163	84	52	35	166
	60	59	24	11	93	67	30	13	130	76	47	20	140	84	51	28	160	82	49	31	158
	55	57	23	9	87	65	28	11	24	73	42	17	130	80	48	25	154	79	46	28	151
	50	54	22	8	81	63	26	10	119	69	39	15	120	79	46	23	148	77	43	26	144
	45	50	20	7	74	60	24	8	114	65	36	14	114	77	43	22	142	74	40	24	136
	40	48	18	6	67	57	22	7	110	62	34	13	107	75	41	20	136	71	37	21	130
	35	45	16	4	60	55	20	5	106	59	31	12	100	72	39	18	129	68	34	20	125
	30	42	14	0	54	52	18	4	98	55	28	11	94	70	36	16	123	63	32	17	119
	25	38	12	0	47	45	16	0	87	51	24	10	87	67	33	13	117	59	29	16	112
	20	34	10	0	38	40	14	0	77	48	21	9	79	61	28	11	110	55	25	11	109
	15	31	8	0	28	36	12	0	69	43	18	7	70	51	25	9	103	48	20	9	96
	10	26	6	0	21	31	10	0	61	36	15	6	62	50	20	6	80	40	17	6	86
	5	16	3	0	15	25	6	0	43	25	9	2	43	40	14	2	61	27	11	3	65
	0	0	0	0	0	0	0	0	0	0	0	0	0	0	0	0	0	0	0	0	0

*Based on scores of over 600 students for each age group (10-18).

From: *AAHPER skills test manual for archery* (1967). Reprinted with permission from AAHPERD.

Validity and Reliability:

Face validity is accepted. A reliability coefficient of .70 was set as the minimum requirement for tests of accuracy in the AAHPER Sports Skills Tests.

Additional Comments:

The chief strength of the AAHPER Archery Skills Test is the availability of national norms that were developed from testing over six hundred students of each gender. It is recommended that the 10-yard distance be eliminated and distances greater than 40 yards be added for older children (Morris, 1977).

Table 2.3
PERCENTILE SCORES FOR AAHPER ARCHERY TEST (GIRLS)*

| | | GIRLS | | | | | | | | | | | | | | |
| Age | | 12 - 13 | | | | 14 | | | | 15 | | | | 16 | | | | 17 - 18 | |
Yards	10	20	Tot.		10	20	Tot.		10	20	Tot,		10	20	Tot.		10	20	Tot.
100	85	60	129		89	70	159		96	81	160		100	91	161		100	95	180
95	69	40	100		74	47	109		82	55	130		87	58	134		87	71	149
90	60	29	89		68	38	99		75	47	112		80	50	115		80	60	129
85	50	22	81		63	35	89		70	43	103		73	44	107		73	52	123
80	46	19	69		58	32	84		66	39	96		67	40	100		69	47	116
75	41	17	64		54	28	79		63	34	89		64	36	96		66	42	109
70	38	15	60		50	25	75		60	32	85		60	32	91		62	40	104
65	35	13	55		48	23	70		56	29	80		56	29	87		58	36	100
60	34	12	50		46	21	66		53	27	77		53	27	80		55	32	95
55	32	10	46		43	20	62		51	25	73		49	25	76		52	29	91
50	30	9	42		41	18	58		49	23	70		46	22	72		48	26	85
45	27	7	38		38	16	54		46	22	66		43	20	67		46	24	78
40	24	6	35		35	14	50		43	20	62		41	18	63		42	21	73
35	22	1	32		33	12	47		40	18	59		38	16	60		40	19	68
30	19	0	28		30	10	45		37	16	55		33	14	56		38	18	64
25	16	0	25		28	8	42		34	13	51		31	12	52		35	16	60
20	14	0	22		25	7	40		31	11	45		29	10	47		31	14	53
15	12	0	17		22	0	34		27	8	40		25	8	41		28	12	45
10	10	0	12		19	0	28		21	6	33		21	6	33		24	9	38
5	6	0	5		12	0	22		13	0	25		16	0	26		19	0	30
0	0	0	0		0	0	0		0	0	0		0	0	0		0	0	0

*Based on scores of over 600 students for each age group (10-18).

From: *AAHPER skills test manual for archery* (1967). Reprinted with permission from AAHPERD.

ARCHERY TEST
(Farrow, 1970)

Purpose:

To evaluate archery ability.

Educational Application:

Although designed for college women, the test is appropriate for junior high and senior high school boys and girls.

Personnel:

One instructor to administer the test while the students serve as scorers.

Equipment and Supplies:

Standard 48-inch target faces, targets, bows, arrows, arm guards and finger tabs. The availability of two bows per target allows two students to be tested on one target simultaneously. Materials for marking the range and recording the scores are necessary accessories.

Facilities and Space:

A facility that requires a maximum shooting distance of 20 yards.

Directions:

The student shoots 24 arrows (four ends) at the 10-yard distance, and the same number at the 20-yard distance.

Scoring Method:

Using the standard target archery scoring system (gold, 9; red, 7; blue, 5; black, 3; white, 1; outside the white or missing the target, 0), the total points accumulated from the 48 arrows shot is the official score. Arrows passing through or bouncing off a target receive a score of seven. A perfect score is 432 points.

Archery References

American Association for Health, Physical Education and Recreation. (1967). *AAHPER skills test manual for archery*. Washington, D.C.: AAHPER.

Bohn, R.W. (1962). *An achievement test in archery*. Unpublished master's thesis, University of Wisconsin, Madison.

Hyde, E.I. (1937). An achievement scale in archery. *Research Quarterly* 8: 108-116.

Ley, K.L. (1960). *Constructing objective test items to measure high school levels of achievement in selected physical education activities*. Unpublished doctoral dissertation, University of Iowa, Iowa City.

McKenzie, R., & Schifflett, B. (1986). *Skill evaluation in a coeducational beginning archery class*. Unpublished paper, San Diego State University.

Morris, H.H. (1977). *A critique of the AAHPER skill test series*. Paper presented at the American Alliance for Health, Physical Education and Recreation National Convention, Seattle.

Reichart, N. (1943). School archery standards. *Journal of Health and Physical Education* 14: 81, 124.

Schifflett, B., & Schuman, B.A. (1982). A criterion-referenced test for archery. *Research Quarterly for Exercise and Sport* 53: 330-335.

Willgoose, C.E. (1961). *Evaluation in health education and physical education*. New York: McGraw.

Zabick, R.M., & Jackson, A.S. (1969). Reliability of archery achievement. *Research Quarterly for Exercise and Sport* 40: 254-255.

Chapter 3

BADMINTON

INTRODUCTION

The sport of badminton has proven to be a fertile subject area for skills tests investigators as evidenced by the extensive number surveyed by the authors. Inasmuch as several of the authenticated badminton tests are similar in design, only a representative sampling is presented in this chapter.

17

FRENCH SHORT SERVE TEST
(Scott et al., 1941)

Purpose:

To measure the ability to accurately serve a shuttlecock with a low and short placement; to measure badminton playing ability when combined with the French Clear Test.

Description:

A rope is stretched 20 inches directly above and parallel to the net. Using the intersection of the short service line and the center service line as a midpoint, a series of two-inch lines in the form of arcs are placed in the right service court at distances of 22, 30, 38 and 46 inches from the midpoint, with each measurement including the width of the two-inch line. It is recommended that the lines be coded in color.

Educational Application:

Designed for college men and women; appropriate for any lower grade level that has developed the basic fundamental techniques associated with the serve.

Time:

A class of 20 students can be tested in one 60-minute period.

Personnel:

One individual to score and record.

Equipment and Supplies:

Badminton racquets, shuttlecocks, badminton net and clothesline rope the length of a regulation net; scoring materials and paint or tape.

Facilities and Space:

Regulation badminton court.

Directions:

The subject being tested may stand anywhere in the right service area diagonally opposite the target. The scorer should stand in the center of the left service court on the opposite court side of the server. It is important that the scorer stand facing the target for proper position in scoring the landing of the shuttlecock and determining whether or not it goes between the net and rope.

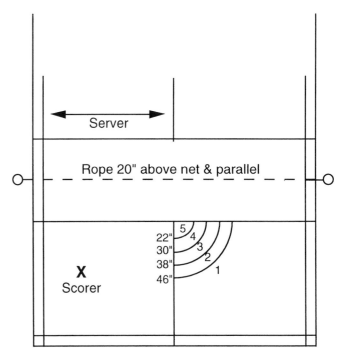

Fig. 3.1 Court markings for French Short Serve Test.

From: Scott, M.G., Carpenter, A., French, E., & Kuhl, L. (1941). Achievement examinations in badminton. *Research Quarterly* 12: 242-253. Reprinted with permission from AAHPERD.

The subject serves 20 legal serves at the target (Figure 3.1). Each serve that passes between the badminton net and the rope adds to the point total, providing the shuttlecock falls somewhere in the proper service court area for doubles play. Illegal serves may be repeated since they are technically considered fouls.

Scoring Method and Norms:

A score is awarded for any legal serve that passes between the net and rope and lands in the proper service court for doubles play.

Points are awarded based on placement of the shuttlecock. The low, short serve is obviously the most desired. The scoring areas are 5, 4, 3, 2 and 1, with the number decreasing as one moves away from the midpoint. Should the shuttlecock land on a line dividing two scoring areas, the subject receives the score of higher value; otherwise, points are awarded according to the area the shuttlecock lands in the target. The total score of 20 trials constitutes the final score.

TABLE 3.1 NORMS FOR FRENCH SHORT SERVE TEST			
T-Score	Short Serve*	Short Serve†	T-Score
80	68	86	80
75	66	79	75
70	59	73	70
65	53	66	65
60	44	59	60
55	37	52	55
50	29	46	50
45	22	39	45
40	13	32	40
35	8	26	35
30	4	19	30
25	1	12	25
20	0	6	20

*Based on performance of 385 college women after a 25-lesson beginning course in badminton.
†Based on performance of 46 college women after a 30-lesson beginning course in badminton.

From: Scott, M.G., Carpenter, A., French, E., & Kuhl, L. (1941). Achievement examinations in badminton. *Research Quarterly* 12: 242-253. Reprinted with permission from AAHPERD.

Validity and Reliability:

From test scores of 29 physical education majors, a validity coefficient of .66 was determined when correlated with the final standings of a ladder tournament. A reliability coefficient of .88 was computed. The odd-even method of obtaining reliability was utilized, followed by the Spearman-Brown Prophecy Formula.

Additional Comments:

To assist the tester in drawing arcs, it is suggested that a string at least 48 inches in length be marked at 22, 30, 36 and 48-inch intervals. Also, colored tape is more feasible for marking the floor than paint, or tape can be color coded once located on the floor.

Dividing the 20 serves into two sets of 10, possibly having 10 serves taken from each service court, is another suggestion.

The French Short Serve Test was originally included in a battery of six tests. It and the French Clear Test proved superior to the others, according to validity coefficient values. When a multiple correlation was used to combine the two test scores, the resulting validity coefficient was .85. Both tests should be administered to measure general badminton playing ability. In using the test combination, the formula used to ensure proper weighting is 1.0 serve and 1.2 clear.

FRENCH CLEAR TEST
(Scott et al., 1941)

Purpose:

To measure the ability to accurately place a clear shot; to measure general badminton playing ability when combined with the French Short Serve Test.

Description:

A line is marked on the floor two feet in front of and parallel to the rear service line in the doubles game. Another line on the same side of the net should be placed two feet behind and parallel to the rear service line in the singles game. The measurements should be taken from the center of the appropriate lines. Both lines should be extended the width of the court to the sideline for doubles play. It is recommended that the lines be color coded for scoring ease. Figure 3.2 should help clarify the floor markings. A rope is stretched across the width of the court at a height of eight feet and a distance of 14 feet from and parallel to the net on the target side.

A two-inch square should be drawn in each of the service courts on the side of the net opposite the target. The center of each square should be 11 feet from the net and three feet from the center line. The measurements should be made from the center of the appropriate line.

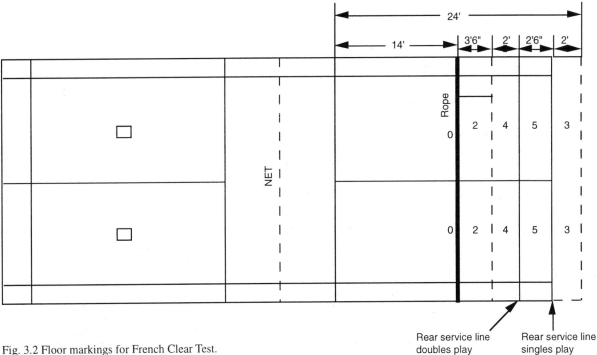

Fig. 3.2 Floor markings for French Clear Test.

From: Scott, M.G., Carpenter, A., French, A., & Kuhl, L. (1941). Achievement examinations in badminton. *Research Quarterly* 12: 242-253. Reprinted with permission from AAHPERD.

Educational Application:

High school and college males and females.

Time:

A class of 20 students can be tested in one 60-minute period.

Personnel:

The instructor or a skilled student may act as server with another student serving as a scorer-recorder.

Equipment and Supplies:

Badminton racquets, shuttlecocks, badminton net, additional set of standards, rope the width of court, and scoring and floor marking materials.

Facilities and Space:

Regulation badminton court.

Directions:

After two practice trials, the subject assumes a position between the two squares located on the side of the net opposite the target. The server, who should demonstrate a minimum of intermediate badminton skill, stands at the intersection of the short service line and center line on the same side of the court with the target. Then the server serves the shuttlecock across the net so that it carries at least even with the two squares. Should the server not serve the shuttlecock far enough or outside the two squares, the subject should not play it. Only shuttlecocks played by the subject count as official trials, and each subject takes 20 clear shot trials. The subject is allowed complete freedom of movement once the shuttlecock has been served. Any carried or slung clear shot may be repeated.

Table 3.2	
NORMS FOR FRENCH CLEAR TEST*	
T-Score	Clear
80	94
75	90
70	86
65	79
60	72
55	64
50	54
45	44
40	32
35	20
30	8
25	2
20	0

*Based on scores of 429 college freshman and sophomore women.

From: Scott, M.G., Carpenter, A., French, E., & Kuhl, L. (1941). Achievement examinations in badminton. *Research Quarterly* 12: 242-253. Reprinted with permission from AAHPERD.

Validity and Reliability:

In a check of the test's validity, a correlation coefficient of .60 was computed. A tournament ranking was the criterion measure. The test subjects were 29 physical education majors.

The reliability was determined by using the odd-even method, with the coefficient stepped up by the Spearman-Brown Formula. A .96 relationship resulted.

Additional Comments:

Two subjects can be tested simultaneously by simply dividing the court in half with the center line utilized. Each subject should stand in the middle of the short service line in his/her respective service court and no closer to the net than the short service line. It is suggested that the 20 trials be divided into two sets of 10 and alternate service courts be used for each 10 hits.

One possible disadvantage of the test might be the idea of having the shuttlecock put into play with a serve. This puts a great deal of responsibility on the server. It is essential that the server be a skilled server and as consistent as possible. The authors recommend that the same server be utilized throughout the test administration, if at all possible, for reliability purposes.

FRENCH-STALTER BADMINTON SKILL TESTS
(French & Stalter, 1949)

Purpose:

To measure general badminton playing ability and to assess individual, basic badminton skills.

Description:

The French-Stalter Badminton Skill Tests comprise a battery of five different skills tests. This series of tests is a follow-up to the French Short Serve and French Clear Tests. French and Stalter wanted to develop a comprehensive battery to measure badminton skill, so they constructed three new tests dealing with footwork, wrist action and smashing ability to include with the two authentic tests previously constructed. Added to the short serve and clear items were the wrist-volley, shuttle and smash tests. Only the last three are discussed here since the first two were presented earlier in this chapter.

Wrist-Volley. Floor markings include a 1 1/2-inch wide line that is six feet from and parallel to the base of the wall. The width of the line is included as part of the six-foot distance.

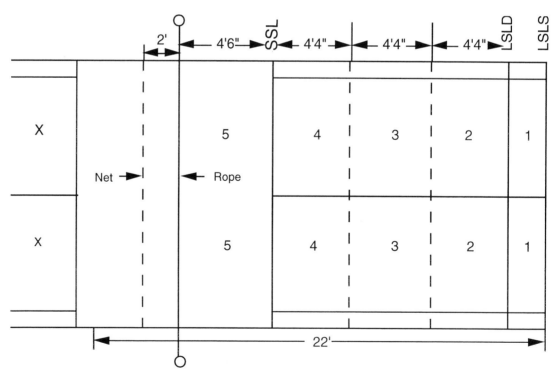

Fig. 3.3 Floor markings for smash test.

From: French, E., & Stalter, E. (1949). Study of skills tests in badminton for college women. *Research Quarterly* 20: 257-272. Reprinted with permission from AAHPERD.

Smash. The tester should begin by marking a 1 1/2-inch wide line on the floor four feet, four inches behind and parallel to the short service line (SSL) as shown in Figure 3.3. A line of the same width is also marked four feet, four inches in front of and parallel to the long service line for doubles (LSLD). The back of the target is represented by the long service line for singles (LSLS). Those lines should be color coded for scoring ease and accuracy. Target areas are numbered 5, 4, 3, 2 and 1 in descending order from the badminton net to the long service line for singles play.

A rope is stretched across the width of the court on the target side from one sideline to the other for doubles play. Two standards hold the rope taut and are positioned two feet from and parallel to the net at a height of seven feet from the floor.

Educational Application:

Originally developed for college women but can be used for both males and females in high school and college.

Time:

Two to four 60-minute class periods to test 20 students, depending upon the number of test items administered.

Personnel:

One or two individuals, again depending on the number of tests used in the battery.

Equipment and Supplies:

Badminton racquets, shuttlecocks, stop watch, badminton net, and additional set of standards necessary for administration of test battery. Accessories include scoring and floor marking materials, plus a rope at least 25 feet long.

Facilities and Space:

A regulation badminton court is needed for the shuttle and smash tests. A smooth wall at least 15 x 15 feet in size and unobstructed floor space of equal dimensions are required for the wrist-volley item.

Directions:

A standardized five-minute practice period is recommended for the wrist-volley item, and two practice trials are suggested for the smash test.

Wrist-Volley. The subject assumes a server's position behind the restraining line, facing the wall with a badminton racquet and shuttlecock in hand. When ready, an audible command to begin is given, and the subject immediately performs a legal serve against the wall. The shuttlecock is continually volleyed against the wall with any desired stroke; in the meantime the subject makes every effort to stay behind the restraining line. Should the shuttlecock come to rest anywhere on the floor area at any time during one of the four 30-second trials, the subject should retrieve it and immediately assume a position behind the restraining line, then put the shuttlecock back into play with a legal serve.

The subject is allowed to move anywhere on the floor area, but points are only scored when the restraining line is not violated. Rest periods should be allowed between trials.

Shuttle. The subject gets ready for the test by standing with a racquet in hand and facing the net. When the audible command to begin is given, he/she commences to run as rapidly as possible back and forth between the sidelines of the singles court, certain to cross over the center line on each trip. The subject may use either a sliding step or a crossover step. The main concern is not the step used, but that the subject keeps his/her body in a favorable position to return the shuttlecock. It is recommended that the scorer stand between the short service line and the net, facing the subject. Four 15-second trials are administered to each subject.

Smash. The server assumes a position behind the short service line on the target side of the net (Figure 3.3). Shuttlecocks should be served with enough force to clear the rope, net, and the short service line on the side opposite the target, and the serve should have enough height so the subject can properly execute an overhead smash shot. If the serve should hit the rope or net or not be long or high enough, it constitutes a fault and is served again.

While being tested the subject stands behind the short service line opposite the target side of the net. The subject receives 20 serves and tries on each to hit a smash shot between the net and the rope, aiming for the area of highest value. The subject should only attempt to hit the good serves. Should the shuttlecock be smashed into the server on the opposite side of the net, the scorer estimates the target area it would have hit, and those points are assigned. A smash hit into the top of the net which falls over to the target side is legitimate.

Scoring Method and Norms:

Wrist-Volley. A point is scored for each legal hit or volley against the wall during the four 30-second trial periods. Any initial serve used to put the shuttlecock into play does not count as a legal hit. The subject's score is the sum total of legal hits for four 30-second trials.

Shuttle. One point is scored each time the subject goes from one side boundary line to the other. A trip across and back counts two points. The score of each 15-second trial is the total number of crossings made. Four trials are permitted, and the final score is the total point accumulation on all four trials.

Smash. Each legitimate smash shot is assigned the point value earned. Shuttlecocks landing on a line dividing target areas are assigned the points associated with the area of higher value. Points are given based on where the shuttlecock initially hits and not where it eventually comes to rest. The scorer records all 20 trials, and a subject's final score is the cumulative total of those trials.

Validity and Reliability:

In correlating test scores with the criterion, a validity coefficient of .78 was obtained for the wrist-volley item. For the same item, a .83 reliability coefficient was determined by the odd-even method and corrected by the Spearman-Brown Formula. Fifty-nine physical education majors served as subjects with judges' ratings used as the criterion measure.

Multiple correlation coefficients for validity and weightings are shown below for the various possible test item combinations for the five-item battery:

Two-item test battery:

2.5 (wrist-volley) + 1.0 (short serve) = .87
1.0 (short serve) + 1.2 (clear) = .85
2.0 (wrist-volley) + 1.0 (clear) = .84

Three-item test battery:

2.0 (wrist-volley) + 1.0 (clear)
+ 1.0 (short serve) = .91

Shuttle + 0.3 (clear)
+ 0.19 (wrist-volley) = .68

Four-item test battery:

Shuttle + 0.19 (wrist-volley)
+ 0.12 (short serve) + 0.11 (clear) = .70

Additional Comments:

The wrist-volley item seems to adequately represent that particular skill, even for evaluation purposes. Other test items should be used only as part of one of the possible batteries, regardless of the purpose.

To speed up the administration of the smash item, it is recommended that two subjects be tested simultaneously on one court. Also, the 20 trials can be divided into two sets of 10 each with the two subjects exchanging sides of the court after completing 10 trials. Additionally for the smash test, it is important that the servers are qualified and retain their assignment throughout the test to ensure maximum consistency in test conditions.

Providing the tester an option of three different scientifically documented test batteries to use, the French-Stalter Badminton Skill Tests demonstrate a uniqueness that is not shown in many other sports skills test batteries. Determination of the multiple correlation coefficients and value weightings made this possible. Variables such as skills stressed, available equipment and supplies, number of students, amount of time available, and desired test difficulty may all be considered before a particular battery is selected for utilization.

Table 3.3	
NORMS FOR WRIST-VOLLEY TEST*	
T-Score	Volley
75	148
73	138
71	128
69	114
65	108
63	106
61	102
59	98
57	92
55	88
53	84
51	82
49	80
45	72
40	62
35	54
30	48

*Based on scores of 91 college freshman and sophomore women.

From: French, E., & Stalter, E, (1949). Study of skill tests in badminton for college women. *Research Quarterly* 20: 257-272. Reprinted with permission from AAHPERD.

Rating	Serve	Clear	Wrist Volley	Smash	Shuttle
			Table 3.4		
		ACHIEVEMENT SCALES FOR FRENCH-STALTER BADMINTON SKILL TESTS			
Superior	57 & up	88 & up	98 & up	89 & up	38 & up
Good	42 - 56	70 - 87	77 - 97	75 - 88	35 - 37
Average	27 - 41	51 - 69	55 - 76	60 - 74	31 - 34
Poor	12 - 26	33 - 50	34 - 54	45 - 59	28 - 30
Inferior	11 & below	32 & below	33 & below	44 & below	27 & below

From: French, E., & Stalter, E. (1949). Study of skill tests in badminton for college women. *Research Quarterly* 20: 257-272. Reprinted with permission from AAHPERD.

LOCKHART-MCPHERSON BADMINTON TEST

(Lockhart & McPherson, 1949)

Purpose:

To determine badminton playing ability.

Description:

A one-foot net line is marked on the wall five feet above and parallel to the floor. A starting line is marked on the floor 6 1/2 feet from and parallel to the base of the wall. A restraining line is also marked on the floor that is only three feet from the base of the wall and parallel to the starting line.

Educational Application:

Originally developed for college women, but Mathews (Mathews, 1973) later adapted it for college men. The test is also considered applicable for junior and senior high school males and females.

Time:

One class of 20 students can easily take the test in a 60-minute period.

Personnel:

One individual to time, score and record.

Equipment and Supplies:

Badminton racquet, indoor shuttlecock, stop watch and scoring materials.

Facilities and Space:

A smooth wall that is at least 10 x 10 feet and floor space of equal dimensions.

Directions:

Each student is allowed a 15-second practice session immediately before being tested.

When ready, the subject assumes a service position behind the starting line and on the starting command, he/she executes a legal badminton serve against the front wall. The shuttlecock is then volleyed as many times as possible during the 30-second time period, with the subject staying behind the restraining line. A legal hit, which counts one point, occurs anytime the subject hits the shuttlecock on or above the net line while remaining anywhere behind the restraining line. The subject may continue to hit the shuttlecock even if the net line or the restraining line has been violated, but no points are scored. Should the shuttlecock come to rest at any time during any one of the 30-second trial periods, the subject needs only to promptly retrieve the shuttlecock, assume a service position behind the starting line and quickly put the shuttlecock into play again with a legal serve against the wall.

Any wood shot, carry or double hit counts as a legal hit providing the subject remains behind the restraining line and the shuttlecock hits on or above the net line.

Scoring Method and Norms:

The subject's score is the sum total of legal hits in the three 30-second trials.

Table 3.5	
NORMS FOR LOCKHART-MCPHERSON BADMINTON TEST*	
T-Score	Volley Test Sum of Three Trials
75	145
70	131
65	114
60	101
55	87
50	73
45	64
40	52
35	45
30	38
25	32
*Based on performance of 178 college women.	

From: Lockhart, A., & McPherson, F.A. (1949). The development of a test of badminton playing ability. *Research Quarterly* 20: 402-405. Reprinted with permission from AAHPERD.

Table 3.6	
ACHIEVEMENT SCALE FOR COLLEGE WOMEN	
Rating	Test Score Sum of Three Trials
Superior	126 & up
Good	90 - 125
Average	62 - 89
Poor	40 - 61
Inferior	39 & below

From: Lockhart, A., & McPherson, F.A. (1949). The development of a test of badminton playing ability. *Research Quarterly* 20: 402-405. Reprinted with permission from AAHPERD.

Validity and Reliability:

An r of .71 was obtained when ratings of three experienced judges were correlated with actual test scores of 68 girls. A .60 coefficient was determined for the relationship between round-robin tournament results of 27 girls and their test scores. Furthermore, an r of .90 was found for the relationship between three judges' ratings and the percentage of games won by the 27 girls in the round-robin tournament.

The .90 reliability coefficient was determined by the test-retest method utilized on a three-day testing period. Fifty girls participated as test subjects.

Additional Comments:

Repeated positive results have been found in studies of the test's validity value, Additionally, high marks are given for the test's reliability, time of administration, ease of administration and scoring.

MILLER WALL VOLLEY TEST
(Miller, 1951)

Purpose:

To measure the ability to hit the clear shot and to determine general badminton playing ability.

Description:

In analyzing one of the United States Amateur Badminton Championship Tournaments, Miller discovered that the clear shot was used more often than any other shot in both singles and doubles play. Based on this knowledge, she proceeded to develop a rather uncomplicated wall volley test that is easily administered.

A one-inch line, 7 1/2 feet above and parallel to the floor, is marked on the wall. The floor marking simply consists of a restraining line located 10 feet back from the base of the wall, with a suggested safety line located three inches behind the restraining line.

Educational Application:

College men and women.

Time:

One class of 20 students can easily take the test in a 60-minute period.

Personnel:

One individual to time, score and record.

Equipment and Supplies:

Badminton racquet, outdoor shuttlecock with sponge ends, stop watch and materials for scoring and marking the floor and wall.

Facilities and Space:

A smooth wall at least 10 x 15 feet and floor space of equal dimensions.

Directions:

Each student is permitted a one-minute practice period immediately before the test begins.

While standing behind the restraining line, the subject serves the shuttlecock in a legal manner against the wall and rallies for 30 seconds with clear shots. Any type of stroke may be used during the testing. The subject should try to volley the shuttlecock against the wall as many times as possible within each of three 30-second time periods. To count as a legal hit or one point, the subject must stay behind the restraining line, and the shuttlecock must hit on or above the high wall line.

A carry or double hit is legal providing the subject does not violate either the restraining or wall line. Although the subject may move anywhere on the court, points are only tallied when he/she remains within the boundaries. Should the shuttlecock come to rest at any time during one of the 30-second trial periods, the subject need only retrieve the shuttlecock, immediately assume a proper position behind the restraining line and again put the shuttlecock into play with a legal serve. Intervening rest periods come between test trials.

Scoring Method:

The subject's score is the sum total of legal hits in the three 30-second trials.

When 115 college men were used as subjects, the resulting range of test scores was 20 to 118. The mean for this group was 76. In another study, scores of 100 university women produced a range of 9 to 113 and a mean of 42.

Validity and Reliability:

A validity coefficient of .83 was determined by correlating the actual scores with the results of a round-robin tournament in which 20 subjects played 380 single games. A reliability coefficient of .94 was determined by use of the test-retest method during a testing period of one week. One hundred college women with varied skill levels served as test subjects.

Additional Comments:

The tester is cautioned that the type of wall surface used can make a difference in subject scores. Therefore, it and the type of shuttlecock used should be consistent throughout a test administration for a class if possible. If any type of shuttlecock other than an outdoor, sponge-tipped kind is used, the rebound from the wall varies significantly. Because of these variables, establishment of local norms should be done with consistency shown in the type of wall surface and shuttlecock used.

It is further suggested that during the three 30-second trials, a person should be placed in charge of providing the subject with helpful information such as saying "back" whenever the subject consistently steps on or over the restraining line.

Miller (Miller, 1964) modified this test by simply changing the restraining line distance to eight feet. The Modified Miller Wall Volley Test, as it is known, was developed for use in a research study which compared the effects of training sessions of diverse time periods on the skill and knowledge achievement of high school girls. The highest reliability coefficient found among student scores in one of the types of training sessions was .93. It was assumed that the test modification also possessed an acceptable degree of validity.

SCOTT-FOX LONG SERVE TEST
(Scott & French, 1959)

Purpose:

To measure the ability to serve high and to the backcourt.

Description:

The floor markings for this test are identical to those described for the French Short Serve Test, except for the location of the target. With the intersection of the long service line and the left side boundary line for singles utilized as a midpoint, a series of arcs are drawn in the left service court at distances of 22, 30, 38 and 46 inches from the midpoint. The measurements include the width of the two-inch line. Each arc should be extended to the outside boundary of the long service line and the sideline (Figure 3.4). The two-inch wide lines can be made of tape or washable paint and should be color coded for scoring ease.

Using an additional set of standards, a rope is stretched across the court 14 feet from and parallel to the net at a height of eight feet. Incidentally, the rope location for this test is identical to that required in the French Clear Test.

Educational Application:

Originally developed for college women; also appropriate for college men and high school boys and girls.

Time:

A class of 20 students can take the test in one 60-minute period.

Personnel:

One scorer-recorder.

Equipment and Supplies:

Badminton racquets, shuttlecocks, badminton net, two sets of standards, rope 20 feet or more in length, plus scoring and floor marking materials.

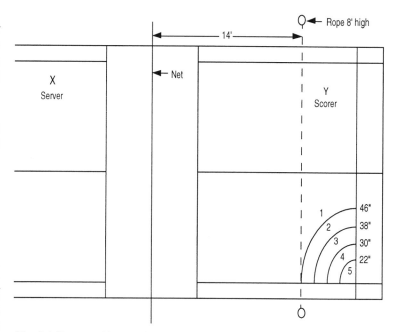

Fig. 3.4 Court markings and rope location for Scott-Fox Long Serve Test.

From: Scott, M.G., & French, E. (1959). *Measurement and evaluation in physical education.* Dubuque, Iowa: Brown. Reprinted with permission from M.G. Scott.

Facilities and Space:

Regulation badminton court.

Directions:

The subject (X) takes a position in the service court diagonally across from the target and may stand at any desired spot providing it is in the proper service court (Figure

3.4). The subject then performs 20 legal serves over the net and rope to the target area. The target is marked in point values of 5, 4, 3, 2 and 1, in decreasing order from the midpoint, Illegal serves may be repeated.

Scoring Method and Norms:

Points are scored when the subject serves a legal serve from the proper service court and the shuttlecock clears the net and rope and lands in the target area. Should a shuttlecock land on a line dividing two target areas, the higher value is awarded. The final score is the sum total of points for the 20 trials. The scorer (Y) should stand on the same side as the target between the rope and the end boundary line and face the target.

Validity and Reliability:

A validity coefficient of .54 was determined by correlating the scores of 45 college women with subjective ratings made by three judges during actual competition. A .77 reliability coefficient was derived by use of the odd-even method and corrected by the Spearman-Brown Formula. Again, the test subjects were 45 college women.

Criterion Measure:

Judges' ratings.

Additional Comments:

The arcs called for in the floor markings can easily be drawn by use of a string at least 46 inches long with marks placed at 22, 30, 38 and 46-inch intervals. It is suggested that tape be used instead of washable paint for the two-inch wide floor lines, Coloring of the tape should be done after it is applied to the floor.

Table 3.7	
NORM FOR SCOTT-FOX LONG SERVE TEST*	
Long Serve	T-Score
35	75
34	68
33	67
32	65
27	60
22	55
18	50
13	44
9	40
5	34
2	31
1	24

*Based on scores of 91 college freshman and sophomore women.

From: Scott, M.G., & French, E, (1959). *Measurement and evaluation in physical education.* Brown: Dubuque, Iowa. Reprinted with permission from M.G. Scott.

To boost the test's value in time of administration, both the right and left service court on one side of the net could be marked off to enable the testing of two subjects at once. Furthermore, the subjects could change sides of the service court after 10 serves.

The Scott-Fox Long Serve Test has been included as part of various test batteries. In a study whereby subjective ratings of judges during tournament play was used as the criterion (Scott & French, 1959), resulting multiple correlation coefficients and weightings were:

5.0 (wrist-volley) + 3.0 (clear) + 1.0 (long serve) $R = .88$
5.0 (wrist-volley) + 1.0 (long serve) $R = .83$
3.0 (clear) + 1.0 (long serve) $R = .71$

Davis (Davis, 1968) felt that the Scott-Fox Long Serve Test and the French Short Serve Test (first test presented in this chapter) should be combined to properly serve as an indicator of serving ability, since under game conditions a player must serve to both sides of the court and use both the short and long serves. Court markings in the Davis Test are similar to those found in the above-mentioned tests, but the serving procedure differs significantly. Initially serving 10 consecutive serves from the right service court while alternating between the short and long serve, the subject then moves to the left service court and repeats the procedure.

Sixty-one freshman and sophomore college males who were enrolled in beginning badminton classes served as subjects. The relationship between their serving scores and the instructor's ratings resulted in a correlation coefficient of .70.

POOLE BADMINTON TEST
(Poole and Nelson, 1970)

Purpose:

To measure performance on the forehand clear shot.

Description:

Floor markings include two parallel lines and two 15 x 15-inch squares (Figure 3.5). The first line is constructed between the short service line (SSL) and the doubles long service line (DLSL) and parallel to them. The second line is located six inches beyond the back boundary line (BBL).

One square (0) is situated in the middle of the center line and 11 feet from the net on the target side. The other square (X) is constructed at the intersection of the doubles long service line and the center line.

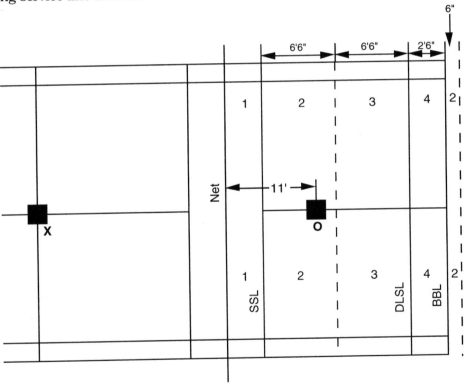

Fig. 3.5 Floor markings for Poole Forehand Clear Test.

From: Johnson, B.L., & Nelson, J.K. (1974). *Practical measurements for evaluation in physical education* (2nd ed.). Minneapolis: Burgess. Reprinted with permission from Burgess International.

Educational Application:

High school and college men and women.

Personnel:

A scorer-recorder plus an assistant.

Equipment and Supplies:

Badminton racquets, shuttlecocks, plus scoring and floor marking materials.

Facilities and Space:

Regulation badminton court.

Directions:

Standing with his/her right foot in the square and holding the badminton racquet face in an upward direction, the subject tosses the shuttlecock high into the air and proceeds to hit 12 consecutive overhead forehand clear shots. A left-handed subject should place his/her left foot in the square and keep it in contact with the floor until the shuttlecock is struck. The shuttlecock should clear the net and the assistant's racquet, plus land in the target area. The assistant serving as the opponent gives an audible signal "low" if the shuttlecock does not pass over the extended racquet.

Twelve forehand clear shots are performed by the subject. The point value of the zone in which the shuttlecock lands is recorded. The final score is the total points for the best 10 out of 12 forehand clear shots. A perfect score is 40 points.

Any shuttlecock landing on a line that divides a target zone is assigned the higher point value, and one point is subtracted from the assigned target value if the shuttlecock does not clear the extended racquet of the "opponent." Only legal serves are scored.

Scoring scales for the forehand clear are presented in Table 3.8. The scales were based on the scores of a limited number of beginning badminton players.

Table 3.8		
FOREHAND CLEAR SCORING SCALE*		
Preliminary Skill Test	Performance Level	Final Skill Test
20 & above	Good	24 & above
13 - 19	Fair	16 - 23
0 - 12	Poor	0 - 15
*Based on scores of a limited number of beginner course students.		

From: Johnson, B.L., & Nelson, J.K. (1974). *Practical measurements for evaluation in physical education* (2nd ed.). Minneapolis: Burgess. Reprinted with permission from Burgess International.

Validity and Reliability:

A validity coefficient of .70 was determined for the forehand clear test, utilizing tournament results as the criterion measure. In a test-retest approach for obtaining reliability, a coefficient of .90 was found for the forehand clear.

Additional Comments:

Norms and scoring scales should be developed at the local level. This is recommended because testers sometimes vary in their approach to testing, plus it neutralizes the need to standardize the height of the individuals serving as "opponents" in the test. The tester should be certain that each student in a class is tested while utilizing the same "opponent" or one of equal height. Poole's innovative idea of using student assistants as "opponents" makes the setting of the test more gamelike.

To insure proper test reliability, the subjects should be trained well in the art of tossing up a shuttlecock to initiate the forehand clear test item. Beginning badminton players should be able to quickly learn this skill.

Poole and Nelson found that the number of recommended trials for the forehand clear item could be reduced without sacrificing test reliability. Using the best six of eight trials as opposed to 10 of 12 in test administration, correlation of the two scoring systems yielded a coefficient of .96.

Badminton References

Beverlein, M.A. (1970). *A skill test for the drop shot in badminton.* Unpublished master's thesis, Southern Illinois University, Carbondale.

Bobrich, M. (1972). *Reliability of an evaluative tool used to measure badminton skill.* Unpublished master's thesis, George Williams College, Chicago.

Boldrick, E.L. (1945). *The measurement of fundamental skills in badminton.* Unpublished master's thesis, Wellesley College, Wellesley, Massachusetts.

Brumbach, W.B. (1967). *Badminton skills and fitness tests.* Unpublished study, University of Oregon, Eugene.

Campbell, V.M. (1938). *Development of achievement tests in badminton.* Unpublished master's thesis, University of Texas, Austin.

Chang, C.J. (1980). *Tests of fundamental badminton skills for college students: Construction, analysis and norms.* Unpublished doctoral dissertation, University of Iowa, Iowa City.

Cotton, D.J., Cobb, P.R., & Fleming, J. (1987). Development and validation of a badminton clear test. Paper presented at the American Alliance for Health, Physical Education, Recreation and Dance National Convention, Las Vegas.

Davis, B. (1946). *The relationship of certain skill tests to playing ability in badminton.* Unpublished master's thesis, Wellesley College, Wellesley, Massachusetts.

Davis, P.R. (1968). *The development of a combined short and long badminton service skill test.* Unpublished master's thesis, University of Tennessee, Knoxville.

French, E., & Stalter, E. (1949). Study of skill tests in badminton for college women. *Research Quarterly* 20: 257-272.

Greiner, M.R. (1964). *Construction of a short serve test for beginning badminton players.* Unpublished master's thesis, University of Wisconsin, Madison.

Hale, P.A. (1970). *Construction of a long serve test for beginning badminton players.* Unpublished master's thesis, University of Wisconsin, Madison.

Hicks, J.V. (1967). *The construction and evaluation of a battery of five badminton skill tests.* Unpublished doctoral dissertation, Texas Women's University, Denton.

Johnson, B.L., & Nelson, J.K. (1974). *Practical measurements for evaluation in physical education* (2nd ed.). Minneapolis: Burgess.

Johnson, B.L., & Nelson, J.K. (1979). Badminton smash test. In *Practical measurements for evaluation in physical education* (3rd ed.). Edina, Minnesota: Burgess.

Johnson, R.M. (1967). *Determination of the validity and reliability of the badminton placement test.* Unpublished master's thesis, University of Oregon, Eugene.

Kowert, E.A. (1968). *Construction of a badminton ability test for men.* Unpublished master's thesis, University of Iowa, Iowa City.

Lockhart, A., & McPherson, F.A. (1949). The development of a test of badminton playing ability. *Research Quarterly* 20: 402-405.

Mathews, D.K. (1973). *Measurement in physical education* (4th ed.). Philadelphia: Saunders.

Mathews, D.K. (1973). Unpublished study. In *Measurement in physical education.* Philadelphia: Saunders.

McDonald, E.D. (1968). *The development of a skill test for the badminton high clear.* Unpublished master's thesis, Southern Illinois University, Carbondale.

Miller, F.A. (1951). A badminton wall volley test. *Research Quarterly* 22: 208-213.

Miller, S.E. (1964). *The relative effectiveness of high school badminton instruction when given in two short units and one continuous unit involving the same total time.* Unpublished master's thesis, University of Washington, Seattle.

Poole, J., & Nelson, J.K. (1970). Construction of a badminton skills test battery. In B.L. Johnson & J.K. Nelson, *Practical measurements for evaluation in physical education* (2nd ed.). Minneapolis: Burgess.

Popp, P. (1970). *The development of a diagnostic test to determine badminton playing ability.* Unpublished master's thesis, University of Washington, Seattle.

Roger, M.J. (1950). *Achievement tests in badminton for college women.* Unpublished master's thesis, University of Iowa, Iowa City.

Sebolt, D. (1986). Sebolt short service test. In T.A. Baumgartner & A.S. Jackson, *Measurement for evaluation in physical education.* (2nd ed.). Dubuque, Iowa: Brown.

Scott, J.H. (1941). *A study in the evaluation of playing ability in the game of badminton.* Unpublished master's thesis, The Ohio State University, Columbus.

Scott, M.G., Carpenter, A., French, E., & Kuhl, L. (1941). Achievement examinations in badminton. *Research Quarterly* 12: 242-253.

Scott, M.G., & French, E. (1959). *Measurement and evaluation in physical education.* Brown: Dubuque, Iowa.

Thorpe, J., & West, C. (1969). A test of game sense in badminton. *Perceptual and Motor Skills* 27: 159-169.

Washington, J. (1968). *Construction of a wall volley test for the badminton short serve and the effect of wall practice on court performance.* Unpublished master's thesis, North Texas State University, Denton.

Chapter 4

BASEBALL

INTRODUCTION

Several factors influence the limited presence of baseball in the curriculum of American schools and universities. The sport closely relates to softball which is routinely offered in physical education programs. Very little carry-over value is exhibited in baseball which is less true of softball. Aside from professional baseball, few opportunities exist for a person to play organized baseball beyond the college years. More playing space is required for baseball than softball, making softball a more logical choice to be inserted into the curriculum.

The baseball skills tests that do exist and are presented in this chapter are helpful tools to Little League coaches for classification purposes and public school physical education teachers for the measurement of achievement.

KELSON BASEBALL CLASSIFICATION PLAN
(Kelson, 1953)

Purpose:

To classify boys for baseball participation at the elementary school and Little League levels. The test could also be used to measure individual and team progress during a season or term of study.

Educational Application:

The test was devised for boys, eight to 12 years in age; however, it has potential for implementation at higher age and ability levels.

Time:

At least 15 to 20 students can be tested in one class session.

Personnel:

One person is needed at the restraining line to check for violations, and a scorer should be located every 25 feet within an area marked off from 50 to 200 feet. Two instructors or coaches would be ideal for the test administration, but one individual of that nature with at least two student assistants should suffice.

Equipment and Supplies:

Little League baseballs, field marking and scoring materials, plus a tape measure.

Facilities and Space:

Level or near level field at least 250 feet in length and 50 feet in width.

Directions:

The throwing area is marked off from 50 to 200 feet with lines every five feet apart. A scorer should be stationed every 25 feet from beginning to end of the throwing area. Since the throws of most students tend to cluster in a predictable range of the throwing area, the test can be adequately administered with fewer scorers than recommended.

In determining the ability to throw for distance, three trial throws are recorded in feet by the scorers. The subjects are permitted to run prior to throwing the ball as long as they do not cross the restraining line. Students should warm up properly before completing the test throws.

Scoring Method and Norms:

The best throw of the three trials is selected as the official score. Sixty-four boys, ages eight to 12, participated in the original study. Eighty-seven additional boys were tested for the distance throw within a year of the original study for the expansion of the developed norms. The classification plan shown in Table 4.1 was devised from the distance throwing scores of the previously mentioned 151 subjects.

Validity and Reliability:

A correlation coefficient of .85 was obtained between the throw for distance test and a composite criterion composed of seasonal batting averages and judges' ratings on four other baseball skills. No reliability coefficient was reported.

Criterion Measure:

A composite score of baseball skills (batting averages and judges' ratings on throwing for accuracy, throwing for distance, catching fly balls and fielding ground balls). Inferior to superior ability was rated from one to five points on all skills, with the batting averages representing batting skill.

Table 4.1	
BASEBALL CLASSIFICATION INDEX FOR BOYS*	
Ability Level	Distance of Throw
Superior	177 feet & over
Above Average	145 - 176 feet
Average	113 - 144 feet
Below Average	80 - 112 Feet
Inferior	79 feet & under
*Based on scores of 151 boys, ages 8-12.	

From: Kelson, R.E. (1953). Baseball classification plan for boys. *Research Quarterly* 24: 304-307. Reprinted with permission from AAHPERD.

Additional Comments:

Of all the well-constructed sports skills tests in existence today, few can match the Kelson Classification Plan in meeting the feasibility criteria for testing. Easy in its administration, economical in time of administration and valid in the determination of baseball ability, the test has demonstrated its value as a worthwhile testing instrument for baseball skill.

Another advantage of the Kelson Test is its potential for adaptation. The test could possibly adapt well to the sport of softball and also to other age and ability levels. The latter adaptation could be made by simply using regulation baseballs instead of the Little League models. Local norms should be developed and used according to particular age and ability levels.

The use of this test for classification purposes seems to have definite advantages over its use in the measurement of achievement. Since baseball throwing for distance seems to be more a result of nature than nurture, its use as an exclusive determinant of achievement is questionable. However, it should not be discarded for grading purposes because the acquired skill a student brings with him/her to any skills class is commonly assigned more value in grading than improvement.

HOOKS BASEBALL TEST BATTERY
(Hooks, 1959)

Purpose:

The original study was designed to determine the relative importance of various structural and strength measures in predicting success in the performance of common baseball skills. The test battery used by Hooks in that study merits consideration for use by coaches and physical education instructors.

Description:

The Hooks Test Battery includes tests for skill in hitting, running, throwing and fielding.

Educational Application:

Original study used college men, but battery is adaptable to high school boys.

Time:

Specific items in the test battery lend themselves well to economy of time in testing; however, to use the whole battery would require at least one 40-minute class period per test item.

Personnel:

More than one instructor would be ideal for judging hitting ability while one instructor with student assistants should suffice for the other test items.

Equipment and Supplies:

Automatic pitching machine plus balls, bats, gloves and stop watch; line marking and scoring materials, plus a rope at least eight to 10 feet in length.

Facilities and Space:

Regulation baseball field.

Directions:

Hitting. The student stands in the batter's box and hits balls pitched by an automatic pitching machine until told to stop. Hooks' rating form may be used or the instructor may choose to develop his/her own.

Running. Utilizing a start commonly recommended for stealing bases and one in which the student feels comfortable, the time recorded to the 10th of a second in running from home plate to second base is the criterion for running ability. The student leaves the batter's box on the command "Go" and is required to touch first and second base.

Throwing. As described in Kelson's Classification Plan (first test presented in this chapter), the baseball throw for distance is used to test throwing ability.

Fielding. Three tests are used in measuring fielding skill: a ball toss test, a ball pick-up test and a test to determine the ability to catch fly balls. The ball toss test begins with the subject stationed directly underneath a rope extended horizontally at a height of 10 feet. On a command to start, the subject tosses the ball over the rope and catches it on the opposite side. This is continued for a period of 30 seconds.

To initiate the ball pick-up test, the tester assumes a position at the highest point of a 90-degree angle with sides extended 8 1/2 feet. The subject takes a crouched position between the two lines and faces the tester. On the command to start, the tester rolls a baseball down one side of the angle for the subject to catch and return. The tester then rolls the ball down the other line of the angle for the subject to field and toss back. The subject returns the ball as many times as possible in 30 seconds.

The test of catching fly balls begins with the subject standing on a line 60 yards from the tester. Eight successive fly balls are hit to the subject. The subject is instructed to catch the balls on the fly and toss them to a student assistant. The subject should disregard any ground balls hit to him.

Scoring Method:

Hitting ability is scored by adding the sum of the instructor's objective ratings. Running ability is scored by recording the best running time of two trials.

The score for throwing is the best of three throws measured to the nearest yard. This test differs from the Kelson Classification Plan as that test is scored by measuring the throws to the nearest foot.

Fielding skill is assigned a score by adding the total of the three fielding tests. The score for the ball toss test is the number of times the subject tosses the ball over the rope in a 30-second time period. The ball pick-up test score reflects the number of times the subject returns the ball to the tester in 30 seconds. The fly ball catching score is the number of balls caught on the fly.

Validity and Reliability:

The major purpose of Hooks' study was not to validate the skills he used to represent baseball ability; therefore, those skills were not correlated with a criterion for baseball playing ability. All the tests show a degree of acceptable face validity, possibly with the exception of the fielding tests, excluding the catching fly balls item.

Additional Comments:

The value of this test could possibly be significantly increased if the test requirements were validated. The apparent face validity of the items should be confirmed.

At first glance the reliability of the ball pick-up test and the test of catching fly balls may seem questionable due to the seemingly strong chance for error in consistency on the part of the tester. However, the high reliability coefficients obtained by Hooks demonstrated a high degree of consistency in test-retest performance of the students on the five baseball skill items.

Baseball References

Cobb, J.W. (1958). *The determination of the merits of selected items for the construction of a baseball skill test for boys of Little League age.* Unpublished doctoral dissertation, Indiana University, Bloomington.

Fry, J.B. (1958). *The relationship between a baseball skill test and actual playing in game situations.* Unpublished master's thesis, Pennsylvania State University, University Park.

Hooks, G.E. (1959). Prediction of baseball ability through an analysis of measures of strength and structure. *Research Quarterly* 30: 38-43.

Kelson, R.E. (1953). Baseball classification plan for boys. *Research Quarterly* 24: 304-307.

Sheehan, F.E. (1954). *Baseball achievement scales for elementary and junior high school boys.* Unpublished master's thesis, University of Wisconsin, Madison.

Chapter 5

BASKETBALL

INTRODUCTION

The sport of basketball is rich in the quantity of developed skills tests, but the quality of many tests is unsubstantiated by scientific evidence. Perhaps more skills tests have been devised in basketball than any other physical education activity.

The tests presented in this chapter are limited primarily to those with value for the measurement of student achievement and classification of students according to ability levels. Some of them are reputed to show value as determinants of potential basketball ability.

JOHNSON BASKETBALL TEST
(Johnson, 1934)

Purpose:

To measure basic shooting, dribbling and throwing skills in boys' basketball.

Educational Application:

High school boys.

Description:

The ability test is composed of a field goal test item, basketball throw for accuracy and dribbling item.

Time:

One 40-minute class period for 15 to 20 students in a mass testing situation.

Personnel:

Instructor and trained assistants to serve as timers and scorers.

Equipment and Supplies:

Three basketballs, four chairs, materials to construct the wall target in the throw for accuracy test, scoring materials and stop watch.

Facilities and Space:

Gymnasium with unobstructed wall space.

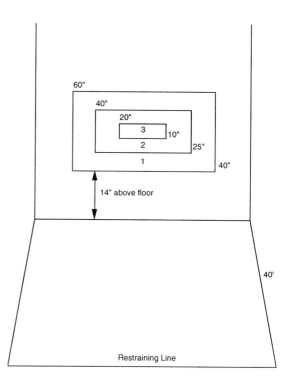

Fig. 5.1 Target for basketball throw for accuracy test.

From: Johnson, L.W. (1934). *Objective tests in basketball for high school boys.* Unpublished master's thesis, University of Iowa, Iowa City. Copyright by author.

Directions:

One practice trial per test item is recommended.

Field Goal Speed. Holding a basketball and standing at a position of his choice, the subject shoots lay-ups as rapidly as possible for 30 seconds.

Throw for Accuracy. The subject completes 10 trials at a target with dimensions as described in Figure 5.1. Either a hook or baseball type throw is recommended.

Dribble. On the starting signal, the subject leaves the starting line by dribbling to the left of the first chair and then to the right of the next chair. This pattern of direction is continued for 30 seconds (Figure 5.2).

Scoring Method and Norms:

The number of shots made in 30 seconds is the score for the field goal speed test. The score for the dribbling item is the number of chairs passed in 30 seconds. Utilizing a 3-2-1 scoring method from inner to outer rectangles, the total number of points represents the score for the throw for accuracy item.

Validity and Reliability:

One hundred and eighty boys were divided into groups referred to as "good" or "poor." The "good" group contained 50 boys and the "poor" group had a total of 130. The individual test items ranged from .65 to .79 in validity values. The reliability values ranged from .73 to .80.

Criterion Measure:

Success in winning a berth on a basketball squad.

Additional Comments:

This well-constructed test originated from a potential battery of 19 items. Norms for the Johnson Test have been established for grades seven through 12. Therefore, it is important to remember that test conditions should be standardized for the particular grade level. For example, Jacobson (Jacobson, 1960) used a 35-foot restraining line in the throw for accuracy test when testing seventh grade boys and a 42-foot line for assessing eighth and ninth grade boys. The original test for high school boys called for a 40-foot restraining line.

Test administrators should also be aware of the potential difference in test scores on the field goal speed item if a net is not used. Norms based on shots made in a netless goal might reflect greater achievement due to the time factor difference.

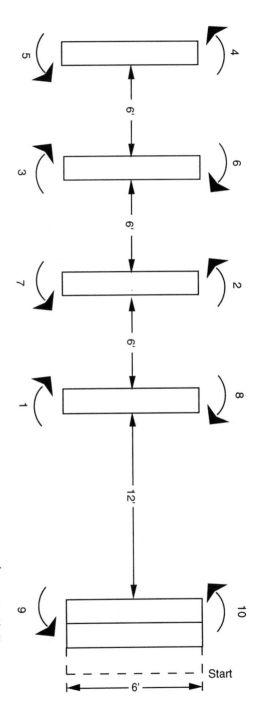

Fig. 5.2 Layout for dribbling test.

From Johnson, L.W. (1934). *Objective tests in basketball for high school boys.* Unpublished master's thesis, University of Iowa, Iowa City. Copyright by author.

	Table 5.1									
	NORMS FOR THE JOHNSON BASKETBALL TEST									
	Throw for Accuracy*			Field Goad Speed Test			Dribble Test			
T-Score	7th Grade	8th Grade	9th Grade	7th Grade	8th Grade	9th Grade	7th Grade	8th Grade	9th Grade	T-Score
85	25	23	25	14	19	22	24	26	26	85
80	23	21	23	13	18	21	23	25	26	80
75	21	19	20	12	16	19	22	24	25	75
70	19	16	18	10	14	17	21	23	24	70
65	16	14	16	9	13	15	20	22	22	65
60	14	12	14	7	11	12	19	20	21	60
55	11	10	11	6	9	10	18	19	20	55
50	9	8	9	5	7	8	17	18	19	50
45	7	5	7	4	6	6	16	17	18	45
40	4	3	4	2	4	4	15	16	17	40
35	2	1	2	1	2	2	14	15	16	35
30							13	14	15	30
25							12	13	14	25
20							11	12	13	20
15							10	11	12	15

*35-foot restraining line for 7th grade boys; 42-foot restraining line for 8th and 9th grade boys.

From: Jacobson, T.V. (1960). *An evaluation of performance in certain physical ability tests administered to selected secondary school boys.* Unpublished master's thesis, University of Washington, Seattle. Copyright by author.

	Table 5.2			
	GRADE RANGES FOR THE JOHNSON BASKETBALL ABILITY TEST			
Event	Grade	(Based on the Raw Scores) 7th Grade	8th Grade	9th Grade
Basketball Throw (In points)	A	18 & over	16 & over	18 & over
	B	13 - 17	11 - 15	13 - 17
	C	7 - 12	6 - 10	7 - 12
	D	1 - 6	1 - 5	1 - 6
	E	0	0	0
Basketball Shooting (Baskets made)	A	10 & over	14 & over	16 & over
	B	7 - 9	10 - 13	12 - 15
	C	4 - 6	6 - 9	7 - 11
	D	1 - 3	2 - 5	2 - 6
	E	0	1 & under	1 & under
Basketball Dribbling (In points)	A	21 & over	23 & over	24 & over
	B	19 - 20	20 - 22	21 - 23
	C	16 - 18	18 - 19	18 - 20
	D	14 - 15	15 - 17	16 - 17
	E	13 & under	14 & under	15 & under
Total Test (Total points)	A	46 & over	48 & over	53 & over
	B	37 - 45	39 - 47	43 - 52
	C	27 - 36	29 - 38	32 - 42
	D	18 - 26	20 - 28	22 - 31
	E	17 & under	19 & under	21 & under

From: Jacobson, T.V. (1960). *An evaluation of performance in certain physical ability tests administered to selected secondary school boys.* Unpublished master's thesis, University of Washington, Seattle. Copyright by author.

YOUNG-MOSER BASKETBALL ABILITY TEST
(Young & Moser, 1934)

Purpose:

To measure basketball playing ability of females.

Description:

Originally published in a five-item test, only three are presented here due to the low reliability values shown for the other two items. The wall speed test measures speed of passing with the moving target item assessing passing accuracy. The bounce and shoot test measures shooting accuracy.

Bounce and Shoot. As shown in Figure 5.3, a perpendicular is dropped from the center of the backboard to the floor. A semicircle with a radius of 15 feet is drawn with the aforementioned point as the center. Other necessary drawings include two radii that form a right angle with each other and a 45-degree angle with the diameter of the semicircle. Also, straight lines are drawn a foot long where the radii and circumferences inter-sect.

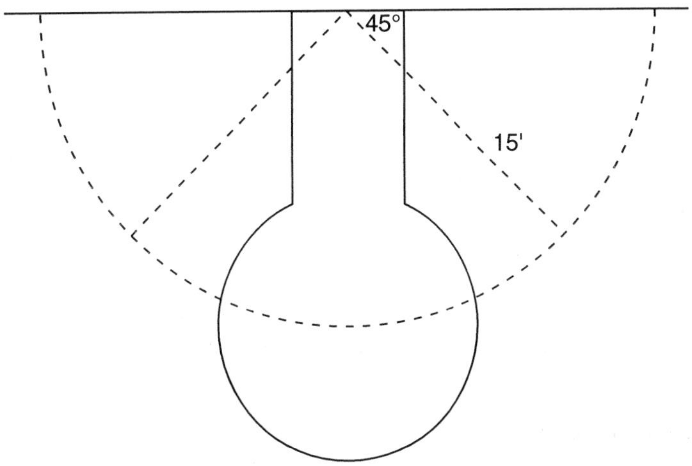

Fig. 5.3 Diagram for bounce and shoot test.

From: Young, G. & Moser, H. (1934). A short battery of tests to measure playing ability in women's basketball. *Research Quarterly* 5: 3-23. Reprinted with permission from AAHPERD.

Moving Target. The target is suspended so that its lower edge is three feet and nine inches from the floor. The point from which it hangs is 11 feet from the floor. The six-inch rope attached to the ring is fastened to the rods that brace the backboard of the basket, at the place were they intersect. (Adjustments must be made for different types of backboard construction.) A line 10 feet from the target is drawn on the floor from which the throws are made (a perpendicular is dropped from the target as it hangs straight, the place where the perpendicular touches the floor is marked and the 10 feet are measured from that point). Two lines, five feet apart, are drawn on the wall behind the target so that the midpoint between them lies directly behind a perpendicular dropped from the center of the target (Figure 5.4).

Educational Application:

High school girls and college women.

Time:

In a mass testing setup, one 60-minute period for 15 to 20 students.

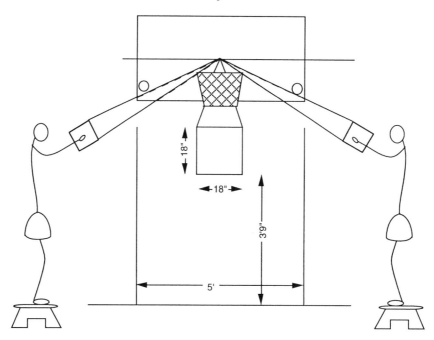

Fig. 5.4 Test layout for moving target item.

From: Young, G., & Moser, H. (1934). A short battery of tests to measure playing ability in women's basketball. *Research Quarterly* 5: 3-23. Reprinted with permission from AAHPERD.

Personnel:

A scorer for each test and a timer for the wall speed pass item. The two assistants designated to swing the target in the moving target test should show thorough familiarity with that assignment prior to testing.

Equipment and Supplies:

At least three basketballs, one stop watch and materials for scoring and construction of target which is made of one-inch board and is 18 inches square.

Facilities and Space:

Gymnasium with flat-surfaced wall.

Directions:

Bounce and Shoot. The shooting accuracy test is initiated with the student facing the basket on the right-hand side and holding the ball. The ball is bounced toward the basket and a lay-up is shot. The same action is repeated on the left side, and the sides are alternated thereafter. Ten trials are allowed.

Moving Target. Standing behind the line with ball in hands, the subject waits for two student assistants to initiate the test for passing accuracy. The students stand on each side of the target with one holding the target at a position whereby the lower inside edge of the target is six feet from the floor at release. The target is held with the palms flat and is released by simply releasing the grasp. The second student catches the target and repeats the procedure in like manner. Release time for the target is not announced, but the subject is given time to get ready. Any type of pass may be used with 10 opportunities given. The subject attempts to hit the swinging target as it passes through the five-foot area marked on the wall.

Wall Speed Pass. To measure the speed of passing, the subject stands behind a six-foot restraining line while facing the wall and holding a basketball. At the sound of a whistle, the subject throws the ball against the wall, catches the rebound and continues this procedure until the 30-second trial is completed. The type of stance and pass used is the student's choice, but she must always keep both feet behind the line preceding each pass. Two trials are given.

Scoring Method:

The number of successful baskets is the bounce and shoot score, while the number of times the ball strikes any part of the target as it passes through the five-foot area is the moving target score. The score for the wall speed pass is the combined number of hits made in the two 30-second trials.

Validity and Reliability:

A correlation coefficient of .86 was found between judges' ratings of playing ability and test scores of the original five items. Reliability estimates of the three test items presented ranged from .89 to .90.

Additional Comments:

The three items presented show merit as tests of specific skill and could have value as part of a more comprehensive battery. The battery lends itself well to time and ease of administration since student assistants can be utilized both extensively and effectively.

WISCONSIN BASKETBALL TEST
(Glassow, Colvin & Schwarz, 1938)

Purpose:

To measure basketball playing ability of college women.

Description:

Bounce and Shoot. As shown in Figure 5.5, an 18-foot dotted line is drawn at a 45-degree angle on each side of the basket. The lines originate from a spot directly below the center of the backboard. Perpendicular to the 18-foot lines are 24-inch lines. One foot behind and 30 inches to the outside of the 18-foot lines, additional 18-inch lines are drawn. A chair with a ball is placed at each of these areas.

Zone Toss. A zone six feet, four inches wide is marked on the floor. An inside dotted line, six inches from each boundary line, is included. Jump standards bisect the zone and are placed parallel to the boundary lines at 10 feet apart with a rope strung between them. The height of the rope is seven feet, one inch from the floor.

Wall Speed. A line is drawn six feet from and parallel to the wall.

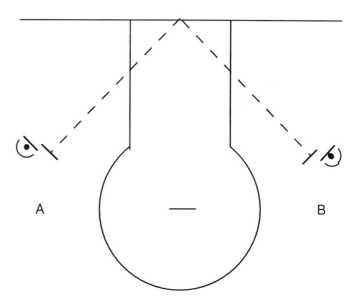

Fig. 5.5 Specifications for bounce and shoot test.

From: Glassow, R.B., Colvin, V., & Schwarz, M.M. (1938). Studies measuring basketball playing ability of college women. *Research Quarterly* 9: 60-68. Reprinted with permission from AAHPERD.

Educational Application:

College women.

Time:

Using a rotational plan, a class of 30 students divided into four stations could be tested in two 40-minute class periods.

Personnel:

The bounce and shoot test requires a timer, scorer and two ball catchers. The zone toss test and wall speed item each requires a timer and scorer.

Equipment and Supplies:

Four basketballs, two stop watches, two chairs, two jump standards, one 12-foot rope, plus floor marking, target and scoring materials.

Facilities and Space:

Gymnasium with at least one flat-surfaced wall.

Directions:

Bounce and Shoot. Standing at the 24-inch line on the B side of the basket, the subject when signaled to begin picks up the ball from the chair, shoots, recovers the rebound and passes the ball back to the catcher at B (Figure 5.5). The subject runs immediately to A, picks up the ball from the chair and repeats the aforementioned action. This action is continued, alternating five times on each side. Each of the 10 repetitions must begin from behind the 24-inch line on the appropriate side.

In addition to regular timing and scoring, the timer notes and records the fouls while the scorer keeps an account of the number of shots and notifies the timer on the ninth shot taken. Fouls include traveling, double bounces and failure to begin from behind the 24-inch line.

Zone Toss. The subject holds the ball, faces the zone and, on the timer's signal, tosses the ball over the rope and retrieves it on the other side. Ten tosses are completed on an alternate basis. Each toss should be made from outside the zone boundaries, but a penalty is not assessed unless the subject's foot crosses the six-inch line. Fouls include tossing the ball under the rope or crossing the six-inch line before the ball is tossed.

Wall Speed Pass. See Young-Moser Basketball Ability Test presented earlier in this chapter.

Scoring Method:

Bounce and Shoot. The time and accuracy scores are combined for each trial. The best two of three trials for score are suggested by the test constructors, but only one trial of 10 shots is recommended when time is a factor. One second is added to the time score for each foul made. The time score is measured to the nearest 10th of a second.

The accuracy score is the number of points made in 10 shots at the basket. Two points are counted for each basket made, one for hitting the rim but missing the basket and zero for missing both the basket and the rim.

The time and accuracy scores are converted to *T*-scores which are added. The sum divided by two is the final score.

Zone Toss. The sum of two trials is recommended for the final score. The developers of the test suggested that the best four trials of six be used, but this arrangement detracts from its feasibility in time of administration. Time to the nearest 10th of a second is measured for the 10 tosses. A second is added for each foul.

Wall Speed. The sum score of the two trials is official. The number of hits in 30 seconds constitutes a trial.

Validity and Reliability:

With 54 college women providing the data, the investigators experimented with five test items. The three items selected showed a multiple R of .66 which was as valid as the five-test combination. Test-retest reliability values ranged from .74 to .82 on the three tests as computed from the test scores of 51 physical education majors.

Criterion Measure:

Judges' ratings of playing ability.

Additional Comments:

Montoye (Montoye, 1970) referred to the common criticism given to the bounce and shoot item, i.e., the variability of the time and accuracy elements. For example, one element could suffer as a result of an intense concentration on the other. He suggested that someone should experiment with a revision of the test which would include a constant time variable in the bounce and shoot item.

Lambert (Lambert, 1969) revised the bounce and shoot item of the Wisconsin Test by omitting the fouls of traveling with the ball, double bounce and failure to start from behind the 24-inch line. Twenty-five women varsity basketball players were tested on the revised version, and some significant findings resulted. The revision was shown to be statistically valid, reliable and administratively feasible. Also, a combination of twice time plus accuracy was determined to be the most valid and reliable method for scoring the bounce and shoot item for either the original or revised version.

DYER-SCHURIG-APGAR BASKETBALL TEST
(Dyer, Schurig & Apgar, 1939)

Purpose:

To measure basketball playing ability of college women and high school girls.

Description:

The four-item test resulted from a fundamental skills analysis which placed basketball skills into general categories of ball handling, shooting and jumping. Several skills test items were experimented with before Dyer and her associates settled upon the four comprising this test. They felt that the four items comprehensively measure motor ability in basketball.

Educational Application:

College women, junior and senior high school girls.

Time:

Two 40-minute class periods for a class of 15 to 20 students.

Personnel:

One examiner per test item with two trained assistants for the moving target test. The Edgren Ball Handling Test may require the use of both a timer and scorer.

Equipment and Supplies:

Four basketballs, three chairs, one stop watch; rope, boards, paper, harness straps, rings, strips of wood and chalk or tape as specified in the test directions; scoring materials.

Facilities and Space:

Gymnasium with unobstructed wall space.

Description and Directions:

Moving Target. A chalk line is drawn 10 feet from and parallel to the plane of target movement. Two lines, five feet apart, are drawn on the wall behind the target so that the center of the target lies midway between them when it is in a motionless state.

The target is 18 inches square and constructed of one-inch boards with a reinforcement of 1 x 4 material; the weight is approximately four pounds. The target is suspended by ropes from a height of 11 feet above the floor; the lower edge is three feet, nine inches above the floor. Harness straps are used in attaching the ropes to the corners at the top of the target and to the point of suspension. The target may be suspended from the back of the basketball backboard, or from any object of proper height (see Figure 5.4 in this chapter).

An assistant prepares the target for motion by pulling it to the side at a position six feet from the floor. The target is held with the palms of the hands and released by simply parting the hands. If the assistant pushes the target, the trial should be repeated. The assistant on the other side repeats the action and the target is released alternately from right to left.

The subject holds the ball behind the 10-foot restraining line and passes the ball at the target as it swings through the five-foot area. The subject receives no warning when the target is released, and the assistant must be certain that the subject is ready before releasing the target. Ten passes are made by each subject.

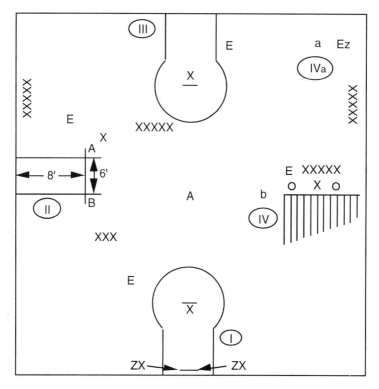

Fig. 5.6 Floor plan for Dyer-Schurig-Apgar Basketball Test.

From: Dyer, J.T., Schurig, J.C., & Apgar, S.L. (1939). A basketball motor ability test for college women and secondary school girls. *Research Quarterly* 10: 128-147. Reprinted with permission from AAHPERD.

Edgren Ball Handling. Standing behind the eight-foot restraining line in area A as illustrated in Figure 5.6, the subject passes the ball against the wall at an angle whereby the ball will rebound in area B. The student runs across the six-foot area to recover the pass. This action is repeated as rapidly as possible until 10 legal passes are recovered. A fumbled or lost ball must be recovered and thrown from the proper area, and any ball recovered in the six-foot area must be dribbled to the proper area before passing again. At least one foot must be outside the six-foot area on all passes. One foot may be in the air during passes but not touching the floor inside the six-foot area. Violations in procedure require that the test item be repeated after a rest period. Each subject performs two test trials with intervening rest periods.

Bounce and Shoot. The subject assumes a position behind the center of the free throw line, then bounces the ball out of the free throw circle and attempts a basket. Alternating right and left, 10 trials are performed. Another student should recover the ball for the subject being tested. A trial is repeated if the subject's feet are not outside the circle or if a dribbling violation occurs.

Free Jump and Reach. A reach scale must be constructed on large size brown paper. The paper is designed in graduated half-inches from 70 to 90 inches and attached to a clear wall space so that the bottom of the scale is 70 inches from the floor.

For use as a jump target, 24 strips of wood are attached to a board that is attached to the wall and hung level with the floor. The strips are graduated in length from one to 24 inches. They are numbered from one to 24 and allowed to hang free from the board. The target is hung by some convenient method in such a way that the shortest strip is unreachable by the tallest female when jumping. The exact distance from the floor to only one strip needs to be determined as the distance of the other strips can be calculated from that measurement.

After a practice trial, the subject faces the reach scale and with her preferred hand reaches as high as possible to place the palm flat on the scale. Undue stretching is not permitted. The middle finger location is recorded to the nearest half-inch to represent the subject's reach height. The examiner should stand on a chair to read the distance, since his/her eyes should be level with or above the particular reach height.

After the reach height is taken, the subject proceeds to the jump target station and stands beneath the target. From a stationary position and again with the preferred hand, she jumps and reaches toward one of the strips, attempting to cause it to swing. The height of the highest strip the subject is able to move is recorded as the jump height.

Scoring Method:

Moving Target. The number of successful target hits in 10 trials.

Edgren Ball Handling. The elapsed time from the starting signal until the tenth throw hits the hands of the subject in area A. The better performance of two trials is recorded.

Bounce and Shoot. Two points for each successful basket and one for hitting the rim but not entering. Sum of points made in 10 trials is official score.

Free Jump and Reach. The difference between the reach and jump height measured to the nearest half-inch is recorded.

Validity and Reliability:

Test scores were accumulated from the performance of students enrolled in two colleges, one high school and one junior high school. Validity coefficients were computed to determine the relationship between the test scores of each school group and each of three performance criteria. These relationships ranged from .76 to .91.

The whole test battery was administered on a test-retest basis to two of the school groups. Reliability coefficients of .89 and .90 were obtained with 39 and 35 students participating in the respective groups.

Criterion Measure:

Three criteria were used: the examiner's rank order list of the students by playing ability in each group; an expert judgment criterion for two groups; and an examiner rating of game play performance for one group.

KNOX BASKETBALL TEST
(Knox, 1947)

Purpose:

To measure basketball ability.

Description:

The four-item test includes a speed dribble item to test dribbling ability; a speed pass to assess passing ability; a dribble-shoot item that tests a combination of ability to dribble and shoot; and a penny-cup test which is designed to measure reaction time. The original intent of the test was for classification purposes, but it seems to have merit as a tool for measurement of achievement. Therefore, it may show value for grading student progress.

Educational Application:

High school boys.

Time:

Two 60-minute class periods for 15 students in a rotational test plan.

Personnel:

A timer and scorer for each test; the instructor should give the verbal commands in the penny-cup item.

Equipment and Supplies:

Ten chairs; three regulation basketballs; four stop watches; three tin cups (coffee cans are suggested, one painted blue, one red and one white); scoring materials; plus an ample supply of tape and pennies.

Facilities and Space:

Gymnasium with unobstructed wall space.

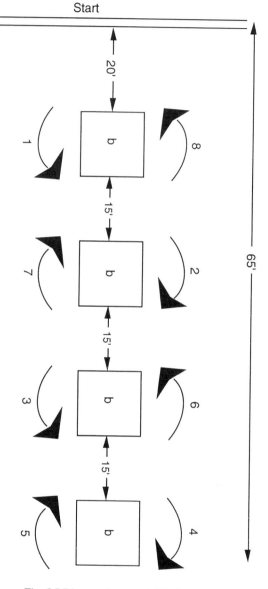

Fig. 5.7 Diagram for speed dribble test.

From: Knox, R.D. (1947). Basketball ability tests. *Scholastic Coach* 17: 45-47. Reprinted with permission from Scholastic Coach.

Directions:

Speed Dribble. Standing in back of the restraining line with hands on knees, the subject begins on the starting command by picking up the ball and dribbling it in the direction shown in Figure 5.7. Time is recorded from the starting signal until the subject crosses the finish line.

Speed Pass. The subject stands behind a line which is marked parallel to the wall and five feet away. Using a chest pass, the subject passes the ball against the wall 15 times as fast as possible. Time is recorded from the starting signal until the ball hits the wall the 15th time. The test is repeated if any rebound requires the student to take more than one step for recovery.

Dribble-Shoot. Utilizing the speed dribble testing procedure with three chairs, the subject must make a basket before the return dribble. More than one shot may be required. The subject chooses the type of shot, but the one-handed lay-up is recommended.

Penny-Cup. The test is initiated with the subject standing on the starting line with his back to the cups and a penny in one hand. On the command to start, the subject turns, runs, and when crossing the signal line, the test administrator gives him a direction signal. The subject proceeds in the direction of the cup corresponding to the signal and places the penny in that cup. A verbal command of "red," "white" or "blue" indicates the desired direction. The elapsed time between the starting signal and the sound of the penny falling into the cup is recorded. The test should be given privately to each individual to ensure consistency in test conditions. Four trials are given.

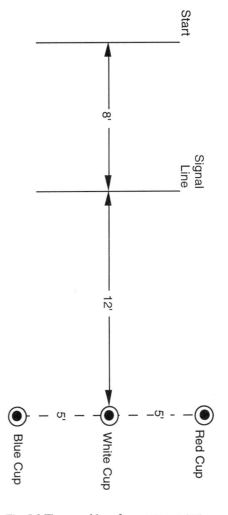

Fig. 5.8 Floor markings for penny-cup test.

From: Knox, R.D. (1947). Basketball ability tests. *Scholastic Coach* 17: 45-47. Reprinted with permission from Scholastic Coach.

Scoring Method:

Speed Dribble. The number of expired seconds from the starting signal until the subject crosses the finish line.

Speed Pass. The number of seconds from the starting command until the ball hits the wall the 15th time.

Dribble-Shoot. The number of seconds taken in completing the test.

Penny-Cup. The total number of seconds required to perform the four test trials.

Validity and Reliability:

The test was validated on the basis of the number of boys selected to high school basketball teams. There was 80 percent agreement between the test scores and squad membership with 81 percent agreement on the ability to make the starting team. Two hundred and sixty boys served as subjects in the test selection.

A reliability coefficient of .88 was derived for the test battery by use of the test-retest method with 50 boys participating. The individual items ranged from a .58 coefficient of correlation on the dribble-shoot item to a .90 relationship for the penny-cup test.

Criterion Measure:

Success in making a 10-man squad and winning a starting berth on a high school basketball team.

Additional Comments:

The results of the Knox Basketball Test are impressive; the 10 best total scores in each school represented in the study were made by the 10 boys who were varsity players, and the five best scores were made by members of the first team. Furthermore, Knox predicted 61 of 68 squad members and 29 of 36 first team members. However, investigators who have studied the Knox Test are not in agreement on its value as a classifier for competition (Boyd, 1955; Glines & Peterson, 1967; Loose, 1961; Randall, 1958). Conclusions from study results ranged from a rating of "high regard" to "little value demonstrated."

KOSKI BASKETBALL CLASSIFICATION TEST
(Koski, 1950)

Purpose:

To classify students into ability groups as measured by dribbling and field goal shooting skills; to serve as an aid in evaluation of student ability.

Description:

The test consists of two items that are commonly included in basketball skills tests, field goal shooting and dribbling. The dribbling item requires 12 folding chairs for use as obstacles. The chairs are placed in two rows of six each with the rows six feet apart. The six-foot distance is measured from the outside leg of one chair to the outside leg of its counterpart. The distance between two chairs is eight feet, as measured from the front leg of one chair to the front leg of the chair directly behind it. The starting point is centered in the middle of the distance between pairs of chairs and located six feet from the first pair (Figure 5.9).

Educational Application:

Designed for college men but appropriate for college women and high school boys and girls.

Time:

If two testers are available, a class of 20 students could be tested in one 40-minute class session.

Personnel:

The instructor of a class should probably serve as scorer for the dribbling test because its degree of difficulty in scoring is greater than the field goal shooting item. Student assistants may serve as timer and scorer for the shooting test.

Equipment and Supplies:

Basketball, two stop watches, 12 folding chairs, scoring materials and line marking materials for the dribbling test. Ordinarily these lines would not be necessary but are advantageous as time savers when a student inadvertently bumps a chair, causing an inconsistency in distance between two chairs. Strips of tape or chalk marks should suffice as distance markers.

Facilities and Space:

A basketball court with a regulation goal.

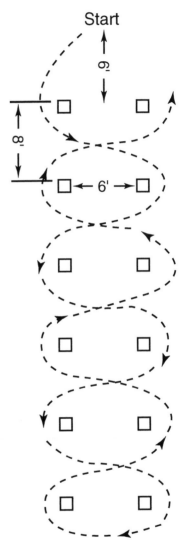

Fig. 5.9 Floor plan for dribbling test.

From: Koski, W.A. (1950). *A basketball classification test.* Unpublished master's thesis, University of Michigan, Ann Arbor. Copyright by author.

Directions:

Dribbling. The subject holds a basketball while assuming a position behind the starting line. On the starting signal, the subject dribbles around the first obstacle on the right and continues in the manner outlined in Figure 5.9 The time period for the test is 30 seconds. When the subject is beside or beyond a chair, it is considered a completed obstacle. A subject that completes the 12 obstacles in less than 30 seconds should continue on as shown in the test diagram.

Field Goal Shooting. The student takes a position in front of the basket while holding a basketball. On the starting signal, the first shot is taken and rebounded. Succeeding shots may be taken anywhere on the floor. This action is continuous for 30 seconds.

Scoring Method:

The number of obstacles the subject passes is the final score in the dribbling test. The number of goals made in 30 seconds constitutes the official shooting test score.

Validity and Reliability:

Coefficients of correlation for validity were .87 for the dribbling test and .78 for the field goal item. The two-item battery showed an *r* of .93. The criterion measure was the subjective ratings of physical education instructors.

Reliability coefficients of .85 for the dribbling test and .78 for the field goal item were determined, using the test-retest method with 71 male college freshmen participating. The two-item battery coefficient was .88.

Additional Comments:

Koski's original intent was to develop a four-item test battery, but two items were eliminated due to low reliability values. The reliability value of the two items finally included in the test, especially that of the field goal test, could probably be strengthened if multiple trials were given instead of only one trial. However, Koski's findings substantiated the scientific authenticity of the two test items included. Authentic basketball tests commonly include dribbling and 30-second field goal tests either identical or related to those in the Koski Test.

STROUP BASKETBALL TEST
(Stroup, 1955)

Purpose:

To measure basketball playing ability of college men and high school boys.

Description:

The three-item battery includes tests for shooting, passing and dribbling skills.

Educational Application:

College men and high school boys.

Time:

Two 60-minute class periods. If an adequate number of testing stations and trained assistants are available, only one period is necessary.

Personnel:

Instructor and two trained assistants per testing station.

Training Involved:

A brief warm-up should be permitted immediately prior to testing. One practice trial is given for the dribbling test.

Equipment and Supplies:

Regulation basketball goal, three basketballs, seven Indian clubs or substitute markers, three stop watches, scoring materials and tape for the wall marking in the passing test item.

Facilities and Space:

Gymnasium with some unobstructed wall space.

Directions:

Goal Shooting. On a starting signal, the student may be standing at any position on the court. He shoots as many baskets as possible in one minute, retrieving the ball himself after each shot.

Wall Passing. At the command to start, the subject while standing behind a six-foot restraining line begins passing the ball against the wall and continues as many times as possible in one minute.

Dribbling. Seven Indian clubs are placed in a line 15 feet apart for a 90-foot distance with the subject stationed at a starting line 15 feet from the first club. On the command to begin, the subject dribbles the ball in zigzag fashion through the clubs. Dribbling is initiated from left to right and the end club must be circled each time. Dribbling continues for one minute.

Scoring Method and Norms:

Goal Shooting. One point for each basket made in a one-minute time period.

Wall Passing. The number of legal passes made in one minute. A pass is disallowed if the subject steps over the restraining line as he passes or if he bats the ball instead of catching it.

Dribbling. The number of clubs the subject passes properly within the one-minute time span. A club must be passed on the proper side to count. Also, no point is given if a club is knocked over.

Validity and Reliability:

The test was validated on the performance of 121 college students. Test scores revealed a correlation coefficient of .83 with student opinion of basketball ability. The test was also validated by a comparison of game scores and average test scores of the competing teams. In a series of 41 games, each 10 minutes in length, the teams with higher skill score average won approximately 84 percent of games played in intraclass competition.

Reliability estimates for the test battery were not reported.

Additional Comments:

The directions for the Stroup Test failed to mention whether or not multiple trials are recommended for the test items. Multiple trials should promote a maximum reliability value because the influence of a learning effect is always a possibility when limited practice and only one trial are permitted in skills tests administration.

Table 5.3
STROUP BASKETBALL TEST SCALE SCORES*

Shooting	Passing	Dribbling	Score	Shooting	Passing	Dribbling	Score
6	53	27	51	26	80		79
7	55		52	27	81	44	80
8	56	28	53		82		81
9	57	29	54	28		45	82
	59	30	55	29	83		83
10	60	31	56		84	46	84
11	61		57	30	85		85
12	62	32	58		86	47	86
13	64	33	59	31	87		87
14	65	34	60	32	88	48	88
	66		61		89	49	89
15		35	62	33	90	50	90
16	67		63	34	91		91
	68	36	64	35	93	51	92
17	69		65	36	94		93
	70	37	66	37	95	52	94
18			67		97		95
19	71	38	68	38	98	53	96
	72		69	39	99		97
20	73	39	70	40	100	54	98
21			71	41	102	55	99
	74	40	72	42	103	56	100
22	75		73	*Based on performance of 121 college men.			
23	76	41	74				
	77		75	From: Stroup, F. (1955). Game results as a criterion for validating basketball skill tests. *Research Quarterly* 26: 353-357. Reprinted with permission from AAHPERD.			
24	78	42	76				
			77				
25	79	43	78				

PIMPA MODIFICATION OF BUNN BASKETBALL TEST
(Pimpa, 1968)

Purpose:

To measure basketball playing ability of high school boys and college men.

Description:

The Pimpa Modification of the Bunn Basketball Test (Bunn, 1959) is used to classify students for instruction and competition. The two-item battery correlated highly with Bunn's six-item test battery for both skilled and unskilled players, making it more functional with regard to time and efficiency of administration. The alternate lay-up test measures the amount of time taken in completing 10 successful alternating lay-up shots. The penny-cup test item measures the subject's level of agility and reaction time.

Educational Application:

Junior and senior high boys and college men.

Time:

Provided an adequate number of testing stations and stop watches are available, a class of 15 to 20 students can be tested in one 60-minute class period.

Personnel:

Two instructors are preferable to maximize the use of time. Student assistants are also needed to serve as timers. One instructor could possibly administer the tests with the help of student assistants.

Equipment and Supplies:

One basketball and goal plus a stop watch or sweep-hand wrist watch for the lay-up item. Three tin cups and several pennies for each testing area in addition to a stop watch for the penny-cup item. Red, white and blue tape or paint is put on the cups. Scoring materials are necessary accessories.

Facilities and Space:

The alternate lay-up test requires a facility with a regulation basketball goal and free of obstacles within a reasonable distance from the basket. An unobstructed floor space at least 30 feet in length and 10 feet in width is needed for the penny-cup test.

Directions:

Alternate Lay-up. Starting on his choice of the side to the basket and a verbal command of "Go," the subject completes 10 successful alternate lay-ups as quickly as possible. The shots are alternated regardless of the circumstances that prevail during the shooting of the 10 lay-ups.

Penny-Cup. The test begins with the subject standing on the starting line with his back to the cups and holding a penny in his hand. With a person stationed behind each cup, preferably an instructor, the student commences on the "Go" signal and runs to the cup to which a direction signal has been given and drops in a penny. The signal is either "red," "white" or "blue." A timer is assigned for each of the three colors.

The time for the particular color measures the time that elapses between the starting signal and the sound of the penny falling into the cup. The time taken to return and prepare for the next trial is not recorded. The process is repeated four times in random order.

Scoring Method:

The alternate lay-up test is scored by recording the amount of time required to make 10 alternate lay-ups. The score for the penny-cup test is the sum of times required in the four trials.

Validity and Reliability:

A correlation coefficient of .88 was obtained between the scores of 50 skilled subjects on the six-item Bunn Test and two-item Pimpa Modification. The relationship of scores on the two tests for 50 unskilled subjects was .95.

Reliability estimates were not reported.

Criterion Measure:

Bunn's Basketball Skill Test was used by Pimpa as the criterion measure. He found that the alternate lay-up and the penny-cup tests appear comprehensive enough to measure general basketball skill.

Additional Comments:

The Pimpa Modification of the Bunn Basketball Test appears to have merit as a test for classification purposes. The test's high relationship with Bunn's rather comprehensive measure of basketball skill substantiates its value as an adequate test of basketball skill, assuming the six-item Bunn Test demonstrates content or face validity.

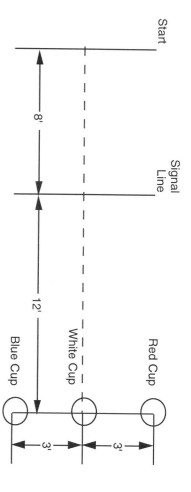

Fig. 5.10 Floor plan for penny-cup test.

From: Pimpa, U. (1968). *A study to determine the relationship between Bunn's Basketball Skills Test and the writer's modified version of that test.* Unpublished master's thesis, Springfield College, Springfield, Massachusetts. Copyright by author.

HARRISON BASKETBALL ABILITY TEST
(Harrison, 1969)

Purpose:
To measure basketball playing ability.

Description:
The four-item test battery measures player proficiency in the basic skills of shooting, passing, dribbling and rebounding. The comprehensive test is well suited for grading and classification purposes.

Educational Application:
Junior and senior high school boys.

Time:
Two 60-minute class periods for a class of 20 students in a multiple-station test design.

Personnel:
One scorer and one timer for each test item.

Equipment and Supplies:
Four basketballs, four stop watches, five chairs or hurdles, marking tape to construct the restraining line for the speed pass test item, and scoring materials.

Facilities and Space:
A basketball facility with unobstructed wall space.

Directions:
Field Goal Test. The subject assumes a position of his choice close to the basket while holding a basketball. On the starting signal, he attempts to make as many baskets as possible in 30 seconds. The type of shot used is the subject's choice. Two trials are given.

Speed Pass Test. On the starting signal, the subject passes the ball against the wall while standing behind an eight-foot restraining line. This action is continued for 30 seconds. The ball must be passed and received from behind the restraining line. The student may use any type of pass he chooses. Two trials are allowed.

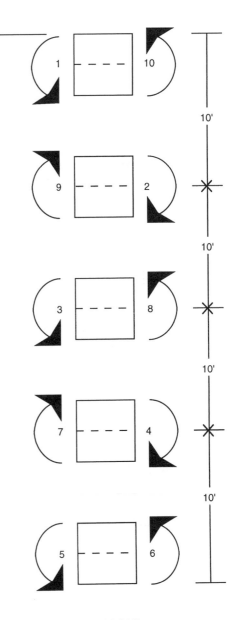

Fig. 5.11 Diagram of dribbling test.

From: Harrison, E. R. (1969).
A test to measure basketball ability for boys. Unpublished master's thesis, University of Florida, Gainesville. Copyright by author.

Dribble Test. Following the dribbling route shown in Figure 5.11, the subject when instructed to begin dribbles the ball for 30 seconds. Two trials are permitted.

Rebound Test. The subject stands near the backboard while holding a basketball. On the signal to start, the subject tosses the ball against the backboard and catches the ball in the air to return it to the backboard. This action is continued for 30 seconds. The subject may catch the ball and return to the floor before making the next toss if he is unable to perform the test item as recommended. Two trials are given.

Scoring Method and Norms:

Field Goal Test. One point is recorded for each successful basket. The better of the two trials is the subject's official score.

Speed Pass Test. One point is scored each time the ball hits the wall with the better of the two test trials recorded as the official score.

Dribble Test. A point is scored each time the midpoint of a chair or hurdle is reached. The better score of the two trials is the official score.

Rebound Test. One point is given for each time the ball hits the backboard. The better of the two trials is recorded.

Validity and Reliability:

A validity coefficient of .89 was obtained between the test battery scores and mean ratings of three criteria consisting of a previously validated battery, a peer rating and a jury rating. The scores of 23 high school varsity basketball players were used in the test battery validation.

Reliability coefficients of the test battery ranged from .91 to .97 for the five subject categories. The 24 students in grade seven produced the .91 coefficient of correlation while the .97 relationship was derived from the test scores of 24 students in grade 10.

Additional Comments:

The Harrison Basketball Ability Test is one of the more comprehensive basketball skill tests as all major skill areas are represented. This, in addition to its impressive validity and reliability values, indicates that the test was well constructed.

The validity and reliability values are particularly impressive since practice trials were disallowed immediately prior to test item administration. Perhaps the practice of counting the better of two trials as the official one for each of the test items compensated for any effect the lack of practice may have had upon the test's scientific authentication.

Table 5.4
T-SCALES FOR THE HARRISON BASKETBALL TEST

T-Scale	Goal Shooting				Speed Pass				Dribble				Rebounding			
	7th	8th	9th	10th	7th	8th	9th	10th	7th	8th	9th	10th	7th	8th	9th	10th
76					37	38	39	42	39	37	40	36	27	29	34	
75																
74																
73		17	18	18	35			41	38						33	32
72	14				34				37	36	39		26		32	
71					33	37			36						31	
70								40				35	25	28	30	31
69											38				29	30
68		16	17	17		36	38	39	35					27		
67	13				32					35		34	24	26		
66				16	31	35		38	34		37				28	29
65	12	15	16											25		
64		14		15			37	37	33				23		27	
63			15	14	30	34				34	36	33				28
62			13				36	36	32						26	
61	11				29	33				33				24		
60				13			35	35				32				27
59			14		28				31	32	35		22			
58		12				32	34								25	26
57	10							34				31		23		
56		11	13			31	33		30	31	34		21			25
55				12	27						33	30			24	
54	9	10				30		33						22		
53			12						29	30	32		20		23	24
52				11			32				31	29				
51	8	9	11					32							22	
50					26	29			28	29		28	19			23
49			10	10			31				30			21		
48									27	28		27			21	
47		8	9	9		28	30	31					18	20		22
46					25					27	29	26	17			
45	6						29				28					21
44			8	8		27		30	26			25		19	20	
43					24		28				27		16			20
42		7						29		26			15			
41				7					25			24			19	
40		7			23	26	27				26			18		19
39		6						28				23	14			
38	4			6					24	25	25			17	18	18
37			6		22	25	26				24	22	13			
36				5				27	23				12	16	17	
35		5			21		25		22			21				17
34		5			20	24				24	23	20	11	15	16	
33				4			24	26	21		22	19	10			
32	3				19											
31					18					23						16
30			4	3		23	23		20	22	21	18	9	14		
29									19				8			
28	2	3	3		17				18	21	20		7		15	
27					16	22	22		17		17		6	13	14	
26							21		16		14		5			
25							20	25			11					
24	1		2	2	15		19		15	20	9	17	4	12		15

From: Harrison, E.R. (1969). *A test to measure basketball ability for boys.* Unpublished master's thesis, University of Florida, Gainesville. Copyright by author.

Basketball References

American Alliance for Health, Physical Education, Recreation and Dance (1984). *AAHPERD skills test manual: Basketball for boys and girls.* Reston, Virginia, AAHPERD.

Barrow, H.M. (1959). Basketball skill test. *The Physical Educator* 16: 26-27.

Broderick, R.J. (1968). *A speed, endurance, accuracy (S.E.A.) test for assessing the basketball playing performance levels of high school boys.* Unpublished specialist's degree research paper, University of Michigan, Ann Arbor.

Boyd, C.A., MacCachren, J.R., & Waglow, I.F. (1955). Predictive ability of a selected basketball test. *Research Quarterly* 26: 364.

Burr, W.P. (1948). *The development of a classification test of basketball ability.* Unpublished master's thesis, Springfield College, Springfield, Massachusetts.

Catlin, O.J. (1966). An individual skills test for basketball. *The NAIA Coach* 1: 6-7.

Chambers, D.E. (1952). Testing for basketball ability. *Scholastic Coach* 22: 36.

Cubberly, H.J., & Cozens, F.W. (1936). The measurement of achievement in basketball. *Spalding's Athletic Library*, New York: American Sports.

Culp, P. (1943). Basketball ability tests. *Scholastic Coach* 12: 11.

Cunningham, P. (1964). *Cunningham basketball test.* Unpublished doctoral dissertation, University of Iowa, Iowa City.

Davis, C.A. (1932). *An experiment in measuring ability and progress in basketball skills.* Unpublished master's thesis, Springfield College, Springfield, Massachusetts.

Dyer, J.T., Schurig, J.C., & Apgar, S.L. (1939). A basketball motor ability test for college women and secondary school girls. *Research Quarterly* 10: 128-147.

Edgren, H.D. (1932). An experiment in the testing of ability and progress in basketball. *Research Quarterly* 3: 159-171.

Fraser, D.C. (1934). *Motor ability test in basketball.* Unpublished master's thesis, Springfield College, Springfield, Massachusetts.

Friermood, H.T. (1934). Basketball progress tests adapted to class use. *Journal of Health and Physical Education* 5: 45-47.

Gaunt, S. (1979). *Factor structure of basketball playing ability.* Unpublished doctoral dissertation, Indiana University, Bloomington.

Gilbert, R.R. (1968). *A study of selected variables in predicting basketball players.* Unpublished master's thesis, Springfield College, Springfield, Massachusetts.

Glassow, R.B., Colvin, V., & Schwarz, M.M. (1938). Studies measuring basketball playing ability of college women. *Research Quarterly* 9: 60-68.

Grandstaff, G. (1969). *Grandstaff-Murphy basketball skills test for high school girls.* Unpublished master's thesis, Chadron State College, Chadron, Nebraska.

Harrison, E.R. (1969). *A test to measure basketball ability for boys.* Unpublished master's thesis, University of Florida, Gainesville.

Hill, L.J. (1956). *Determining basketball ability through the use of basketball skill tests.* Unpublished master's thesis, Washington State University, Pullman.

Hopkins, D.R. (1977). Factor analysis of selected basketball skill tests. *Research Quarterly* 48: 535-540.

Hopkins, D.R. (1979). Using skill tests to identify successful and unsuccessful basketball performers. *Research Quarterly* 50: 381-387.

Hughes, L. (1957). *Comparison of the validation of six selected basketball ability tests.* Unpublished master's thesis, Pennsylvania State University, University Park.

Jacobson, T.V. (1960). *An evaluation of performance in certain physical ability tests administered to selected secondary school boys.* Unpublished master's thesis, University of Washington, Pullman.

Johnson, L.W. (1934). *Objective tests in basketball for high school boys.* Unpublished master's thesis, University of Iowa, Iowa City.

Jones, E. (1941). *A study of knowledge and playing ability in basketball for high school girls.* Unpublished master's thesis, University of Iowa, Iowa City.

Knox, R.D. (1937). *An experiment to determine the relationship between performance in skill tests and success in playing basketball.* Unpublished master's thesis, University of Oregon, Eugene.

Knox, R.D. (1947). Basketball ability tests. *Scholastic Coach* 17: 45-47.

Koski, W.A. (1950). *A basketball classification test.* Unpublished master's thesis, University of Michigan, Ann Arbor.

Lambert, A.T. (1969). *A basketball skill test for college women.* Unpublished master's thesis, University of North Carolina, Greensboro.

Lehsten, N. (1948). A measurement of basketball skills in high school boys. *The Physical Educator* 5: 103-105.

Leilich, A.R. (1952). *The primary components of selected basketball tests for college women.* Unpublished doctoral dissertation, Indiana University, Bloomington.

Loose, W.A. (1961). *A study to determine the validity of the Knox Basketball Test.* Unpublished master's thesis, Washington State University, Pullman.

Matthews, L.E. (1963). *A battery of basketball skills tests for high school boys.* Unpublished master's thesis, University of Oregon, Eugene.

Miller, W.K. (1954). Achievement levels in basketball skills for women physical education majors. *Research Quarterly* 25: 450-455.

Money, C.V. (1933). Tests for evaluating the abilities of basketball players. *Athletic Journal* 14: 18-19.

Nelson, J.K. (1974). *The measurement of shooting and passing skills in basketball.* Unpublished study, Louisiana State University, Baton Rouge.

Peters, G.V. (1964). *The reliability and validity of selected shooting tests in basketball.* Unpublished master's thesis, University of Michigan, Ann Arbor.

Pimpa, U. (1968). *A study to determine the relationship between Bunn's Basketball Skill Test and the writer's modified version of that test.* Unpublished master's thesis, Springfield College, Springfield, Massachusetts.

Randall, C.R. (1958). *Determining the validity of the Knox Basketball Test.* Unpublished master's thesis, Washington State University, Pullman.

Schwartz, H. (1937). Knowledge and achievement tests in girls basketball on the senior high level. *Research Quarterly* 8: 143.

Sobo, D.D. (1960). *A comparison of the performance of basketball teams of high school age selected by test results and by the judgment of the coach.* Unpublished master's thesis, Northern Illinois University, DeKalb.

Stroup, F. (1955). Game results as a criterion for validating basketball skill tests. *Research Quarterly* 26: 353-357.

Stubbs, H.C. (1968). *An explanatory study of girls' basketball relative to the measurement of ball handling ability.* Unpublished master's thesis, University of Tennessee, Knoxville.

Thornes, M.A.B. (1963). *An analysis of a basketball shooting test and its relationship to other basketball skill tests.* Unpublished master's thesis, University of Wisconsin, Madison.

Voltmer, E.F., & Watti, T. (1947). A rating scale for player performance in basketball. *Journal of Health and Physical Education* 2: 94-95.

Walter, R.J. (1968). *A comparison between two selected evaluative techniques for measuring basketball skill.* Unpublished master's thesis, Western Illinois University, Macomb.

Wilbur, C.D. (1959). Construction of a simple skills test. *DGWS Basketball Guide.* Washington, D.C.: AAHPER.

Young, G., & Moser, G. (1934). A short battery of tests to measure playing ability in women's basketball. *Research Quarterly* 5: 3-23.

Chapter 6

BOWLING

INTRODUCTION

Skills tests per se are not necessary for bowling since the game in itself represents objective measurement. Furthermore, the instructional approach commonly used in bowling allows for constant evaluation of student progress. As a result, the primary emphasis in the evaluation of bowling skill has been the development of achievement scales or norms. Bowling norms are especially valuable for score comparison purposes because of the high level of consistency shown in test conditions.

PHILLIPS-SUMMERS BOWLING NORMS
(Phillips & Summers, 1950)

Purpose:

To measure bowling achievement of college women of varying ability levels.

Description:

The Phillips-Summers Bowling Norms classify beginning bowling students into eight levels of ability. The ability levels range from 50-59.5 for the first level to 120-129.5 for the highest level. Student progress may be measured at the end of 10, 15, 20 and 25 lines.

Educational Application:

College women.

Time:

A half-semester or two-thirds of a quarter term would be required for a class of 15 to 20 students to bowl 25 lines.

Personnel:

One bowling instructor and students serving as scorers.

Equipment and Supplies:

One bowling ball per student and scoring materials.

Facilities and Space:

Bowling alley.

Directions and Scoring Method with Norms:

Five lines are bowled by each student to obtain an average for ability classification. Assessment of the student's progress is made at the completion of 10, 15, 20 and 25 lines. The student's bowling average at each progress assessment is compared to the established norms.

The norm values are expressed in both quantitative and qualitative terms with ranges of bowling averages categorized as superior, good, average, poor and inferior (Table 6.1). The performance ratings were determined by the number of standard deviation units a score departed from the mean. Each performance rating and its range of deviation from the mean are as follows.

Superior - 1.8 standard deviations above mean.
Good - Between 0.6 and 1.8 standard deviations above mean.
Average - Between 0.6 standard deviations below and 0.6 standard deviations above mean.
Poor - Between 0.6 and 1.8 standard deviations below mean.
Inferior - 1.8 standard deviations below mean.

To determine the amount of progress made by a student, an average of her bowling score is taken at the end of five lines and checked with the performance rating that corresponds with the average. The same procedure is taken for the average of the first 10 lines bowled. Thereafter, only the particular line interval is averaged. For example, lines 11 through 15 are averaged as are intervals of 16 to 20 and 20 to 25.

The Phillips-Summers Bowling Norms were developed from the scores of 3,634 women students from 22 colleges.

Additional Comments:

A key feature of the Phillips-Summers Bowling Norms is the demonstrated value the scale provides as a motivator for improvement in bowling performance. Its design removes some of the pressure of peer competition and promotes a concentration on self-improvement. The norms seem to illustrate a well-conceived method of evaluating bowling skill at the beginner level.

Table 6.1

PHILLIPS-SUMMERS BOWLING NORMS*

Level of Ability, 50-59.9

Rating	Lines 1-10	Lines 11-15	Lines 16-20	Lines 21-25
Superior	75 & up	102 & up	109 & up	113 & up
Good	69 - 74	89 - 101	96 - 108	99 - 112
Average	61 - 68	75 - 88	81 - 95	84 - 98
Poor	55 - 60	62 - 74	67 - 80	70 - 83
Inferior	54 & below	61 & below	66 & below	69 & below
N	99	64	59	40
M	64.5	81.4	87.8	90.1
S.D.	5.1	10.7	11.5	11.7

Level of Ability, 60-69.9

Rating	Lines 1-10	Lines 11-15	Lines 16-20	Lines 21-25
Superior	85 & up	109 & up	114 & up	115 & up
Good	78 - 84	96 - 108	100 - 113	102 - 114
Average	70 - 77	81 - 95	85 - 99	88 - 101
Poor	63 - 69	68 - 80	71 - 84	76 - 87
Inferior	62 & below	67 & below	70 & below	75 & below
N	322	206	151	114
M	73.5	88.0	92.2	94.8
S.D.	6.0	11.3	11.6	10.7

Level of Ability, 70-79.9

Rating	Lines 1-10	Lines 11-15	Lines 16-20	Lines 21-25
Superior	93 & up	117 & up	118 & up	124 & up
Good	86 - 92	101 - 116	103 - 117	109 - 123
Average	78 - 85	85 - 100	88 - 102	92 - 108
Poor	71 - 77	70 - 84	74 - 87	76 - 91
Inferior	70 & below	69 & below	73 & below	75 & below
N	611	378	280	213
M	81.3	92.7	95.2	99.7
S.D.	5.7	12.7	12.0	13.1

Continued on the next page

Table 6.1 - Continued			
PHILLIPS-SUMMERS BOWLING NORMS*			
Level of Ability, 80-89.9			
Rating	**Lines 1-10**	**Lines 11-15**	**Lines 16-20**	**Lines 21-25**
Superior	101 & up	119 & up	120 & up	125 & up
Good	94 - 100	106 - 118	106 - 119	111 - 124
Average	86 - 93	91 - 105	91 - 105	96 - 110
Poor	79 - 85	78 - 90	77 - 90	82 - 95
Inferior	78 & below	77 & below	76 & below	81 & below
N	818	492	337	249
M	89.3	97.8	98.2	102.8
S.D.	5.8	11.1	11.6	11.7

Level of Ability, 90-99.9

Rating	**Lines 1-10**	**Lines 11-15**	**Lines 16-20**	**Lines 21-25**
Superior	110 & up	126 & up	127 & up	131 & up
Good	102 - 109	111 - 125	112 - 126	116 - 130
Average	93 - 101	96 - 110	97 - 111	100 - 115
Poor	86 - 92	82 - 95	82 - 96	86 - 99
Inferior	85 & below	81 & below	81 & below	85 & below
N	797	502	342	255
M	97.2	103.4	104.2	107.8
S.D.	6.5	11.8	12.1	12.2

Level of Ability, 100-109.9

Rating	**Lines 1-10**	**Lines 11-15**	**Lines 16-20**	**Lines 21-25**
Superior	117 & up	130 & up	134 & up	134 & up
Good	110 - 116	117 - 129	119 - 133	120 - 133
Average	102 - 109	103 - 116	104 - 118	105 - 119
Poor	95 - 101	89 - 102	90 - 103	91 - 104
Inferior	94 & below	88 & below	89 & below	90 & below
N	552	369	247	200
M	105.6	109.1	111.1	112.1
S.D.	6.0	11.0	11.9	11.6

Level of Ability, 110-119.9

Rating	**Lines 1-10**	**Lines 11-15**	**Lines 16-20**	**Lines 21-25**
Superior	125 & up	135 & up	139 & up	139 & up
Good	118 - 124	122 - 134	125 - 138	124 - 138
Average	110 - 117	107 - 121	110 - 124	109 - 123
Poor	103 - 109	94 - 106	96 - 109	95 - 108
Inferior	102 & below	93 & below	95 & below	94 & below
N	310	209	153	119
M	113.6	114.1	116.8	116.3
S.D.	5.8	11.2	11.8	11.8

Level of Ability, 120-129.9

Rating	**Lines 1-10**	**Lines 11-15**	**Lines 16-20**	**Lines 21-25**
Superior	135 & up	145 & up	146 & up	150 & up
Good	127 - 134	132 - 144	133 - 145	135 - 149
Average	118 - 126	117 - 131	120 - 132	118 - 134
Poor	110 - 117	104 - 116	107 - 119	103 - 117
Inferior	109 & below	103 & below	106 & below	102 & below
N	125	93	60	50
M	122.4	124.0	126.0	126.0
S.D.	6.6	11.0	10.4	12.8

*Based on scores of 3,634 college women.

From: Phillips, M., & Summers, D. (1950). Bowling norms and learning curves for college women. *Research Quarterly* 21: 377-385. Reprinted with permission from AAHPERD.

MARTIN BOWLING NORMS
(Martin, 1960)

Purpose:

To measure bowling achievement of college students of different skill levels.

Description and Scoring Method with Norms:

Each student without prior bowling experience is automatically placed in the beginner level of ability. Other students in the class bowl five lines for average which places them in one of three ability groups:

	Men	Women
Beginning	120 or under	98 or under
Intermediate	121 to 145	99 to 119
Advanced	146 and over	120 and over

After a student completes 26 lines of bowling (omitting the first five lines), his/her average is computed. The student's rate of improvement is determined by checking the performance rating that coincides with his/her final average (Table 6.2). The performance ratings are categorized as superior, good, average, poor and inferior.

The Martin Bowling Norms were derived from the bowling averages of 704 freshman and sophomore male and female college students enrolled in bowling classes. The averages were accumulated over a period of three years.

Table 6.2 MARTIN BOWLING NORMS* Scores						
	Beginning		**Intermediate**		**Advanced**	
Rating	**Men**	**Women**	**Men**	**Women**	**Men**	**Women**
Superior	127 & above	113 & above	150 & above	125 & above	162 & above	None
Good	116 - 126	101 - 112	140 - 149	120 - 124	157 - 161	
Average	107 - 115	93 - 100	126 - 139	115 - 119	152 - 156	
Poor	96 - 106	81 - 92	115 - 125	110 - 114	147 - 151	
Inferior	95 & below	80 & below	114 & below	109 & below	146 & below	
N	162	292	155	58	37	
Range	86 - 132	70 - 123	107 - 155	101 - 135	143 - 174	
M	111.26	97.31	134.42	117.11	154.46	
SD	8.22	8.18	7.33	4.02	4.41	

*Based on scores of 704 college students.

From: Martin, J.L. (1960). Bowling norms for college men and women. *Research Quarterly* 31: 113-116. Reprinted with permission from AAHPERD.

Educational Application:

College men and women.

Time:

About one-half semester or two-thirds of a quarter term for a class of 15 to 20 students meeting twice weekly.

Personnel:

An instructor with students serving as scorers.

Equipment and Supplies:

One bowling ball per student and scoring materials.

Facilities and Space:

Bowling alley.

Additional Comments:

The set of norms shows value as a motivator for student improvement in bowling performance. The inclusion of both men and women in the development of the norms is a notable advantage of the Martin Norms since college bowling classes are commonly coeducational in design and reality.

MARTIN-KEOGH BOWLING NORMS
(Martin & Keogh, 1964)

Purpose:

To measure bowling achievement of college students of different skill levels.

Description and Scoring Method with Norms:

Prior to the recording of scores for those students classified as inexperienced, four to six class periods of instruction are recommended. The inexperienced classification includes students who have bowled less than 10 games and have received no formal instruction. The students who possess more experience than the above description also participate in four to six class periods of instruction before bowling the games to be included in a final average.

The average of the first two games bowled after the practice period and the average of the final two games at the end of the instructional term constitute the basis for the norms. The norms are categorized as superior, good, average, poor and inferior.

These norms were based upon scores made by 320 men and women students who enrolled for bowling classes on an elective basis. As reflected in Table 6.3, the means and standard deviations of the scores for nonexperienced men students were 110.3 and 17.9, 113.1 and 19.3. For the experienced men students, the values were 143.4 and 30.7, 151.7 and 23.3. The nonexperienced women students showed values of 89.0 and 22.6, 112.2 and 14.6; for experienced women students, values of 121.9 and 19.7, 128.7 and 18.3 were achieved.

Educational Application:

College men and women.

Time:

The amount of time required for each student in a class of 15 to 20 students to bowl a minimum of 26 games, based on the assumption that the class meets twice weekly.

Personnel:

An instructor with students serving as scorers.

Equipment and Supplies:

One bowling ball per student and scoring materials.

Facilities and Space:

Bowling alley.

Additional Comments:

It is important to remember that the Martin and Keogh Norms were collected from college bowling classes consisting of students who completed the courses for elective credit. This is especially notable since in this study the initial averages of the nonexperienced men and women students were 22 and 15 points greater than for those groups of the same classification in the Martin Norms study. The higher averages are probably a result of greater motivation and interest shown by the students taking bowling for elective credit as opposed to those students completing the course simply to complete a required credit.

| | Nonexperienced | | | | Experienced | | | |
| | Men | | Women | | Men | | Women | |
Item	Initial	Final	Initial	Final	Initial	Final	Initial	Final
				Table 6.3				
			MARTIN-KEOGH BOWLING NORMS*					
				Scores				
Superior[†]	133	157	117	131	181	182	148	152
Good	122 - 132	146 - 156	103 - 116	122 - 130	162 - 180	167 - 181	135 - 147	140 - 151
Average	99 - 121	122 - 145	76 - 102	103 - 121	125 - 161	138 - 166	110 - 134	117 - 139
Poor	88 -98	110 - 121	62 - 75	95 - 102	106 - 124	123 - 137	97 - 109	105 - 116
Inferior[‡]	87	109	61	94	105	122	96	104
N	38	38	67	67	139	139	76	76
Range	57 - 147	104 - 182	61 - 122	77 - 147	100 - 222	100 - 221	83 - 180	82 - 172
M	110.3	113.1	89.0	112.2	143.4	151.7	121.9	128.7
SD	17.9	19.3	22.6	14.6	30.7	23.3	19.7	18.3

*Based on scores of 320 college students.
[†] and above.
[‡] and below.

From: Martin, J.L., & Keogh, J. (1964). Bowling norms for college students in elective physical education classes. *Research Quarterly* 25: 325-327. Reprinted with permission from AAHPERD.

Bowling References

Johnson, N.J. (1962). *Tests of achievement in bowling for beginning girl bowlers.* Unpublished master's thesis, University of Colorado, Boulder.

Martin, J.L. (1960). Bowling norms for college men and women. *Research Quarterly* 31: 113-116.

Martin, J.L., & Keogh, J. (1964). Bowling norms for college students in elective physical education classes. *Research Quarterly* 25: 325-327.

Olson, J.K., & Liba, M.R. (1967). A device for evaluating spot bowling ability. *Research Quarterly* 38: 193-201.

Phillips, M., & Summers, D. (1950). Bowling norms and learning curves for college women. *Research Quarterly* 21: 377-385.

Chapter 7

CANOEING

INTRODUCTION

Canoeing and other related activities have shown a popularity gain in recent years largely due to the prevalent "back to nature" trend. However, canoeing will probably never reach the popularity level of some sports in the physical education curriculum because it exemplifies a course offering which requires a special type of teaching environment, namely a large body of water, that may be unavailable.

Instructors of canoeing are advised to consider the sport's only apparent scientifically documented skills test (Critz, 1948).

CRITZ CANOEING TEST
(Critz, 1948)

Purpose:

To determine the general ability to handle a canoe.

Description:

The subject paddles a canoe as fast as possible in a figure-eight path around two buoys set 525 feet apart.

Educational Application:

Originally used to evaluate college women, but it is applicable to any canoeist, regardless of gender or educational level.

Time:

Two 60-minute class periods for a class of 20 students.

Personnel:

One person to serve as both timer and scorer.

Equipment and Supplies:

Canoes, two buoys, paddles, stop watch and scoring materials.

Facilities and Space:

A body of water at least 550 feet in length.

Directions:

Prior to being tested for score, the subject should demonstrate proper familiarity with the required test skills.

In preparation for the test, the tester places the two buoys 525 feet apart. The subject takes a position at the stern of the boat with a paddle in hand. Assuming a position at the bow of the canoe, the tester does not paddle but merely rides along to keep the canoe on a more even keel.

The subject assumes a rowing position behind the buoy selected as the starting point. On an audible command, she/he paddles the canoe as rapidly as possible to the buoy, circles it and paddles back to the starting point. It is recommended that the canoe be put in motion far enough behind the starting point so that it is moving when that buoy is reached. The subject may start out paddling on either the port or starboard side of the canoe, but she/he must remain in that position for the entire test. Whatever side the subject chooses in passing the buoy at the half-way point of the test course, she/he must follow the figure-eight path around the buoys.

Scoring Method and Norms:

As the bow of the boat passes the first buoy or starting point, the timer begins recording the time and continues until the course is completed when the bow of the boat passes the same buoy where the test was initiated. The elapsed time is the official score.

Table 7.1
ACHIEVEMENT SCALE FOR CRITZ CANOE TEST

Excellent	-	4 min. to 5 min. & 29 sec.
Good	-	5 min. & 30 sec. to 6 min. & 59 sec.
Average	-	7 min. to 8 min. & 29 sec.
Fair	-	8 min. & 30 sec. to 9 min. & 59 sec.
Poor	-	10 min. or slower

From: Critz, M.E. (1948). *An objective test for beginning canoeists.* Unpublished master's thesis, University of Iowa, Iowa City. Copyright by author.

Validity and Reliability:

A validity value of .64 was determined by correlating the *T*-scores on the test times with judges' ratings. Each of 104 college women was rated on stroking form and general ability to handle a canoe.

On successive days with similar wind and current conditions, 23 college women were tested to determine the reliability of the test. The resulting coefficient was .92.

Additional Comments:

The Critz Canoeing Test was well conceived by test feasibility standards. However, a possible limitation is the amount of time required to administer the test. Giving the test to one student at a time takes a minimum of two 60-minute class periods for a class of 20 students. To reduce the test administration time, two subjects may be tested simultaneously by staggering the starts. As one subject makes the turn around the second buoy, another student could begin with this testing method, continuing until all the students are tested.

Critz indicated that any modification of the test course distance should be restricted to an increase in its length. A shorter course would not allow the lesser skilled canoeist to stray far from the course, thus causing a cluster effect or grouping of scores. This would naturally affect the validity of the test.

Each tester is encouraged to develop his/her own set of achievement scales, based on the test population, course condition and canoe design.

Canoeing Reference

Critz, M. E. (1948). *An objective test for beginning canoeists.* Unpublished master's thesis, University of Iowa, Iowa City.

Chapter 8

DIVING

INTRODUCTION

The Bennett Test (Bennett, 1942) is the only scientifically documented skills test the authors were able to locate.

Foster (Foster, 1956) conducted an interesting study involving a part method of judging divers. His part method consisted of having each judge rate only one part of a dive, with each dive being divided into three parts: the approach and take-off; height and mechanics of the dive; and alignment and entry. Foster concluded that the part method gave very close relative rankings, higher total scores and a greater range of scores.

BENNETT DIVING TEST
(Bennett, 1942)

Purpose:

To determine the diving ability of beginning divers.

Description:

Originally developed to test the diving skill of beginners, the 50-item test requires each subject to complete as many dives as possible for score and may be used to test diving skill beyond the beginner level.

Educational Application:

Elementary school, high school and college males and females.

Time:

A class of 20 students can probably be tested in two 60-minute class periods.

Personnel:

A scorer-recorder.

Equipment and Supplies:

Diving boards of one and three meters; score cards.

Facilities and Space:

Swimming pool with diving area.

Directions:

The test should be administered toward the end of a beginners' class to assure that each student has developed some competency in basic skills such as the approach and take-off.

Progressing from the simple to the more difficult dives, with the more difficult dives being divided into parts, each subject starts with the first dive and moves through the list as far as possible. A diver may progress to the next dive, however, without either trying or successfully completing the previous dive. None of the dives is weighted since the progressive steps are considered approximately equal and the value of each dive in points is the same.

Certain terms need to be clearly defined for the students, since the successful completion of each dive is dependent to a large degree on their understanding of the following definitions:

1.   Headfirst: implies the hands, head, hips, knees and feet enter the water in consecutive order. Anything short of a "belly flop" is classified as a headfirst entry.

2.   Belly flop: occurs when the hands, head, hips, knees and feet enter the water simultaneously or nearly so.

3.   Straight headfirst: means a near perfect vertical headfirst dive with the feet

entering the same or nearly the same opening in the water as the head. The body should be straight with no bend.

4. Feetfirst: implies the feet, knees, hips, shoulders and head enter the water in consecutive order.

5. Straight feetfirst: means a near perfect vertical feetfirst entry with the head entering the same opening in the water as the feet. There should be no body bend and the hands should be touching the sides of the body.

Test Items:

1. Standing dive from pool edge: enter straight headfirst.

2. Standing dive from pool edge with return to surface: enter straight headfirst, keeping hands and arms in same relative position until return to surface.

3. Standing dive from pool edge to bottom of pool: enter straight headfirst and touch the bottom at an 11-foot depth.

4. Sitting tuck position with fall into the water from the one-meter board: remain completely tucked (hands grasping shins and forehead on knees which are drawn up to chest) until under the water. Any starting position.

5. Standing dive from board: enter straight headfirst.

6. Standing feetfirst dive: body must be in the straight feetfirst position in air and at entry. Jump from board, do not step.

7. Forward approach: must include at least three steps and a hurdle, landing on both feet. Accompanying arm motion must be smooth; no pauses in entire approach. Toes must be pointed to the board during the hurdle before landing on the end of the board.

8. Running feetfirst dive: combine requirements of numbers seven and six.

9. Springing the board: rise from the board at least six inches with five consecutive jumps, using the arms to help in gaining height.

10. Rocking chair: sit on the end of the board facing the water, and by rocking backward with feet over head, gain enough momentum to rock forward headfirst into the water. Enter headfirst.

11. Springing the board with a double tuck position: same as number nine except that a tuck position must be assumed when in the air. Knees must be bent when hands touch shins in tuck position. Do four consecutive tucks.

12. Running front tuck dive: enter straight headfirst after assuming a tuck position in the air (knees bent, hands on shins).

13. Forward dive over pole hip high: enter straight headfirst, clearing the pole.

14. Elementary front jackknife dive (standing): bend enough at the hips to have the hands below the knees (though not necessarily touching the legs) at the time of the bend. Enter headfirst.

15. Running jackknife dive: enter straight headfirst. Keep knees together and straight after leaving the board. Wrists below knees at time of jackknife bend.

16. Advanced jackknife dive: same as number 15 except that diver must actually touch ankles or top of arch and must enter water within six feet of the end of the board.

17. Elementary back jackknife dive (taken to the side of the board): enter headfirst with the head entering the water behind the starting point. Must have some bend at hips.

18. Back jackknife dive: same as number 17 except that the dive is taken straight back from the end of the board.

19. Advanced back jackknife dive: same as number 18 except that there must be a straight headfirst entry and knees must be kept together and straight after leaving the board.

20. Back approach: must include at least three steps, correct direction of turn (free leg swings out over the water, not over the board), and no hesitations.

21. Back spring to the water feetfirst: use arms in the spring-up from the board; jump, do not step, from the board, and enter the water straight feetfirst.

22. Back spring to the board: from the back stance, spring upward from the board (using arms smoothly to assist) with knees straight and toes pointed to the board. Toes must be at least six inches above the board when in the air. Return to the board.

23. Back bend: from the back stance position, bend backward and enter the water headfirst.

24. Elementary back dive: same as number 23, but hold straight headfirst position in air and at entry.

25. Back dive: same as number 24 but use some preparatory spring with smooth use of arms.

26. Advanced back dive: same as number 25, but done in two parts; (1) keep the head up, eyes forward, as body is rising from the board, then (2) head is thrown back when the crest of the height is reached. Enter straight headfirst within six feet of the board (no twist). Toes pointed throughout the dive.

27. Standing forward dive with an arch: when in the air look distinctly forward and up. Look down just before entering straight headfirst. Lead with hands throughout the dive.

28. Butterfly dive: same as number 27, either running or standing, but with hands on hips when in the air. Enter straight headfirst.

29. Running swan dive: must have the body arched in the air. No body bends, arms above shoulder height and extended to sides, head up. The regular position of the swan dive in the air must be attained even if only for a moment. Enter headfirst.

30. Advanced running swan dive: same as number 29, entering straight headfirst.

31. Running forward half twist, feetfirst: turn at least 180 degrees and enter straight feetfirst.

32. Quarter twist: assume a distinct swan position in the air, followed by a turn on the long axis of the body of at least 90 degrees. (Shoulders determine degree of turn.) Enter headfirst.

33. Half twist: same as number 31, but turn at least 180 degrees.

34. Jackknife with a quarter twist: assume a distinct jackknife position in the air, followed by a turn of at least 90 degrees. Enter headfirst.

35. Elementary jackknife with a half twist: same as number 33 but turn at least 180 degrees.

36. Neck stand: lie with back to board and head at the "water" end of the board. Bring the feet up over the head, aim them toward the water and enter the water feetfirst. Hands must be at sides at time of feetfirst entry.

37. Handstand dive: enter straight headfirst. Entire body must clear the board.

38. Handstand feetfirst dive: enter feetfirst, after assuming the handstand position on board and holding on until feet complete the arc and point toward the water.

39. Rocking chair (three-meter board): enter headfirst.

40. Neck stand (three-meter board): enter feetfirst, see number 36.

41. Forward fall dive (three-meter board): from an erect forward standing position with arms extended over head, fall forward, entering the water headfirst. Remain perfectly still throughout the fall.

42. Backward fall dive (three-meter board): same as number 41 except that the fall is taken from a backward standing position.

43. Tuck and roll with a spring from edge of pool (a forward somersault in the air from the edge of the pool, turning in the tuck position): turn at least far enough forward so that the head clears the water and the back strikes the water first.

44.   Forward somersault (one-meter board): turn a forward somersault in the air so that the feet hit the water first.

45.   Backward somersault: turn a backward somersault in the air so that the feet hit the water first.

46.   Half gainer: only requirement is to enter headfirst.

47.   Full gainer: only requirement is to enter feetfirst.

48.   Back half twist: from the back stance position, make a half twist, entering the water straight headfirst. Do not twist until after leaving the board.

49.   Forward 1 1/2 somersault: only requirement is to enter headfirst.

50.   Perform any of the standard dives (including also the handstand dive and the handstand feetfirst dive) from the three-meter board. No requirements as to form except that the dive is recognizable to the judges and has a headfirst or feetfirst entry depending on the dive selected. If, for instance, a jackknife dive is done with very little bend at the hips, it would not be evident to the judges whether it was intended to be a jackknife or a plain forward dive.

Scoring Method:

Each dive attempted is assigned a score of either one or zero, depending only on the successful completion of the dive. The final score is the sum total of points accumulated on the 50 test items successfully completed.

Validity, Reliability and Objectivity:

The group of test subjects used in this study consisted of 26 college women who completed elementary diving classes. A validity coefficient of .94 was determined by comparing the results of this test with a rating of eight selected dives by three expert judges who used the official 10-point rating scale and degree of difficulty as discussed in the Official Collegiate Scholastic Swimming Guide at the time of the test.

A reliability coefficient of .95 was determined by the split-half method and stepped up by the Spearman-Brown Formula. An objectivity value of .89 was determined by having three judges rate four divers simultaneously on 42 dives each or a total of 168 dives. Two of the judges were experienced and together had an objectivity coefficient of .93.

Additional Comments:

The Bennett Diving Test is a highly regarded, scientifically documented diving test that is simple enough for true beginners, yet diversified enough for the rapid learners or intermediate divers. This test is unlimited for a beginning class since all the standard dives may be attempted from the high board.

A legitimate concern might arise when the tester realizes that no distinction is made between the subjects that pass a test item on their first attempt and those who require additional attempts. The authors suggest that a limit be set either on the time or number of attempts required to complete a particular test item. Placing higher value on successful completion of a dive on the first attempt is another possibility.

In addition to its value as an evaluation tool, the Bennett Test has proven valuable as a teaching aid. It is useful in the classification of students by skill level, and its design allows the student a natural progression from simple to more difficult skills. Local norms should be developed by age group and ability level.

Diving References

Bennett, L.M. (1942). A test of diving for use in beginning classes. *Research Quarterly* 13: 109-115.

Foster, J.T. (1956). *Alternate procedures for judging and scoring competitive diving.* Unpublished master's thesis, University of Iowa, Iowa City.

Chapter 9

EQUITATION

INTRODUCTION

Equitation or horseback riding is an age-old art that dates back to early civilizations. As expected, the techniques and equipment associated with the equestrian art have been refined considerably through the years. Today, many of the nation's colleges and universities offer equitation courses, yet the authors were able to locate only one skills test in physical education literature. A reason for this might be that students are usually evaluated on the basis of horsemanship, and this umbrella term encompasses general knowledge, skill both on and off the animal and other related areas. Also, subjective evaluations are common in a sport in which form is of primary importance in the evaluation process.

CRABTREE RIDING TEST
(Crabtree, 1943)

Purpose:

To judge riding performance in competition.

Description:

The Crabtree Riding Test consists of eight items.

Educational Application:

Junior high, high school and college males and females.

Time:

One class of 20 students can take the test in two 60-minute periods.

Personnel:

One judge.

Equipment, Supplies and Other Physical Needs:

Horse, riding equipment and score card.

Facilities and Space:

Riding area of sufficient size to properly administer each test item.

Directions:

At the discretion of the tester, practice may be allowed prior to the test. The subject prepares and mounts the horse, then begins to execute the following performance items:

Item	Points	Description
Mounting	3	Reins (1 1/2); ease and coordination (1 1/2)
Dismounting	3	Reins (1 1/2); ease and coordination (1 1/2)
Walk	5	Hands (1); circle (1); reverse (1); form (2)
Trot Collected	11	Change diagonals (2); figure-eight (2); circle (1); reverse (1); elbows (1); hands (1); legs (1); heels (1); rhythm (1)
Extended	3	Seat (1); hands (1); control (1)
Canter Collected	8	Right lead (1); left lead (1); figure-eight (2); seat (2); hands (2)
Extended	3	Seat (1); hands (1); control (1)

| General Horsemanship | 4 | A general opinion item |

Scoring Method:

Points are scored for each of the eight test items based on the quality of the performance. Forty points is the maximum score.

Validity and Reliability:

Not reported.

Additional Comments:

In addition to its apparent value as a comprehensive test of riding ability, the Crabtree Riding Test serves well as a teaching and learning aid for the instructor and student. When students train for the test, they receive practice in all essential riding skills, and the test items provide a basic content checklist for the instructor in teaching the riding component of horsemanship.

Equitation Reference

Crabtree, H.K. (1943). An objective test for riding. *Journal of Health and Physical Education* 15: 419.

Chapter 10

FENCING

INTRODUCTION

Of the few available skills tests in fencing, the better ones were developed in the 1960s. Three tests from that era are presented in this chapter.

EMERY FENCING PERFORMANCE TEST
(Emery, 1960)

Purpose:
To measure general fencing ability.

Description:
The test is a seven-item rating scale for beginning fencers with each required skill assigned a numerical value of one to three points.

Educational Application:
High school and college females.

Time:
One 60-minute time period to test 20 students.

Personnel:
One judge.

Equipment and Supplies:
Fencing foils and score cards.

Facilities and Space:
Fencing area.

Directions:
The test should be administered near the end of the beginners' course so the students can have maximum exposure in performing the required skill items.

Subjects are tested one at a time. Each attempts to successfully complete the seven test items. Item evaluations by the judge are based on the quality of performance, not the time required to perform the particular skill.

Test Items:
1. On-Guard

    A. Foil Arm
        (1)   Elbow comfortable distance from waist
        (2)   Pommel flat on wrist
        (3)   Hand supinated
        (4)   Point in line with opponent's eyes

    B.   Non-foil Arm
        (5)   Upper arm parallel with floor
        (6)   Forearm at right angles
        (7)   Hand relaxed toward head

    C.   Upper Body
- (8) Hand supinated
- (9) Trunk erect, head toward opponent
- (10) Hips tucked under

    D.   Lower Extremities
- (11) Feet at right angles
- (12) Distance two foot lengths
- (13) Right foot toward opponent
- (14) Knees over insteps
- (15) Right knee toward opponent

2.   Advance

    A.   Lower Extremities
- (1) Right foot lifts first, heel touches first
- (2) Left foot one movement
- (3) Both feet move close to floor, no sliding

3.   Lunge

    A.   Foil Arm
- (1) Extended shoulder height
- (2) Hand supinated

    B.   Non-foil Arm
- (3) Arm straightened
- (4) Palm turned up

    C.   Lower Extremities
- (5) Right foot forward, straight line toward opponent
- (6) Right knee over instep, toward opponent
- (7) Left foot flat on floor
- (8) Left knee and leg straight

4.   Disengage
- (1) On-guard position
- (2) Foil arm extended
- (3) Drop foil arm around opponent's bell guard in same movement as arm extension
- (4) Lunge
- (5) Movement continuous and done with fingers

5.   Parry-Lateral
- (1) On-guard position
- (2) Hand half-supination throughout
- (3) Middle of blade against middle of opponent's blade
- (4) Blade moved enough to cover line being attacked
- (5) Hand level, no change

6. Parry-Counter
    (1) On-guard position
    (2) Circle made by finger action
    (3) Small circle
    (4) Last three fingers
    (5) Counter parry quarte counterclockwise
    (6) Counter parry sixte clockwise
    (7) Hand level, no change

7. Riposte-Simple
    (1) On-guard position
    (2) Follows successful parry, no delay
    (3) Arm extended if needed
    (4) Lunge if needed

Scoring Method and Norms:

Each subject receives either one, two or three points for each of the seven skill items, depending upon the quality of performance. If the tester declares that no more than one part of a skill is lacking in quality, the student should be awarded three points. A score of 21 is maximum.

Validity and Reliability:

A coefficient of .80 was determined when judges' ratings were correlated with rating scale scores. A reliability estimate was not reported.

Additional Comments:

The value of the Emery Fencing Test should be further substantiated. A study of the test's reliability value is one obvious need. Of equal importance is the need to study the objectivity value of this particular fencing test. Consistency among judges in their performance evaluations is imperative if a test of this type is to demonstrate any significant worth.

	Table 10.1								
	ACHIEVEMENT STANDARDS FOR EMERY FENCING PERFORMANCE TEST								
Raw Score	21	20	19	18	17	16	15	14	13
Letter Grade	A	B	B	C	C	C	D	D	F
T-score	74	68	62	56	48	44	38	32	26

From: Emery, L. (1962). Criteria for rating selected skills of foil fencing. *DGWS Bowling-Fencing-Golf Guide* (1960-62). Washington, D.C.: AAHPER. Reprinted with permission from AAHPERD.

BOWER FENCING TEST
(Bower, 1961)

Purpose:

To determine general foil fencing ability.

Description:

In order to provide a comprehensive measure of general fencing ability, Bower included both offensive and defensive skill items in her test. Each subject attempts to attack a defender and also defend an attack in completing the test requirement.

Educational Application:

College men and women.

Time:

Twenty students can be tested in 60 minutes.

Personnel:

One scorer-recorder.

Equipment and Supplies:

Regular fencing attire including costume, gloves, jacket and mask; fencing foil; scoring and floor marking materials.

Facilities and Space:

A fencing room or area with a smooth floor and a flat wall surface.

Directions:

A few minutes should be set aside in several class periods to prepare the students properly for the test requirements.

To initiate the testing, the defender takes an on-guard position with his/her rear foot against the wall. The attacker determines his/her lunging position by making a full lunge which reaches the defender and results in a slight bend of the foil blade. Once the correct attack distance is determined, the scorer draws a chalk line along the inner border of the attacker's rear foot. This line is the starting line and the attacker's back foot must remain behind this line before starting his/her attack. Another line is drawn five inches nearer the wall from the starting line and is designated as the foul line.

More than one test group may perform for score simultaneously. Each group contains an attacker, a defender and a scorer. The attacker makes five attacks at his/her own pace with each attack beginning behind the starting line. He/she may choose any acceptable attack to use. At the conclusion of each attack, the rear foot must be on the floor behind the foul line.

The defender may use any parry or parries he/she so chooses. After five consecutive attacks, the subjects switch positions with five attacks then made by the new attacker. The scorer marks two different sets of chalk lines for each attacker.

Scoring Method:

Standing slightly behind and one yard to the right of the attacker, the scorer decides whether or not a point is landed on the attack, or if there is a complete miss. He/she must also make sure the rear foot of the attacker remains behind the foul line. This assures a proper lunge attack.

One point is scored by the attacker for each disengage which lands on a valid target area. No points are scored on an incorrect attack, or an attack that lands off target and is not parried.

One point is scored by the defender for each successful counter parry. Should the defender parry the blade with a counter parry so the attack lands foul, it is considered a good parry and a point is awarded the defender. No points are scored for an incorrect parry. Also, a direct parry which stops the attack earns no score.

Scores should be called out after each attack to keep the fencers informed of their running scores. There is a total of 10 possible points for each test, five on attack and five on defense.

Validity and Reliability:

Fifty-one college students enrolled in two beginning coeducational foil fencing classes were the subjects for the Bower study. In comparing test results with round-robin tournament rankings, a validity coefficient of .80 was obtained. Utilizing the test-retest method for obtaining reliability, a .82 coefficient of correlation resulted.

Additional Comments:

The mass testing capability of the Bower Test adds greatly to its value as a feasible test of general foil fencing ability. Also, the test is unusually easy to administer. There is a plus connected with the practice requirement: The students are drilled in both basic offensive and defensive fencing skills which contributes to improvement in overall fencing ability. On the negative side, the extra practice time required in regular class sessions makes the test somewhat less attractive.

SAFRIT FENCING TEST
(Safrit, 1962)

Purpose:

To measure the speed of the lunge recovery; to determine general fencing ability.

Description:

The Safrit Fencing Test originally was designed to measure the speed of the lunge recovery along with appropriate form checks and an accuracy measure of the lunge by utilizing a wall target.

The latter item demonstrated a low reliability value and was not considered to be a practical test. Therefore, discussion of the Safrit Test is limited to the lunge recovery speed item.

Educational Application:

College women.

Time:

One 60-minute period for a class of 20 students.

Personnel:

One scorer and possibly a timer, depending upon the equipment used in testing.

Equipment and Supplies:

Automatic Performance Analyzer* (optional), fencing foils, stop watches measuring one-hundredth of a second and scoring materials.

Facilities and Space:

Proper floor space for lunging and a flat, smooth wall surface.

Directions:

Subjects should be tested only after demonstrating reasonable familiarity with the test requirements. The subject stands far enough from the wall so that a lunge recovery can be executed with the tip of the foil touching the wall. She assumes an on-guard position with the forward foot on a mat which is used with a rather elaborate piece of equipment called the "Automatic Performance Analyzer." This apparatus measures reaction time, movement time or total time of a simple or complex movement. It was used in the original Safrit Fencing Test but is not an absolute necessity. Stop watches that measure one-hundredth of a second may also be used. A mat is not needed if stop watches are used. On an audible command, the subject makes a lunge against the wall. The clock starts when the forward foot of the subject is lifted off the mat or floor and stops after the lunge when the forward foot has recovered and is placed back on the mat so that the body weight is equally distributed over both feet. Subjects must be balanced before the clock is stopped. Five trials are given.

*The Automatic Performance Analyzer, Model 631, by George J. Dekan, Dekan Athletic Equipment, Inc., Carol Stream, Illinois.

Form is also an important part of the test, so appropriate form checks are made by the tester. They include:

1. upward bend of the blade
2. foil arm extension
3. back knee extension
4. back and front foot position

Scoring Method:

Two scores are recorded for each of five trials. A time score is recorded based on the elapsed time from the instant the forward foot is lifted until the forward foot has fully recovered and the subject is again in a balanced position. The score for each form check is five if the form is correct and zero if the form is not correct. With five form checks per trial, 25 points is maximum, and 125 are possible for all five trials.

Validity and Reliability:

Forty-three beginning fencers in three collegiate classes provided the test data in the Safrit study. None had any previous fencing experience.

Face validity is accepted for the test, and the reliability coefficients ranged from .81 to .85, depending upon the number of trials given and the amount of time allowed between trials.

Additional Comments:

Reliability of the test should be confirmed with the use of stop watches because of the inaccessibility of the Automatic Performance Analyzer.

Fencing References

Bower, M.G. (1961). *A test of general fencing ability*. Unpublished master's thesis, University of Southern California, Los Angeles.
Busch, R.E. (1966). *The construction of a fencing test using a moving target*. Unpublished master's thesis, University of North Carolina, Greensboro.
Cooper, C.K. (1968). *The development of a fencing skill test for measuring achievement of beginning collegiate women fencers in using the advance, beat and lunge*. Unpublished master's thesis, Western Illinois University, Macomb.
Emery, L. (1962). Criteria for rating selected skills of foil fencing. *DGWS Bowling-Fencing-Golf Guide* (1960-62). Washington, D.C.: AAHPER.
Fein, J.T. (1964). *Construction of skill tests for beginning collegiate women fencers*. Unpublished master's thesis, University of Iowa, Iowa City.
Kuhajda, P.F. (1970). *The construction and validation of a skill test for the riposte-lunge in fencing*. Unpublished master's thesis, Southern Illinois University, Carbondale.
Safrit, M.J. (1962). *Construction of skill tests for beginning fencers*. Unpublished master's thesis, University of Wisconsin, Madison.
Schutz, H.J. (1940). *Construction of an achievement scale in fencing for women*. Unpublished master's thesis, University of Washington, Seattle.
Swanson, A.H. (1967). *Measuring achievement in selected skills for beginning women fencers*. Unpublished master's thesis, University of Iowa, Iowa City.

Chapter 11

FIELD HOCKEY

INTRODUCTION

Skills tests construction for field hockey has not kept pace with its popularity as an outdoor team sport for females. However, the three tests that follow afford the instructor a comprehensive tool for evaluating field hockey ability.

STRAIT FIELD HOCKEY TEST
(Strait, 1960)

Purpose:

To measure field hockey ability.

Description:

The field markings include a 10-foot starting line with a stake (A) placed at the midpoint of the line (Figure 11.1). Two 10-foot parallel sidelines are also constructed. Stake B is placed in the ground at 42 feet and directly across from stake A with line markings constructed similar to those surrounding stake A. A backboard (F) with minimum dimensions of 12 x 18 feet is located at a spot indicated by Figure 11.1. Four one-foot squares (C, D, E and F) are also part of the field markings.

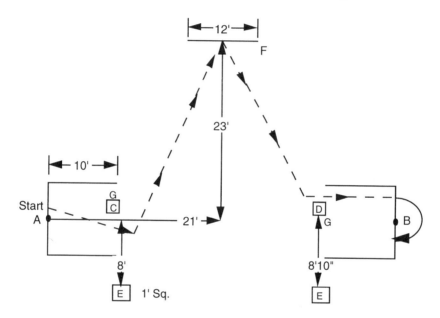

Fig. 11.1 Field markings for Strait Field Hockey Test.

From: Strait, C.J. (1965). *The construction and evaluation of a field hockey skills test.* Unpublished master's thesis, Smith College, Northampton, Massachusetts. Copyright by author.

Educational Application:

College women.

Time:

Twenty students can be tested in two 60-minute class periods.

Personnel:

A scorer-timer and one stick holder.

Equipment and Supplies:

Hockey sticks, balls, stop watch, backboard, scoring and field marking materials.

Facilities and Space:

A grass field with minimum measurements of 52 x 62 feet.

Directions:

After a practice trial, the subject stands behind the starting line while holding a field hockey stick. Behind the starting line and in front of the subject, a ball is placed. On an audible signal, the subject dribbles the ball away from stake A toward square C (Figure 11.1). A designated person (G) is standing at square C, holding a hockey stick. A legal dodge must be executed around the motionless assistant, and the ball is quickly recovered and driven to the backboard (F). The ball rebounding from the backboard is fielded and dribbled to stake B. A circular tackle is made around stake B, and the subject then repeats the same procedure as she heads back to stake A. This means the subject leaves stake B by dribbling the ball toward square D. A dodge is executed around square D and is followed by a drive and dribble and ends with a circular turn around stake A. The subject then begins the complete circuit again, and the watch is stopped when the student passes stake A the second time. The assistant (G) must remember to stand on square C at the beginning of the test and quickly shift to square D in time for the subject's return trip. This shifting continues for the second half of each trial.

Should a driven ball miss the backboard by passing it, the subject proceeds to the nearest ball enclosure (E) for another ball and continues the test circuit. Assuming the driven ball fails to reach the backboard, the subject continues to play the same ball by driving it again. Her feet must stay in the lane boundaries during the dribble or the trial is repeated.

Scoring Method:

The score for one trial is the time required to complete two continuous circuits beginning at stake A and ending when the subject dribbles past stake A for the second time. The final score is the best of three trials. A rest and recovery interval should be given to each subject between trials.

Validity and Reliability:

In correlating test scores with judges' ratings, a coefficient of .76 was obtained. The judges used a five-point scale developed by Strait. This scale shows potential as an aid in evaluating individual progress or achievement. It has value for self-testing and motivation purposes.

Utilizing the test-retest method, a .87 correlation coefficient was determined.

Rating Scale:

Excellent - 5 points
1. Stick work is superior
2. Footwork is consistently controlled
3. Ball control is excellent
4. Passes are well timed and accurate
5. Very rarely fouls
6. Positions herself well
7. Cuts to receive passes
8. Takes advantage of nearly all opportunities

Good - 4 points
1. Shows ability to make proper use of the stick
2. Feet are used to good advantage most of the time
3. Ball is usually under control
4. Passes are well timed and accurate
5. Rarely fouls
6. Positions herself well most of the time
7. Is able to see opportunities and take advantage of them
8. Cuts to receive passes

Average - 3 points
1. Drives and fielding are good, but lacks fine control of the ball for consistent dodges and tackles
2. Full use is not made of the feet
3. When in possession of the ball, occasionally loses it because of poor control
4. Some passes are good, but others are not well timed or accurate
5. Fouls moderately often
6. Is not sure as to where her position should be many times
7. Misses some available opportunities
8. Does not consistently cut for passes

Low - 2 points
1. Drives are not strong
2. When fielding, often misses the ball
3. Rarely tries dodges
4. Tackles unsuccessfully
5. Feet are sometimes in the way
6. Has small degree of ball control
7. Passes are poorly timed and not accurate
8. Fouls fairly often
9. Lacks good positioning
10. Usually fails to take advantage of opportunities
11. Is slow in getting to the ball

Poor - 1 point
1. Lacks general control of the stick
2. Feet are in the way
3. Ball is rarely under control
4. Passes are poorly timed and are not well directed
5. Fouls often
6. Appears not to realize the benefits of good positioning
7. Rarely takes advantage of opportunities
8. Usually does not move to meet the ball
9. Lacks body control, in general

Additional Comments:

Simulating a gamelike condition, this test naturally shows value as both a practice and testing device. Its validity value is sufficient enough to measure individual achievement.

HENRY-FRIEDEL FIELD HOCKEY TEST
(Henry, 1970)

Purpose:
To evaluate dribbling, dodging and shooting ability.

Description:
Field specifications for the combined dribbling, dodging and shooting test are shown in Figure 11.2.

Educational Application:
Designed for college and high school field hockey players, the test is appropriate for measuring general field hockey ability of junior and senior high school students.

Personnel:
One timer-scorer, a person to roll the balls to the student being tested, and a third individual to serve as a stationary object.

Equipment and Supplies:
Field hockey sticks and balls, goal cage, measuring tape, cones, stop watch, field marking and scoring materials.

Facilities and Space:
A 25 x 10 yard area.

Directions:
The subject holds a hockey stick and positions herself in the goal cage behind the starting line. On an audible signal, she runs toward the target area located 15 yards away. When the student crosses the seven-yard mark, a ball is rolled from one of the 10-yard sideline marks. The rolled ball should pass through the target within one foot in either direction of both corners, and stop within one foot inside the sideline of the testing area. Fielding the ball on the run within the two-yard square target area, the student dribbles toward a stationary

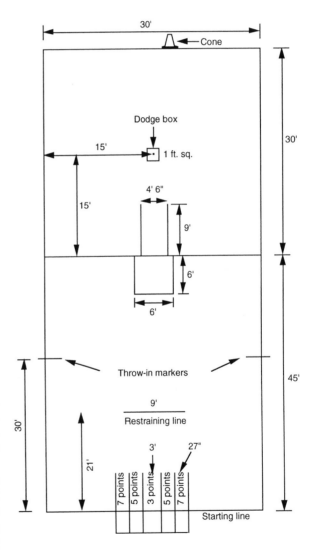

Fig. 11.2 Field markings for Henry-Friedel Field Hockey Test.

From: Henry, M.E. (1970). *The validation of a test of field hockey skills*. Unpublished master's thesis, Temple University, Philadelphia. Copyright by author.

individual standing in the one-foot square dodge area, and makes a right dodge around that person. The stationary person should vacate the testing area immediately after the testing student moves by. The student continues to dribble toward the end line, simulates a circular tackle in going around the cone and proceeds to dribble back downfield making sure to move within the 1 1/2-yard line. While behind the restraining line and within the lane line, the student drives the ball toward the goal. When a driven ball crosses the starting line or the sideline or comes to a stop in the testing area, the clock is stopped.

Ten time trials are scored, five for balls rolled in from the left side, and five rolled in from the right. One practice trial is permitted from each side, allowing a retrial if the ball does not pass through the target area.

Scoring:

The student receives an accuracy score and a speed score. The accuracy score is the total points accumulated in 10 trials. The point value assigned to the lane the ball passes through in the cage goal is recorded for each trial (Figure 1.12). Balls passing outside the cage goal are awarded one point, and balls not reaching the starting line or going over the sideline earn no points.

For the speed score, the time that elapses from the starting signal until the ball crosses the goal line, sideline, or stops within the testing area, is recorded in seconds and 10ths of seconds. A one-second penalty is assessed for the following: incorrect right dodge; omission of dodge; "sticks" on drive; using reverse sticks during circular tackle; driven ball over sideline; driven ball not reaching starting line; not fielding accurately rolled ball within target area. The total time for the 10 trials is the final speed score.

Validity and Reliability:

.70 to .89 for validity and .71 to .81 for test-retest reliability.

CHAPMAN BALL CONTROL TEST
(Chapman, 1982)

Purpose:

To measure stick movement ability
in field hockey.

Description:

Figure 11.3 depicts the necessary
floor target measurements for administering the Chapman Test.

Personnel:

One timer and one scorer-recorder.

Equipment and Supplies:

Field hockey sticks, balls, measuring
tape, marking tape, stop watch and
scoring materials.

Facilities and Space:

An area about 15 x 15 feet per testing
station.

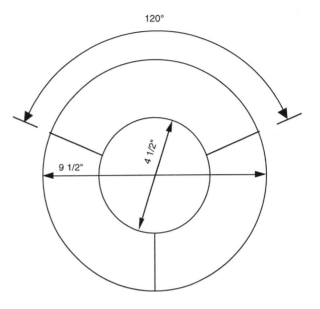

Fig. 11.3 Target measurements for Chapman Field Hockey
Test.

From: Chapman, N.L. (1982). Chapman ball control test -
field hockey. Reprinted with permission from *Research
Quarterly for Exercise and Sport* 53: 239-242. Copyright
1982 by the American Alliance for Health, Physical
Education, Recreation and Dance, 1900 Association Drive,
Reston, VA 20191.

Directions:

Following a short practice period, the
student stands just outside the larger
circle with a field hockey stick in
hand. On an audible signal, the
student taps a ball through or in and
out of the center circle. Each time this
is done, the ball must roll outside the larger circle. Legal target hits are illustrated in
Figure 11.4. Three 15-second trials are required.

Scoring Method:

A ball passing through or into the center circle counts as one point. Also, a point is
scored if the ball passes from the center circle to outside the larger circle through a
segment different from the one it entered (Figure 11.4). Balls tapped on the segment
area or with the rounded side of the stick receive no points. The total points earned in
the three 15-second trials is the final score.

Validity and Reliability:

Two methods of obtaining validity estimates resulted in coefficients of .63 (logical validity)
and .64 (concurrent validity). Utilizing intraclass reliability, a coefficient of .89 was
determined.

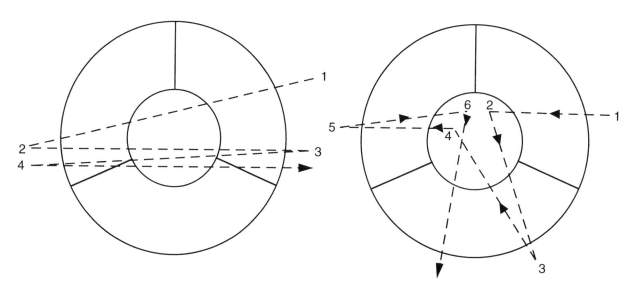

Fig. 11.4 Scoring methods for Chapman Field Hockey Test.

From: Chapman, N.L. (1982). Chapman ball control test - field hockey. Reprinted with permission from *Research Quarterly for Exercise and Sport* 53: 239-242. Copyright 1982 by the American Alliance for Health, Physical Education, Recreation and Dance, 1900 Association Drive, Reston, VA 20191.

Field Hockey References

Chapman, N.L. (1982). Chapman ball control test - field hockey. *Research Quarterly for Exercise and Sport* 53: 239-242.

Friedel, J.E. (1956). *The development of a field hockey skill test for high school girls.* Unpublished master's thesis, Illinois State University, Normal.

Henry, M.E. (1970). *The validation of a test of field hockey skills.* Unpublished master's thesis, Temple University, Philadelphia.

Illner, J.A. (1968). *The construction and validation of a skill test for the drive in field hockey.* Unpublished master's thesis, Southern Illinois University, Carbondale.

Kelly, E.D., & Brown, J.E. (1950). The construction of a field hockey test for women physical education majors. *Research Quarterly* 23: 322-329.

Lucey, M.A. (1934). *A study of reliability in relation to the construction of field hockey tests.* Unpublished master's thesis, University of Wisconsin, Madison.

Perry, E.L. (1969). *An investigation of field hockey skills tests for college women.* Unpublished master's thesis, Pennsylvania State University, University Park.

Schmithals, M., & French, E. (1940). Achievement tests in field hockey for college women. *Research Quarterly* 9: 84-92.

Stewart, H.E. (1965). *A test for measuring field hockey skill of college women.* Unpublished doctoral dissertation, Indiana University, Bloomington.

Strait, C.J. (1965). *The construction and evaluation of a field hockey skills test.* Unpublished master's thesis, Smith College, Northampton, Massachusetts.

Chapter 12

FIGURE SKATING

INTRODUCTION

Few American universities include figure skating as part of their educational curriculum. Consequently, only a limited number of skills tests have been constructed for the sport, and most of those were not scientifically evaluated.

CARRIERE SKATING TEST
(Carriere, 1969)

Purpose:

To determine basic figure skating ability.

Description:

The Carriere Skating Test contains 40 items which are progressively more difficult and provides a comprehensive measure of basic figure skating skills.

Educational Application:

College men and women.

Time:

A class of 20 students can be tested in two 60-minute class periods.

Personnel:

One scorer-recorder.

Equipment and Supplies:

Skates and scoring materials.

Facilities and Space:

Ice rink or other similar skating area.

Directions:

It is best to administer the test in a rink with regular ice hockey markings to ensure uniformity. The ice markings should include the following:

1. Hockey blue line to goal line - 60 feet
2. Face-off mark to other face-off mark - 60 feet
3. Face-off circle diameter - 20 feet
4. Face-off mark diameter - 2 feet

The subjects should try to successfully execute as many of the 40 test items as possible. The items do not have to be attempted or successfully completed in any particular order and may be attempted any number of times. All of the items are of equal value.

Certain terms and abbreviations need to be clarified before the testing begins since successful execution depends to a great extent on the subject's understanding of the terminology. The subjects and tester should refer to a book by Ogilvie (Ogilvie, 1968) for more specific and technical information.

Abbreviations

R - right	F - forward	I - inside edge
L - left	B - backward	O - outside edge

Terms:

1. Inside shoulder: shoulder toward inside of curve.
2. Employed skate: skate on ice.
3. Free skate: skate off ice.
4. Free arm: arm that is forward when the free leg is back.
5. Leading leg: when skating backwards, means the free leg is extended in back of the body.
6. Continuous axis: an imaginary line running the length of the rink.
7. Lobe: any step or sequence of steps on one side of the continuous axis.
8. Transverse axis: an imaginary line intersecting the continuous axis at a right angle.

Test Items:

Forward:
1. Skate 60 feet in any manner.
2. Stroke and parallel glide alternately for 60 feet; start with T push-off.
3. T push-off and cover 60 feet with three more strokes.
4. Take three strokes (R-L-R or L-R-L) and glide 30 feet on one skate with skating knee slightly bent (not straight) and head up.

Backward Sculling:

Each sculling motion must start with feet less than six inches apart.
5. Scull with both feet for 60 feet in a straight line.
6. Scull around face-off circle with R scull and L glide. Repeat with L scull and R glide.
7. Scull straight with alternate feet for 60 feet; gliding skate must remain on red or blue line.
8. Scull straight with alternate feet and glide straight on either skate for 30 feet with skating knee slightly bent, back straight, arms down and out to the side.

Stops:

9. Skate five strokes forward and execute three consecutive stops using either snowplow, T, or parallel stops.
10. Skate forward from one face-off circle and stop on the other face-off mark.

Turns:

Each turn must start from head and shoulders.
11. Forward to backward turn on two feet: skate four F strokes, parallel glide on both skates, half turn R and stop. Repeat with half turn L.
12. Forward to backward three turn on both feet and backward to forward turn changing from one foot to the other around face-off circle. Preliminary strokes, parallel glide, clockwise (RFO and LFI), three turn to RBI and LBO, shift weight to left skate, and turn to RFO. Repeat counterclockwise.

Forward Curves:

13. Four alternate, parallel glide half-circles (10-foot radius): push off on RFO from line; glide with feet parallel around half-circle and back to line; change at line to LFO and parallel glide; change again to RFO and LFO at line. Lean with body straight from ankles up.

14. Ten alternate single strokes along straight line: push off on RFO, curve back to line, shift to LFO (and back) four times.

15. Ten alternate single FI strokes along straight line: same as item 14 but on single inside edges.

Backward Curves:

16. Four alternate, backward, parallel glide half-circles (five-foot radius): like item 13 but backward; push off on RBO from line, glide around half-circle with feet parallel, change at line to LBO and parallel glide; repeat. No toe scratches.

17. Ten alternate single BO strokes along straight line: push off on RBO and curve back to line, shift to LBO, etc.

18. Ten alternate single BI strokes along straight line: same as item 17 but on single inside edges.

Forward Crossovers:

19. Five forward crossovers around face-off circle, clockwise and counterclockwise (preliminary strokes permissible), and stop (no stepping).

20. T push off, complete circuit of face-off circle with four (or less) crossovers, clockwise or counterclockwise. Must show a bent skating knee, outward thrust with trailing skate, outside arm and shoulder forward and inside arm back.

Advanced Turns:

21. RFO three turn and LFO three turn: start with two or three preliminary strokes, turn from RBO to RBI and hold RBI for three seconds, then parallel glide, and stop. Repeat with LBO to LBI turn. Movement must be straight or around face-off circle.

22. Four consecutive, alternate, small three turns in a straight line and stop: T push off, RFO to RBI to LFO and LBI and repeat, stop.

23. Controlled three turn, RFO to RBI or LFO to LFI: T push off, glide for three seconds on RFO preparing to turn with arms and shoulders, turn to RBI and glide for three seconds going back to line, and stop. Skater must prepare for turn with arms and shoulders and come out strongly checked (free arm, shoulder and hip back).

24. Forward inside open Mohawk: start with three or four preliminary strokes from LFO, glide for three seconds on RFI, change to LFI (inside R) and glide for three seconds, then parallel glide, skate backward to starting line and stop. May be done to opposite side.

Advanced Stops:

26. Forward T stop: skate three or four strokes, short glide and stop, alternate R and L braking skate behind at R angle and parallel to shoulders. No ankle dragging on inside edge of blade, arms held down and out to the side.

27. Parallel side stop (hockey stop): take 10 to 15 strokes with increasing speed, parallel glide and stop (hold position one second). Shoulders must face the direction of travel; skates are parallel and knees strongly bent.

Jumps:

28. Three bunny hop jumps: executed consecutively or alternated with one or two strokes between each jump. Free leg thrown forward, landing on toe pick, then push from toe pick into that of skating foot blade, stroke and stop.
29. Waltz jump: start with preliminary strokes, glide on a FO, swing free leg forward and push up with skating foot, make half turn in air, land on opposite BO, glide and stop. Free arm forward and head facing the initial direction. The jump is done on a curve.

Spins:

30. Three complete two-foot spins and stop. Spin on the flat of the blades without traveling on ice.

Intermediate and Advanced:

31. Five backward crossovers around face-off circle, clockwise and counterclockwise. When skating counterclockwise the left foot never loses contact with the ice and vice versa for clockwise (no toe scratch).
32. Six alternate sequences of progressive and chasse steps along the blue line with a count of six for each sequence (2-1-3). Curves should be equal size and about a third of a circle of 10-foot radius.
33. Six alternate FO swing rolls. Same as item 32 but the free leg is extended and swinging from the back to the front of the body. Free toe pointed down and turned slightly out.
34. Forward change of edges on one foot: a moving start or start from rest may be used to change from RFO edge to RFL. Curves should be equal sizes and change on blue or red line.
35. Shoot the duck: take as many preliminary strokes as desired before going into a sitting position with free leg extended in front, head up, back straight. Glide for five seconds and come back to initial upright position, stroke and stop.
36. Forward spiral: start off with preliminary strokes, glide on one foot, bring extended free leg up and behind. Head and free foot should be at least at the level with the upper part of the seat. Arms are extended to the side of the body. Glide for five seconds; bring free foot on ice, stroke and stop.
37. Four alternate FI curves along an axis (blue or red line): push off from rest. Free shoulder and arm are held low and in leading position. Skating shoulder and arm are held back. The free foot is in front at the middle of the curve. Approaching the long axis, square shoulder to the line of travel. Size of the curves same as item 32.
38. Four alternate BO curves along axis (blue or red line): push off from rest. Free shoulder and arm in front, skating shoulder arm in leading position. Body rotates; free leg is behind at the middle of the curve. Approaching the long axis, free side is in open position. Size of curves same as item 32.
39. Full circle on one foot (outside edge): push off from rest position to a forward outside edge, complete the face-off circle circuit on one foot and stop.

40. Forward outside eight: push off on a right forward outside complete circle and stroke into the left forward outside edge crossing the transverse axis. Stay close to the marker on the ice (a range of one foot is allowed only).
Diameter of circles: 15 feet.

Scoring Method:

Each maneuver attempted is assigned a score of either one or zero, depending only upon the successful completion of that particular item. The final score is the sum total of points accumulated on the 40-item or point test. It might help the tester to know that the number of test items successfully completed in the Carriere study ranged from 10 to 34. None of the subjects passed items 39 or 40.

An item is failed for improper execution involving such mistakes as:
1. falling or having to recover;
2. not covering distance in specified time;
3. not holding stop for three seconds;
4. using a toe pick (unless specifically allowed);
5. not changing feet on the line when specified.

Validity and Reliability:

The original test group consisted of 49 male and female college students from two ice skating classes. Seven students ultimately did not have their data included so the test group ended with 42 subjects.

The .90 validity value was determined by correlating the sum of three judges' ratings and the number of items passed. The .97 reliability coefficient was computed by the split-half method and corrected by the Spearman-Brown Prophecy Formula.

Objectivity:

The objectivity was determined by having the test originator, a student from the skating class and a student assistant from another skating class judge three students when performing 11 randomly selected items.

Additional Comments:

A questionnaire was given to the subjects at the end of the previously mentioned skating classes, and 82 percent thought the test helped motivate them to learn and progress at their own pace. This test is particularly valuable in the assessment of individual progress and achievement.

The test items show a degree of flexibility in range of difficulty enough to motivate the lesser experienced skaters and challenge the intermediate and advanced ones.

No distinction is made between the subjects that pass a test item on their first attempt and those that require additional attempts. When the test is used as an evaluation tool, the authors suggest that the tester limit the number of attempts per student or set some type of time limit. This would naturally place a higher value on successful completion of a maneuver on the first try. It would also reduce the time involved in the testing process.

Figure Skating References

Carriere, D.L. (1969). *An objective figure skating test for use in beginning classes.* Unpublished master's thesis, University of Illinois, Urbana.

Leaming, T.W. (1959). *A measure of endurance of young speed skaters.* Unpublished master's thesis, University of Illinois, Urbana.

Moore, K.F. (1967). *An objective evaluation system for judging free skating routines.* Unpublished master's thesis, Michigan State University, East Lansing.

Ogilvie, R.S. (1968). *Basic ice skating skills.* New York: Lippincott.

Recknagel, D. (1945). A test for beginners in figure skating. *Journal of Health and Physical Education* 16: 91-92.

Chapter 13

FOOTBALL

INTRODUCTION

In the same length of time, probably no other American sport has grown in popularity as much as football. The sport literally became a cultural phenomenon in the latter half of the 20th century, enjoying success at all organized levels.

Normally thought of in terms of tackle football, the type found in physical education programs is either flag or touch football. From elementary school to college, these are rather common and popular offerings in the physical education curriculum. However, the majority of football skills tests either pertain to tackle football or lack scientific documentation. Those that follow in this chapter have either been authenticated in value or at least are widely accepted and used.

BORLESKE TOUCH FOOTBALL TEST
(Borleske, 1936)

Purpose:

To measure basic skills and classify students for instruction and competition in touch football.

Description:

Borleske constructed an 18-item test battery which was later reduced to five and then three items. Using a criterion of expert judgment, validity coefficients of .93 and .88 were derived for the five- and three-item batteries, respectively.

Comprising the smaller battery are the forward pass for distance, punt for distance and run for time tests. Each item in the smaller battery is included in the five-item battery, and a description of all five follows.

Forward Pass for Distance. No special field markings are needed if the test is administered on a regulation football field. Otherwise, yard markers spaced at five-yard intervals are used.

Punt for Distance. Field markings same as for the forward pass for distance item.

Run for Time. A 50-yard distance is marked off if a regulation football field is unavailable.

Catching Forward Pass. Regulation football field or an area designed as for the forward pass for distance test.

Pass Defense Zone. The field or testing area is marked off into four equal rectangles or quadrants. Each has a measurement of 42 x 36 feet (Figure 13.1).

Educational Application:

College men.

Time:

One class of 20 students can be tested in one or two 60-minute class periods for the three-item battery, depending on the number of test stations available. Twenty students can complete the five-item battery in two or three 60-minute periods, depending again on how many test stations are available.

Personnel:

One to five scorers, depending on the particular test battery used and number of test stations utilized simultaneously. Student assistants also play an instrumental role in the test administration.

Equipment and Supplies:

Footballs, stop watch, scoring and field marking materials.

Facilities and Space:

Regulation football field or an outdoor field or playing area of similar size.

Directions:

A warm-up of one minute is recommended for each student immediately prior to three of the test items. None is recommended for the catching forward pass and pass defense zone tests.

Forward Pass for Distance. The subject receives the ball from center while standing at the end line and executes three forward passes for distance. The forward pass should be as straight as possible and at right angles to the end line. The subject remains behind the end line when executing the forward pass. He allows ample space behind the end line for proper execution of the pass without going over that line.

Borleske recommended that the subjects throw in pairs with one throwing and the other marking and retrieving the thrown ball. Each subject alternates throws with his partner. The subject is not required to throw the ball if the center pass is not a good one.

Punt for Distance. The administration of this test is similar to that of the forward pass for distance item except that the subject receives the ball seven yards behind the end line where the center snaps the ball. Subjects punt the ball within two seconds after receiving the center snap.

Run for Time. Subjects line up in a three-point stance five yards from the center. When the ball is snapped, the subject proceeds to sprint 50 yards. The 50-yard distance is measured from the point where the run initiated.

Only one trial is given to each subject. The trial is repeated when a bad center snap occurs. The ball may be carried by the subject in any desired manner.

Catching Forward Pass. Subjects run three different pass patterns and catch a forward pass. The running patterns vary, and it is important that the subject follow the designated pass route as closely as possible. Pass patterns are as follows:

a. Square-out pattern - subject goes 10 yards straight down the field from the center, cuts right at a 90-degree angle and runs toward the sideline.

b. Post or flag pattern - subject goes 10 yards down the field from the center, cuts left at a 35-degree angle and continues to run.

c. V pattern - subject goes 15 yards down the field at a 45-degree angle from the center, cuts right at another 45-degree angle and continues the run across the field parallel to the end line.

The forward pass should be caught while the subject is running the pattern. Three "fair" trials are given for each subject. A "fair" trial is one in which the pass is thrown accurately enough for the subject to have a reasonable opportunity to catch the ball. A bad pass results in a retrial. If the subject can touch the ball with a reasonable effort, it counts as a fair trial.

Pass Defense Zone. The subject takes a position in one of the four quadrants (Figure 13.1). A center (C) snaps the football to a passer (P) who is standing 10 yards to the rear. Three receivers (R) run predetermined pass patterns. Three pass plays are executed and each has either one, two or three receivers running to the same quadrant as the

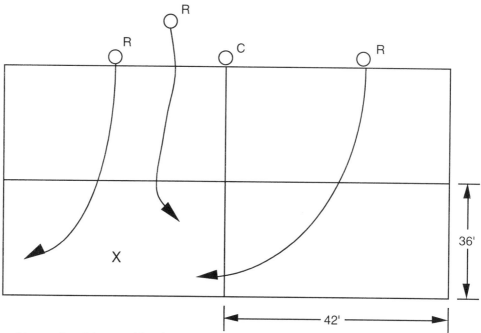

Fig. 13.1 Field markings and participant positions in pass defense zone test.

From: Borleske, S.E. (1936). *A study of achievement of college men in touch football.* Unpublished master's thesis, University of California, Berkeley. Copyright by author.

defensive subject (X). The order of plays may be varied, but it is absolutely necessary that the number of eligible receivers varies for each of three plays. The passer and receivers should huddle before each play so patterns can be assigned.

The subject or defensive player should play a zone defense, and when the pass is thrown, he attempts to either knock the ball away from the receiver or intercept it. More credit is naturally given for an interception.

A defender is penalized if defensive pass interference occurs. Only one trial is allowed for each play unless a poor pass is thrown that neither the receiver nor a defensive player can reach. The subject is cautioned to stay in the assigned quadrant and only defend receivers who enter that particular quadrant.

Scoring Method and Norms:

Forward Pass for Distance. Each subject is allowed three trials, and the final score is the best of the three throws measured to the nearest yard.

Punt for Distance. Same as for the forward pass for distance test.

Run for Time. Each subject is allowed one trial, and the final score is the time elapsed from the instant the player receives the ball until the 50-yard line is crossed.

Catching Forward Pass. Subjects are allowed three "fair" trials when completing the pass patterns. Each pass caught and retained by the subject counts 10 points with a perfect score being 30 points.

Pass Defense Zone. The subject completes one trial for each of the three plays. Should the receiver catch the pass and it is ruled a legal completion under football rules, no points are given to the subject. One-third of the total earned points are deducted from the score for each defensive pass interference that occurs.

Two points are awarded if the defensive player knocks down the ball when one receiver is in the quadrant, and four points are given if the ball is intercepted under that circumstance. Six points are awarded if the defensive player knocks down the ball with two receivers in the quadrant, and eight points are given if the ball is intercepted in the same situation. Ten points are awarded if the defensive player either knocks down or intercepts the pass with three receivers in the quadrant.

The maximum score a defensive player can achieve is 22 points.

Conversion of raw scores to *T*-scores enables an instructor to classify students according to ability levels for the purpose of grading.

Validity and Reliability:

The Borleske Touch Football Test was administered to five college physical education classes, consisting of 87 men. Validity coefficients for specific items were not reported. However, the three-item and five-item battery coefficients were .88 and .93, respectively, utilizing judges' ratings as the criterion measure. Reliability coefficients were not reported.

Additional Comments:

The forward pass and punt for distance items plus the run for time test are all easy to administer with minimum equipment involved. These items are very conducive to a multistation testing plan.

In addition to the practice needed by the subject in preparation for the catching forward pass item, it is also imperative that the passer be consistent and accurate in throwing; otherwise, the fatigue factor may significantly affect results. Running pass patterns is time-consuming and can be tiring for the subject, even when receivers are alternated.

For the pass defense zone test, a center is needed who can snap the ball in a consistent and accurate manner. The same is true for the passer. Receivers should readily comprehend and master the assigned pass patterns.

	Table 13.1				
	T-SCORES FOR BORLESKE TOUCH FOOTBALL TEST*				
T-Score	Forward Pass-Yds.	Punting - Yds.	Running - Sec.	Catching - Points	Past Defense- Points
76					
75	56 - 58	50.6 - 53.5			8.0 - 8.49
74					
73	53 - 55		5.36 - 5.55		
72					7.0 - 7.99
71		47.6 - 50.5			
70					6.5 - 6.99
69	50 - 52	44.6 - 47.5			6.0 - 6.49
68					5.5 - 5.99
67					5.0 - 5.49
66	47 - 49				4.5 - 4.99
65			5.56- 5.75		
64					4.0 - 4.49
63	44 - 46				
62		41.6 - 44.5			
61			5.76 - 5.95		
60				9.51 - 10.0	
59	41 - 43				
58					3.5 - 3.99
57					3.0 - 3.49
56		38.6 - 41.5	5.96 - 6.15		
55				7.01 - 9.50	2.5 - 2.99
54	38 - 40				
53					2.0 - 2.49
52			6.16 - 6.35		
51		35.6 - 38.5		6.51 - 7.00	
50	35 - 37				
49					1.5 - 1.99
48		32.6 - 35.5	6.36 - 6.55		
47					1.0 - 1.49
46	32 - 34			3.51 - 6.50	0.5 - 0.99
45		29.6 - 32.5			
44			6.56 - 6.75		
43				3.01 - 3.50	
42	29 - 31				
41			6.76 - 6.95		
40		26.6 - 29.5			0.0 - 0.49
39	26 - 28				
38		23.6 - 26.5	6.96 - 7.15	0.51 - 3.00	
37		20.6 - 23.5			
36	23 - 25				
35		17.6 - 20.5	7.16 - 7.35		
34	20 - 22			0.00 - 0.50	
33					
32			7.36 - 7.55		
31	17 - 19				
30		14.6 - 17.5			
29					
28			7.56 - 8.95		
27	14 - 16	11.6 - 14.6			
26					
25	11 - 13		8.6 - 11.5		

*Based on scores of 87 college men.

From: Borleske, S.E. (1936). *A study of achievement of college men in touch football.* Unpublished master's thesis, University of California, Berkeley. Copyright by author.

Table 13.2	
GRADING SCALE FOR BORLESKE TOUCH FOOTBALL TEST	
Classification	Points
Superior	314 and over
Above Average	274 - 313
Average	232 - 273
Below Average	191 - 231
Inferior	190 and below

From: Borleske, S.E. (1936). *A study of achievement of college men in touch football.*
Unpublished master's thesis, University of California, Berkeley. Copyright by author.

JACOBSON-BORLESKE TOUCH FOOTBALL TEST
(Jacobson, 1960)

Purpose:

To measure general ability in touch football.

Description:

Jacobson designed an instrument to objectively evaluate touch football skills of junior high school boys. The three-item test battery of the Borleske Touch Football Test was selected for investigation because it was the only test of demonstrated value constructed prior to 1960.

The investigator proceeded to administer the three-item test battery (forward pass for distance, punt for distance and run for distance) to junior high boys' physical education classes. An average of 55 boys per class existed, and there were four classes of seventh, eighth and ninth graders, for a total of 12 classes containing 660 students.

Educational Application:

Junior high school boys.

Time:

One class of 20 students can be tested in one or two 60-minute class periods for the three-item battery, depending on the number of test stations available. Twenty students can complete the five-item battery in two or three 60-minute periods, depending again on how many test stations are available.

Personnel:

One to five scorers, depending on the particular test battery used and number of test stations utilized simultaneously. Student assistants also play an instrumental role in the test administration.

Equipment and Supplies:

Footballs, stop watch, scoring and field marking materials.

Facilities and Space:

Regulation football field or an outdoor field or playing area of similar size.

Directions:

The punt for distance and run for time tests are administered according to the directions of the Borleske Test, but directions for the forward pass for distance item differ somewhat from Borleske's original test. One to six passers are tested at once, and the student throws three consecutive passes. Also, the center snap is eliminated, and a trial may be repeated when the passer steps over the restraining line.

Scoring Method and Norms:

Each of the three test items is scored as indicated in the Borleske Test.

Table 13.3 includes the *T*-scores for each of the three test items when applied to seventh, eighth and ninth grade boys. The tester may wish to use the data found in Table 13.4 for classification and/or grading purposes.

Table 13.3
T-SCORES FOR JACOBSON-BORLESKE TOUCH FOOTBALL TEST*

T-Score	Pass for Distance			Punt for Distance			Run for Speed			*T*-Score
	7th Grade	8th Grade	9th Grade	7th Grade	8th Grade	9th Grade	7th Grade	8th Grade	9th Grade	
85	41	48	53	38	43	47				85
80	39	45	50	36	40	44	6.3	5.8	5.7	80
75	36	41	46	33	37	41	6.7	6.2	6.0	75
70	34	38	43	31	34	38	7.0	6.6	6.3	70
65	31	35	39	28	31	34	7.3	7.0	6.7	65
60	28	32	36	26	28	32	7.7	7.4	7.0	60
55	25	29	33	23	25	28	8.0	7.7	7.3	55
50	23	26	29	20	22	25	8.3	8.1	7.6	50
45	20	23	26	18	19	22	8.6	8.5	7.9	45
40	18	20	23	16	16	19	9.0	8.9	8.3	40
35	15	17	19	13	13	16	9.3	9.2	8.6	35
30	13	14	16	11	10	13	9.6	9.6	8.9	30
25	10	10	13	8	7	10	10.0	10.0	9.2	25
20	8	8	10	6		7	10.3	10.4	9.5	20
15	5	6					10.6	10.7	9.9	15

*Based on scores of 220 boys in each of the above grades.

From: Jacobson, T.V. (1960). *An evaluation of performance in certain physical ability tests administered to selected secondary school boys*. Unpublished master's thesis, University of Washington, Seattle. Copyright by author.

Validity and Reliability:

Scientific documentation data of the Borleske Test were accepted for this test since only minor modifications were made in the test items.

Additional Comments:

Jacobson made a valuable contribution to skills testing literature by formulating the two sets of scales which should greatly aid instructors of touch football classes at the junior high level.

Like Borleske, Jacobson failed to document the reliability value of the three test items. This is an area that needs exploration.

		Table 13.4		
	GRADING SCALE FOR JACOBSON-BORLESKE TOUCH FOOTBALL TEST			
Event	Grade	7th Grade	8th Grade	9th Grade
Pass for Distance (Measured in Yards)	A	33 & over	38 & over	42 & over
	B	27 - 32	30 - 37	34 - 41
	C	21 - 26	23 - 29	26 - 33
	D	15 - 20	15 - 22	18 - 25
	E	14 & under	14 & under	17 & under
Punt for Distance (Measured in Yards)	A	30 & over	34 & over	37 & over
	B	24 - 29	26 - 33	30 - 36
	C	18 - 23	19 - 25	22 - 29
	D	12 - 17	12 - 18	15 - 21
	E	11 & under	11 & under	14 & under
Running Speed (Measured in Seconds)	A	7.1 & under	6.7 & under	6.4 & under
	B	7.2 - 7.8	6.8 - 7.6	6.5 - 7.1
	C	7.9 - 8.7	7.7 - 8.5	7.2 - 7.9
	D	8.8 - 9.5	8.6 - 9.4	8.0 - 8.7
	E	9.6 & over	9.5 & over	8.8 & over
Total Test (Measured in T-Scores)	A	195 & over	193 & over	195 & over
	B	166 - 194	165 - 192	165 - 194
	C	137 - 165	137 - 164	136 - 164
	D	108 - 136	108 - 136	106 - 135
	E	107 & under	107 & under	105 & under

From: Jacobson, T.V. (1960). *An evaluation of performance in certain physical ability tests administered to selected secondary school boys.* Unpublished master's thesis, University of Washington, Seattle. Copyright by author.

AAHPER FOOTBALL SKILLS TESTS
(AAHPER, 1965)

Purpose:

To measure the fundamental skills associated with football.

Description:

The AAHPER Football Skills Tests result from the Sports Skills Test Project sponsored by the organization now known as the American Alliance for Health, Physical Education, Recreation and Dance. Each of the 10 tests is designed to measure a specific football skill. They are regarded as not only a tool for evaluation but also as a practice device for the purpose of player improvement.

This particular test can be used for either tackle, touch or flag football, with the exception of the blocking item. Special test layout markings are restricted to those test items described below.

Forward Pass for Distance. A restraining area is formed which consists of two parallel lines drawn six feet apart.

Blocking. A starting line is drawn, and a blocking bag is positioned 15 feet away. A second bag is located 15 feet directly to the right of bag one, and a third bag is stationed 15 feet from the second at a 45-degree angle toward the starting line.

Forward Pass for Accuracy. Requirements for this item include a target, 8 x 11 feet in size. The target has three concentric circles of two, four and six feet in diameter, from inside to outside. Circle lines should be coded with colors to promote scoring ease. The canvas target may be hung between the goal posts with the narrow end tied over the cross bar. The bottom of the outer circle is located three feet above the ground, and the canvas is stretched tight.

A restraining line is drawn 15 feet away from the target.

Ball Changing Zigzag Run. Five chairs are placed 10 feet apart in a straight line with the first chair positioned 10 feet from the starting line. The chairs face away from the starting line.

Catching Forward Pass. Thirty feet and straight away from the starting line, an appropriate marker signifies the "turning point" for the subject to cut around as part of the test requirement. Directly to its right at 30 feet is a "receiving point," which should be some marker that in no way could possibly interfere with the subject in catching the ball.

Pull-out. A finish line is drawn 30 feet away and parallel to the scrimmage line.

Educational Application:

Junior and senior high school boys.

Time:

A class of 20 students can be tested in approximately five 60-minute class periods.

Personnel:

One scorer-timer per test station plus assistants wherever indicated in test directions.

Equipment and Supplies:

Footballs, stop watch, blocking bags, goal posts, 8 x 11 canvas target, chairs, kicking tee, hurdles, white handkerchief, scoring and field marking materials.

Facilities and Space:

Regulation football field properly marked off, or a playing field of similar size.

Directions, Scoring Method and Norms:

One practice pass is recommended for each subject immediately before being tested on the forward pass for distance item. A warm-up is suggested in preparation for the 50-yard dash, and a practice trial is allowed for the blocking, forward pass for accuracy, football punt for distance, ball changing zigzag run, pull-out, kick-off and dodging run items. A practice pass pattern for both the right and left direction is recommended for the catching forward pass test.

Forward Pass for Distance. Each subject is given three trials to pass the ball as far as possible. The subject may take one or more running steps but must stay within the six-foot restraining area and not step over the second restraining line or the goal line. A wire stake is used to mark the longest pass.

The score is the longest throw of three trials. The distance is measured to the last foot passed at right angles to the throwing line.

Fifty-Yard Dash with Football. The student stands behind the starting line while holding a football. The starter gives the audible signal "Go" and drops a white handkerchief. This signals the timer to start the watch. The subject proceeds to sprint the 50-yard distance while carrying the ball.

Two trials are allowed with a rest period in between, and the score is the best of the two trials timed to the nearest 10th of a second.

Blocking. The student takes a position behind the starting line. When the audible signal "Go" is given, the watch is started and the student proceeds to sprint to the first blocking bag.

Once the subject has cross-body blocked the first bag, he should quickly scramble to his feet and sprint toward the second bag and then the third, repeating the same action at each. Once all the bags have been properly cross-body blocked, the subject sprints over the starting line which terminates the trial.

Two test trials are given with an intervening rest period. Each of the three bags must be cross-body blocked to the ground which means a bump does not count. The score is the lowest time recorded for the two trials when measured to the nearest tenth-second.

Forward Pass for Accuracy. Positioned behind the restraining line, the subject should take two or three running steps behind and parallel to the line, hesitate and throw at the target. The subject may run to either the right or left, but the restraining line must not be crossed. The pass should have some "zip" on it or be of "good speed."

Ten test trials are given and the score is the total number of points accumulated on all 10 trials. The target areas yield one, two or three points, and a ball striking a dividing line receives the higher point value.

Football Punt for Distance. Directions and scoring method same as for forward pass for distance item.

Ball Changing Zigzag Run. The student stands behind the starting line with a football under the right arm. Positioned to the right of the first chair and responding to the audible signal "Go," he proceeds to sprint to the right side of the first chair. When the first chair is passed, the subject changes the ball to the left arm and runs to the left of the second chair. The subject continues to run between the chairs, changing the ball from one side to the other. The ball should always be kept under the outside arm, with the inside arm extended in an imaginary stiff-arm position. The fifth or end chair should be circled from right to left and the subject continues back through the chairs as before with the trial ending when he crosses the starting line.

The chairs should not be hit for any reason. Two test trials are administered with a rest period between them. The score is the best time in two trials which are timed to the nearest tenth-second.

Catching Forward Pass. The student assumes a position immediately behind the scrimmage line and nine feet to the right of center. When the audible signal "Go" is given, the center snaps the ball directly back to the passer while the subject proceeds to run to the designated "turning point." The subject cuts around the "turning point" to the right and runs to the "receiving point."

The passer should receive the center snap, take one step and pass the ball at head height and directly over the "passing point." The subject attempts to catch as many of the passes as possible. Poorly thrown passes or passes not thrown over the "passing point" do not count as test trials.

Ten test trials on both the right and left side are given. The running pattern and procedure are the same for each side. The score is the sum of total passes caught from each side. One point is scored for each pass reception.

Pull-out. The test subject assumes a set position (three- or four-point stance) while facing straight ahead, and his hands are placed on a line running between the goal posts. The subject is located exactly half the distance between the two posts.

When the audible signal "Go" is given, the subject immediately pulls out or off the line of scrimmage and proceeds to run behind and parallel to the line until reaching the right-hand goal post. The subject makes a sharp turn around the right goal post and sprints directly downfield to the finish line.

Each subject is allowed two test trials with a rest period between. The final score is the best of two trials timed to the nearest 10th of a second.

Kick-off. Directions and scoring method are the same as for the first item above with two exceptions. First, there is no restraining area, so the approach run may be as long as the subject desires. Second, the ball is placed on the kicking tee with a slight backward tilt.

Dodging Run. Holding a football and standing behind a point designated on the starting line to the right of the first hurdle, the subject responds to the audible signal "Go" by sprinting to the left of the second hurdle which is located five yards in front of the starting point. The subject continues to run around the right side of the third hurdle, which is located to the right of the second hurdle and two yards farther up the field. The fourth hurdle is passed on the left and located to the left of the third hurdle which is also two yards farther up the field. Circling the fifth hurdle right to left, the subject continues to run between the hurdles while progressing back to the first hurdle. That hurdle is circled from right to left, and a repeat trip is made with the test trial ending when two complete round trips are completed. The fifth hurdle is located to the right of the fourth hurdle and again is two yards on up the field.

Two trial runs are given with a rest period scheduled between them. The tester should note that the subject is not required to switch the ball from side to side as the run is being made. If the ball is dropped, the run does not count. The final score is the best time recorded for the two trials which are timed to the nearest 10th of a second.

Ten-Item Battery. Percentile scores of boys, ages 10 to 18, are shown in Tables 13.5 through 13.14. Subjects ranging from 600 to 900 in number were tested on each item.

Validity and Reliability:

Face validity is claimed for each item. Reliability standards were established at a minimum level of .80 for the tests or events scored on the basis of distance, and not less than .70 for the tests measuring accuracy or form.

The test items were administered to students from schools located in several different cities throughout the United States. All had recently experienced a complete instructional unit on the test contents.

Additional Comments:

The administrative feasibility of the AAHPER Football Test is questionable when used only as an evaluation tool. Learning drills could be developed for each item to periodically measure student progress.

The face validity assumption should be confirmed for the ball changing zigzag run, pull-out and dodging items because they only approximate actual football skill requirements. Other criticisms leveled at the AAHPER Football Test include its omission of a time limit in the punt for distance item, the scoring difficulty that the blocking test presents, and that the pass catching item is too time-consuming. Also, a ball snapping item should be included in the battery to make it a fully comprehensive measure of football ability (Morris, 1977).

Table 13.5
FORWARD PASS FOR DISTANCE Test Scores in Feet

Percentile	10	11	12	Age 13	14	15	16	17-18	Percentile
100th	95	105	120	150	170	180	180	180	100th
95th	71	83	99	115	136	135	144	152	95th
90th	68	76	92	104	118	127	135	143	90th
85th	64	73	87	98	114	122	129	137	85th
80th	62	70	83	95	109	118	126	133	80th
75th	61	68	79	91	105	115	123	129	75th
70th	59	65	77	88	102	111	120	127	70th
65th	58	64	75	85	99	108	117	124	65th
60th	56	62	73	83	96	105	114	121	60th
55th	55	61	71	80	93	102	111	117	55th
50th	53	59	68	78	91	99	108	114	50th
45th	52	56	66	76	88	97	105	110	45th
40th	51	54	64	73	85	94	103	107	40th
35th	49	51	62	70	83	92	100	104	35th
30th	47	50	60	69	80	89	97	101	30th
25th	45	48	58	65	77	85	93	98	25th
20th	44	45	54	63	73	81	90	94	20th
15th	41	43	51	61	70	76	85	89	15th
10th	38	40	45	55	64	71	79	80	10th
5th	33	36	40	46	53	62	70	67	5th
0	14	25	10	10	10	20	30	20	0

From: AAHPER (1965). *Skills test manual: Football.* Washington, D.C.: AAHPER. Reprinted with permission from AAHPERD.

Table 13.6
FIFTY-YARD DASH WITH FOOTBALL Test Scores in Seconds and Tenths

Percentile	10	11	12	Age 13	14	15	16	17-18	Percentile
100th	7.3	6.8	6.2	5.5	5.5	5.8	5.5	5.0	100th
95th	7.7	7.4	7.0	6.4	6.4	6.2	6.0	6.0	95th
90th	7.9	7.6	7.2	6.8	6.6	6.3	6.1	6.1	90th
85th	8.1	7.7	7.4	6.9	6.8	6.4	6.3	6.2	85th
80th	8.2	7.8	7.5	7.0	6.9	6.5	6.4	6.3	80th
75th	8.3	7.9	7.5	7.1	7.0	6.6	6.5	6.3	75th
70th	8.4	8.0	7.6	7.2	7.1	6.7	6.6	6.4	70th
65th	8.5	8.1	7.7	7.3	7.2	6.8	6.6	6.5	65th
60th	8.6	8.2	7.8	7.4	7.2	6.9	6.7	6.6	60th
55th	8.6	8.3	7.9	7.5	7.3	7.0	6.8	6.6	55th
50th	8.7	8.4	8.0	7.5	7.4	7.0	6.8	6.7	50th
45th	8.8	8.5	8.1	7.6	7.5	7.1	6.9	6.8	45th
40th	8.9	8.6	8.1	7.7	7.6	7.2	7.0	6.8	40th
35th	9.0	8.7	8.2	7.8	7.7	7.2	7.1	6.9	35th
30th	9.1	8.8	8.3	8.0	7.8	7.3	7.2	7.0	30th
25th	9.2	8.9	8.4	8.1	7.9	7.4	7.3	7.1	25th
20th	9.3	9.1	8.5	8.2	8.1	7.5	7.4	7.2	20th
15th	9.4	9.2	8.7	8.4	8.3	7.7	7.5	7.3	15th
10th	9.6	9.3	9.0	8.7	8.4	8.1	7.8	7.4	10th
5th	9.8	9.5	9.3	9.0	8.8	8.4	8.0	7.8	5th

From: AAHPER (1965). *Skills test manual: Football.* Washington, D.C.: AAHPER. Reprinted with permission from AAHPERD.

					Table 13.7				
					BLOCKING				
					Test Scores in Seconds and Tenths				

| | | | | Age | | | | | |
Percentile	10	11	12	13	14	15	16	17-18	Percentile
100th	6.9	5.0	5.5	5.0	5.0	5.0	3.0	5.0	100th
95th	7.5	6.6	6.6	5.9	5.8	6.0	5.9	5.5	95th
90th	7.7	7.1	7.3	6.5	6.2	6.2	6.1	5.7	90th
85th	7.9	7.5	7.6	6.7	6.6	6.3	6.3	5.8	85th
80th	8.1	8.0	7.7	6.9	6.8	6.5	6.5	6.0	80th
75th	8.3	8.3	7.9	7.2	7.0	6.7	6.7	6.2	75th
70th	8.5	8.6	8.1	7.4	7.1	6.9	7.0	6.3	70th
65th	8.9	9.1	8.4	7.6	7.3	7.0	7.2	6.5	65th
60th	9.3	9.5	8.6	7.7	7.5	7.2	7.4	6.7	60th
55th	9.6	9.7	8.8	7.9	7.7	7.4	7.6	7.0	55th
50th	9.8	9.9	9.0	8.1	7.8	7.5	7.8	7.2	50th
45th	10.1	10.2	9.2	8.3	8.0	7.8	8.0	7.4	45th
40th	10.5	10.4	9.5	8.4	8.1	7.9	8.3	7.6	40th
35th	10.7	10.6	9.6	8.6	8.3	8.2	8.6	7.8	35th
30th	11.0	10.9	9.7	8.9	8.5	8.3	8.8	8.0	30th
25th	11.3	11.1	9.9	9.1	8.7	8.5	9.1	8.2	25th
20th	11.6	11.3	10.2	9.4	9.0	8.8	9.5	8.5	20th
15th	12.0	11.6	10.5	9.8	9.2	9.0	9.0	9.0	15th
10th	12.8	12.0	10.9	10.2	9.5	9.4	10.6	9.4	10th
5th	14.4	13.1	11.6	11.2	10.3	10.4	10.7	10.8	5th
0	17.5	18.0	15.0	15.0	15.0	13.0	15.0	14.0	0

From: AAHPER (1965). *Skills test manual: Football*. Washington, D.C.: AAHPER. Reprinted with permission from AAHPERD.

					Table 13.8				
					FORWARD PASS FOR ACCURACY				
					Test Scores in Points				

| | | | | Age | | | | | |
Percentile	10	11	12	13	14	15	16	17-18	Percentile
100th	18	26	26	28	26	26	28	28	100th
95th	14	19	20	21	21	21	21	22	95th
90th	11	16	18	19	19	19	20	21	90th
85th	10	15	17	18	18	18	18	19	85th
80th	9	13	16	17	17	17	17	18	80th
75th	8	12	15	16	16	16	16	18	75th
70th	8	11	14	15	15	15	15	17	70th
65th	6	10	13	14	14	14	15	16	65th
60th	5	9	12	13	13	13	14	15	60th
55th	4	8	11	13	13	13	13	15	55th
50th	3	7	11	12	12	12	13	14	50th
45th	2	6	10	11	11	11	12	13	45th
40th	2	5	9	11	10	11	12	12	40th
35th	1	5	8	10	9	9	11	12	35th
30th	0	4	7	9	8	9	10	11	30th
25th	0	3	6	8	8	8	9	10	25th
20th	0	2	5	7	7	7	8	9	20th
15th	0	1	4	5	5	6	7	8	15th
10th	0	0	3	4	4	5	6	7	10th
5th	0	0	1	2	2	3	4	5	5th
0	0	0	0	0	0	0	0	0	0

From: AAHPER (1965). *Skills test manual: Football*. Washington, D.C.: AAHPER. Reprinted with permission from AAHPERD.

Table 13.9

FOOTBALL PUNT FOR DISTANCE
Test Scores in Feet

				Age					
Percentile	10	11	12	13	14	15	16	17-18	Percentile
100th	87	100	115	150	160	160	160	180	100th
95th	75	84	93	106	119	126	131	136	95th
90th	64	77	88	98	110	119	126	128	90th
85th	61	75	84	94	106	114	120	124	85th
80th	58	70	79	90	103	109	114	120	80th
75th	56	68	77	87	98	105	109	115	75th
70th	55	66	75	83	96	102	106	110	70th
65th	53	64	72	80	93	99	103	107	65th
60th	51	62	70	78	90	96	100	104	60th
55th	50	60	68	75	87	94	97	101	55th
50th	48	57	66	73	84	91	95	98	50th
45th	46	55	64	70	81	89	92	96	45th
40th	45	53	61	68	78	86	90	93	40th
35th	44	51	59	64	75	83	86	90	35th
30th	42	48	56	63	72	79	83	86	30th
25th	40	45	52	61	70	76	79	81	25th
20th	38	42	50	57	66	73	74	76	20th
15th	32	39	46	52	61	69	70	70	15th
10th	28	34	40	44	55	62	64	64	10th
5th	22	27	35	33	44	54	56	53	5th
0	11	9	10	10	10	10	10	10	0

From: AAHPER (1965). *Skills test manual: Football.* Washington, D.C.: AAHPER. Reprinted with permission from AAHPERD.

Table 13.10

BALL CHANGING ZIGZAG RUN
Test Scores in Seconds and Tenths

				Age					
Percentile	10	11	12	13	14	15	16	17-18	Percentile
100th	7.2	7.4	7.0	6.0	6.5	6.0	6.0	6.0	100th
95th	9.9	7.7	7.8	8.0	8.7	7.7	7.7	8.4	95th
90th	10.1	8.1	8.2	8.4	9.0	8.0	8.0	8.7	90th
85th	10.3	8.6	8.5	8.7	9.2	8.3	8.4	8.8	85th
80th	10.5	9.0	8.7	8.8	9.4	8.5	8.6	8.9	80th
75th	10.7	9.3	8.8	9.0	9.5	8.6	8.7	9.0	75th
70th	10.9	9.6	9.0	9.2	9.6	8.7	8.8	9.1	70th
65th	11.1	9.8	9.1	9.3	9.7	8.8	8.9	9.2	65th
60th	11.2	10.0	9.3	9.5	9.8	8.9	9.0	9.3	60th
55th	11.4	10.1	9.5	9.6	9.9	9.0	9.1	9.4	55th
50th	11.5	10.3	9.6	9.7	10.0	9.1	9.3	9.6	50th
45th	11.6	10.5	9.8	9.8	10.1	9.2	9.4	9.7	45th
40th	11.8	10.6	10.0	10.0	10.2	9.4	9.5	9.8	40th
35th	11.9	10.9	10.1	10.2	10.4	9.4	9.7	9.9	35th
30th	12.2	11.1	10.3	10.3	10.5	9.6	9.9	10.1	30th
25th	12.5	11.3	10.5	10.3	10.7	9.9	10.1	10.3	25th
20th	12.8	11.6	10.8	10.8	10.9	10.1	10.3	10.5	20th
15th	13.3	12.1	11.1	11.1	11.2	10.3	10.6	10.9	15th
10th	13.8	12.9	11.5	11.4	11.5	10.6	11.2	11.4	10th
5th	15.8	14.2	12.3	12.1	12.0	11.5	12.2	12.1	5th
0	24.0	15.0	19.0	20.0	14.5	20.0	17.0	15.0	0

From: AAHPER (1965). *Skills test manual: Football.* Washington, D.C.: AAHPER. Reprinted with permission from AAHPERD.

					Age					
Percentile	10	11	12	13	14	15	16	17-18	Percentile

Table 13.11

CATCHING FORWARD PASS
Test Scores in Number Caught

Percentile	10	11	12	13	14	15	16	17-18	Percentile
100th	20	20	20	20	20	20	20	20	100th
95th	19	19	19	20	20	20	20	20	95th
90th	17	18	19	19	19	19	19	19	90th
85th	16	16	18	18	18	19	19	19	85th
80th	14	15	18	17	18	18	18	18	80th
75th	13	14	16	17	17	18	18	18	75th
70th	12	13	16	16	16	17	17	17	70th
65th	11	12	15	15	15	16	16	16	65th
60th	10	12	14	15	15	16	16	16	60th
55th	8	11	14	14	14	15	15	15	55th
50th	7	10	13	13	14	15	15	15	50th
45th	7	9	12	13	13	14	14	14	45th
40th	6	8	12	12	12	13	13	13	40th
35th	5	7	11	11	11	12	12	13	35th
30th	5	7	10	10	10	11	11	12	30th
25th	4	6	10	9	9	10	10	11	25th
20th	3	5	8	8	8	9	9	10	20th
15th	2	4	7	7	8	8	8	9	15th
10th	1	3	6	6	6	7	6	8	10th
5th	1	1	5	4	4	6	4	6	5th
0	0	0	0	0	0	0	0	0	0

From: AAHPER (1965). *Skills test manual: Football.* Washington, D.C.: AAHPER. Reprinted with permission from AAHPERD.

Table 13.12

PULL-OUT
Test Scores in Seconds and Tenths

					Age					
Percentile	10	11	12	13	14	15	16	17-18	Percentile
100th	2.5	2.2	2.2	2.4	2.2	2.0	2.0	1.8	100th
95th	2.9	2.5	2.8	2.8	2.7	2.5	2.5	2.6	95th
90th	3.2	2.7	3.0	2.9	2.8	2.6	2.6	2.7	90th
85th	3.3	2.8	3.0	3.0	2.9	2.7	2.7	2.8	85th
80th	3.4	2.9	3.1	3.0	3.0	2.8	2.9	2.8	80th
75th	3.5	2.9	3.1	3.1	3.0	3.0	2.9	2.9	75th
70th	3.5	3.0	3.2	3.1	3.0	3.0	3.0	2.9	70th
65th	3.6	3.1	3.3	3.2	3.1	3.0	3.0	3.0	65th
60th	3.6	3.2	3.3	3.2	3.1	3.1	3.1	3.0	60th
55th	3.7	3.3	3.4	3.3	3.2	3.1	3.1	3.1	55th
50th	3.8	3.4	3.4	3.3	3.2	3.2	3.2	3.1	50th
45th	3.8	3.5	3.5	3.4	3.3	3.2	3.2	3.1	45th
40th	3.9	3.6	3.5	3.4	3.3	3.3	3.3	3.2	40th
35th	3.9	3.7	3.6	3.5	3.4	3.3	3.3	3.2	35th
30th	4.0	3.8	3.7	3.5	3.4	3.4	3.3	3.2	30th
25th	4.0	3.9	3.8	3.6	3.5	3.5	3.4	3.3	25th
20th	4.1	4.0	3.9	3.7	3.5	3.6	3.5	3.4	20th
15th	4.2	4.1	3.9	3.8	3.6	3.7	3.7	3.5	15th
10th	4.3	4.2	4.1	3.9	3.7	3.9	3.9	3.6	10th
5th	4.4	4.4	4.2	4.0	4.0	4.1	4.3	3.9	5th
0	5.5	5.0	5.0	5.0	5.0	5.0	5.0	5.0	0

From: AAHPER (1965). *Skills test manual: Football.* Washington, D.C.: AAHPER. Reprinted with permission from AAHPERD.

					Age				
Percentile	10	11	12	13	14	15	16	17-18	Percentile

Table 13.13

KICK-OFF
Test Scores in Feet

Percentile	10	11	12	13	14	15	16	17-18	Percentile
100th	88	110	120	129	140	160	160	180	100th
95th	69	79	98	106	118	128	131	138	95th
90th	64	72	83	97	108	120	125	129	90th
85th	59	68	78	92	102	114	119	124	85th
80th	58	64	74	86	97	108	114	119	80th
75th	55	60	70	81	94	104	108	113	75th
70th	53	58	67	78	90	100	104	108	70th
65th	50	56	65	75	86	96	99	105	65th
60th	47	54	64	72	84	93	97	103	60th
55th	46	52	60	69	81	90	95	98	55th
50th	45	50	57	67	77	87	93	95	50th
45th	43	48	54	64	74	83	90	92	45th
40th	40	46	52	62	71	79	87	88	40th
35th	39	44	48	59	68	76	83	84	35th
30th	37	42	45	56	65	72	79	79	30th
25th	35	40	42	52	62	69	75	74	25th
20th	32	37	38	48	58	64	70	70	20th
15th	30	34	34	42	52	59	65	64	15th
10th	26	30	29	36	45	50	60	57	10th
5th	21	24	22	26	38	40	47	43	5th
0	5	10	0	0	0	10	10	10	0

From: AAHPER (1965). *Skills test manual: Football.* Washington, D.C.: AAHPER. Reprinted with permission from AAHPERD.

Table 13.14

DODGING RUN
Test Scores in Seconds and Tenths

Percentile	10	11	12	13	14	15	16	17-18	Percentile
100th	21.0	18.0	18.0	17.0	16.0	16.0	16.0	16.0	100th
95th	24.3	20.4	23.8	23.3	22.6	22.4	22.3	22.2	95th
90th	25.8	21.6	24.6	24.2	23.9	23.5	23.3	23.2	90th
85th	26.3	22.5	25.0	24.8	24.6	24.1	23.9	23.7	85th
80th	26.4	23.5	25.2	24.9	24.7	24.6	24.3	24.1	80th
75th	27.5	24.0	25.3	25.3	25.2	24.9	24.7	24.4	75th
70th	27.8	25.0	25.8	25.7	25.2	25.2	25.0	24.7	70th
65th	28.1	25.7	26.3	26.1	26.1	25.5	25.3	25.0	65th
60th	28.4	26.3	26.6	26.5	26.3	25.8	25.5	25.3	60th
55th	28.7	26.9	26.9	26.8	26.6	26.1	25.8	25.6	55th
50th	28.9	27.4	27.3	27.2	26.9	26.4	26.1	26.0	50th
45th	29.3	28.0	27.6	27.5	27.2	26.7	26.3	26.3	45th
40th	29.7	28.3	27.9	27.9	27.5	27.0	26.7	26.6	40th
35th	30.1	28.8	28.4	28.3	27.9	27.4	27.0	26.9	35th
30th	30.5	29.2	28.8	28.7	28.3	27.8	27.3	27.2	30th
25th	30.9	29.8	29.2	29.1	28.7	28.2	27.7	27.6	25th
20th	31.1	30.4	29.8	29.5	29.3	28.6	28.1	28.0	20th
15th	31.8	31.1	30.4	30.1	29.9	29.1	28.8	28.7	15th
10th	32.7	32.0	31.3	30.8	30.7	29.8	29.6	29.2	10th
5th	33.6	33.5	33.0	32.3	31.8	31.0	30.6	30.4	5th
0	40.0	40.0	41.0	40.0	36.0	36.0	36.0	36.0	0

From: AAHPER (1965). *Skills test manual: Football.* Washington, D.C.: AAHPER. Reprinted with permission from AAHPERD.

Football References

AAHPER. (1965). *Skills test manual: Football.* Washington, D.C.: AAHPER.

Borleske, S.E. (1936). *A study of achievement of college men in touch football.* Unpublished master's thesis, University of California, Berkeley.

Brace, D.K. (1943). Validity of football achievement tests as measures of motor learning as a partial basis for the selection of players. *Research Quarterly* 14: 372.

Brechler, P.W. (1940). *A test to determine potential ability in football (backs and ends).* Unpublished master's thesis, University of Iowa, Iowa City.

Cormack, H.P. (1940). *A test to determine potential ability in football (linemen).* Unpublished master's thesis, University of Iowa, Iowa City.

Cowell, C.C., & Ismail, A.H. (1961). Validity of a football rating scale and its relationship to social integration and academic ability. *Research Quarterly* 33: 461-457.

Edwards, R.L. (1960). *A method for selecting linemen for high school football.* Unpublished master's thesis, University of Utah, Salt Lake City.

Hatley, F.J. (1942). *A battery of functional tests for the prediction of football potentiality.* Unpublished master's thesis, University of Iowa, Iowa City.

Jacobson, T.V. (1960). *An evaluation of performance in certain physical ability tests administered to selected secondary school boys.* Unpublished master's thesis, University of Washington, Seattle.

Lee, R.C. (1965). *A battery of tests to predict football potential.* Unpublished master's thesis, University of Utah, Salt Lake City.

May, L.D. (1972). *A study of the measurement of potential football ability in high school players.* Unpublished master's thesis, Texas Tech University, Lubbock.

McDavid, R.F. (1978). Predicting potential in football players. *Research Quarterly* 49: 98-104.

McElroy, H.N. (1938). A report of some experimentation with a skill test. *Research Quarterly* 9: 82-88.

McGauley, T. (1959). *A scoring device for analyzing individual defensive football performance.* Unpublished master's thesis, South Dakota State University, Brookings.

Micheli, R.P. (1977). *Development of a battery of tests to predict football ability at the college level.* Unpublished doctoral dissertation, University of Arkansas, Fayetteville.

Morris, H.H. (1977). *A critique of the AAHPER Skill Test Series.* Paper presented at the AAHPER National Convention, Seattle.

Wallrof, P.J. (1965). *Methods for rating defensive proficiency of high school football players.* Unpublished master's thesis, University of Washington, Seattle.

Chapter 14

GOLF

INTRODUCTION

A large number of skills tests have been developed for the sport of golf. This seems somewhat ironic because objective measurement of a participant's ability level occurs each time the game is played. Even though the score provides a valid measure of golfing skill, having students play an actual round of golf for grading purposes is not absolutely necessary. A good indication of playing proficiency may be obtained by the use of available skills tests as they simulate game conditions well and generally possess a high degree of face validity.

Both indoor and outdoor tests exist for golf, with the outdoor variety generally more preferable when the necessary equipment and facilities are available. Examples of each type of test are found in this chapter.

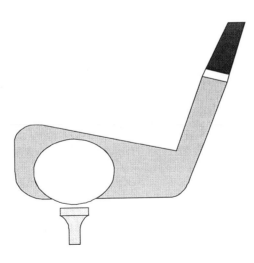

VANDERHOOF GOLF TEST
(Vanderhoof, 1956)

Purpose:

To measure general golfing ability.

Description and Directions:

The Vanderhoof Golf Test is designed for indoor use and utilizes a plastic golf ball. Originally, a subject's skill with a 2-wood, 5-iron and 7-iron was measured by the test. All three involve the same area specifications, and the drive item (2-wood) proved to be the best single indicator of playing ability. The 5- and 7-iron items are very similar, with the latter showing less value as an instrument to measure general golfing ability according to results of the Vanderhoof study.

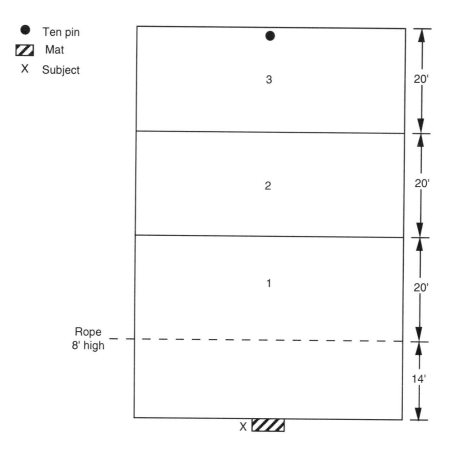

Fig. 14.1 Scoring area for Vanderhoof Golf Test.

From: Vanderhoof, E.R. (1956). *Beginning golf achievement tests*. Unpublished master's thesis, University of Iowa, Iowa City. Copyright by author.

Should both the drive test and 5-iron item be given, the formula to be used is 1.3 drive + 1.0 5-iron. Only the drive test is discussed in this chapter since both the 7-iron and 5-iron tests are administered exactly as the drive test, except that no tee is used. The target area or gymnasium floor is marked off with three equal scoring areas that are each 20 feet in length. The subject stands at a designated tee area and attempts to drive each ball under a rope that is eight feet high and located 14 feet from and parallel to the line from which the balls are being hit.

Two or three practice balls may be hit during the warm-up period for the test. When the subject (X) is ready, she proceeds to drive 15 consecutive balls from the practice tee toward the target area while aiming for the ten pin. Figure 14.1 further clarifies the test layout.

Educational Application:

College women.

Time:

Twenty students can be tested in one 60-minute period.

Personnel:

One scorer-recorder.

Equipment and Supplies:

Two-woods, mat with permanent tee, plastic golf balls, two standards, rope at least 20 feet long, ten pin or similar object such as a cone, scoring and floor marking materials.

Facilities and Space:

Indoor area such as a gymnasium or fieldhouse with a minimum space of 74 x 13 feet for each testing station. There should be no overhead obstructions.

Scoring Method and Norms:

A numerical score from zero to three is assigned to each ball that passes under the rope on the fly and lands in the designated target area. The final score is the sum of the points accumulated for all 15 trials. Two topped balls in succession count as only one trial with a zero score.

Validity and Reliability:

One hundred and ten university women students who had received 15 lessons of group instruction served as subjects in this study. A validity coefficient of .71 was reported, with judges' ratings of playing form used as the criterion measure. The .90 reliability coefficient was computed on odd-even sums and corrected by the Spearman-Brown Formula.

Table 14.1	
NORMS FOR VANDERHOOF DRIVE TEST*	
T-Score	Raw Score (Total of 15 trials)
75	45
70	41
65	38
60	33
55	28
50	24
45	19
40	13
35	9
30	7
25	4
*Based on scores of 110 college women.	

From: Vanderhoof, E.R. (1956). *Beginning golf achievement tests*. Unpublished master's thesis, University of Iowa, Iowa City. Copyright by author.

Additional Comments:

Besides measuring general golf ability, the Vanderhoof Test serves well as a practice device for students and as a measure of student improvement. In addition, the test may be used to detect possible inconsistencies in the swing. Should the tester signify on the student's score card the spot where each ball lands, a pattern might possibly develop, and directional errors could then be corrected, accordingly.

Multiple test stations are suggested to reduce the time of test administration, but this may require an additional scorer for each. Also, Davis (Davis, 1960) indicated that a rope is not needed for the test, since similar results were obtained without the use of a rope. Furthermore, it is important that the tester use only one type of plastic golf ball per test group, since a different type of ball may produce notably different results.

DAVIS FIVE-IRON TEST
(Davis, 1960)

Purpose:

To determine general golf ability and ability to hit a full-swinging 5-iron shot.

Description:

Davis developed an outdoor golf skills test utilizing a full-swinging 5-iron golf shot that measures both distance and accuracy. A driving range or playfield area is marked off as a target zone. One target of 120 yards in width is divided into three equal sections. Another target of 150 yards in length is divided into 15 intervals measuring 10 yards each. Each target section is assigned numerical value with the middle area (II) naturally having the higher scoring intervals. Refer to Figure 14.2 for clarification of the scoring areas.

Educational Application:

College women.

Time:

Class of 20 students can easily be tested in one 60-minute period.

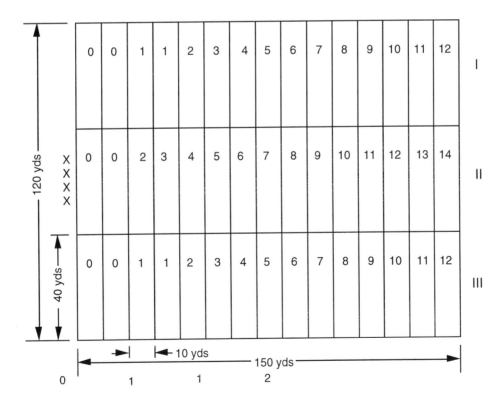

Fig. 14.2 Field markings for Davis Five-Iron Test.

From: Davis, C.M. (1960). *The use of the golf tee in teaching beginning golf.* Unpublished master's thesis, University of Michigan, Ann Arbor. Copyright by author.

Personnel:

One scorer-recorder.

Equipment and Supplies:

Five-irons, colored and plain balls, scoring and field marking materials.

Facilities and Space:

Outdoor driving range or similar hitting area with a minimum measurement of 150 x 120 yards.

Directions:

Two practice hits are permitted immediately prior to testing, but a reasonable number of practice swings is encouraged.

To get ready for testing, four subjects (X) line up directly behind the hitting line (Figure 14.2). Two trials of 10 balls each are taken by each student with a rest period between trials. Each subject hits five balls from each of the four test stations. Eight plain balls are needed for practice hits and four sets of different colored or coded balls for the test trials.

Scoring Method:

The final score is the point total obtained when multiplying the number of balls in each scoring zone by the numerical value assigned to the particular zone. It is important to remember that each ball is scored according to the spot at which it comes to rest, and not where it initially lands. After each 10-ball trial, the balls in each zone are gathered in the center and appropriately scored.

It is recommended that each scoring zone be labeled with a set of 4 x 8-inch signs placed on stakes.

Validity and Reliability:

Face validity was claimed for the test. In testing 67 university women, a reliability coefficient of .80 was found when using the split-half procedure for obtaining reliability.

Additional Comments:

The field size and marking requirement may create some concern for potential testers as the area called for in the test design is obviously larger than most playing fields. Construction of the 45 target zones demands a good deal of marking time. Combine that with the signs and stakes that are to be placed in each scoring zone, and administrative time starts to become a prohibitive factor in the Davis Test.

In order to save on actual testing time, it is recommended that the scoring be conducted after all 20 shots are completed, instead of after the suggested 10.

BENSON GOLF TEST
(Benson, 1963)

Purpose:

To determine overall golf playing ability.

Description:

Benson developed an outdoor golf skills test in which skill with a 5-iron is measured. Flight distance and deviation from the intended flight of the golf ball are each considered in the test score.

The driving range or designated hitting area is dotted with distance signs placed at 25-yard intervals starting from the hitting line. Nine deviation signs are placed five yards apart on each side of a line that marks the middle of the hitting area. The deviation signs are 150 yards from and parallel to the hitting line and are numbered one to nine (Figure 14.3).

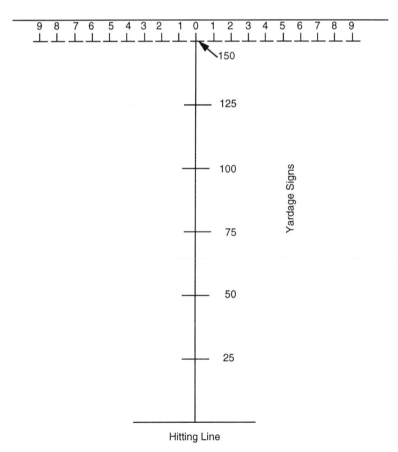

Fig. 14.3 Field markings for Benson Golf Test.

From: Benson, D.W. (1963). *Measuring golf ability through use of a number five-iron test.* Unpublished study presented at the California Association for Health, Physical Education and Recreation Annual Convention, Long Beach. Copyright by CAHPERD.

Educational Application:

Males and females from junior high school through college.

Time:

One 60-minute class period for 20 students.

Personnel:

One scorer-recorder.

Equipment and Supplies:

Golf balls, 5-irons, marking flags or signs, and scoring materials.

Facilities and Space:

Outdoor driving range or similar hitting area that has minimum measurements of 150 x 100 yards.

Directions:

Assuming a proper position directly behind the hitting line, the subject proceeds to take 20 consecutive shots or test trials for score. The tester or scorer stands approximately three yards behind the hitting line and the test subject.

Scoring Method:

The 20 distance and deviation scores are separately averaged, providing official results for distance and flight accuracy.

Validity and Reliability:

Correlation of official scores for a round of golf with the distance and flight deviation scores produced a coefficient of .94. Reliability coefficients of .90 and .70 were derived for the distance and deviation scores, respectively.

Additional Comments:

Preparation for the Benson Test is not as cumbersome as some of the other available outdoor tests. Marking the field should require no more than 30 minutes.

The low reliability value of the flight deviation item prohibits the use of its score alone in determining general golf ability. For that purpose, it should always be used along with the distance score.

NELSON GOLF PITCHING TEST
(1967)

Purpose:

To measure the ability to use short irons in pitching.

Description:

The outdoor golf test measures ability in hitting short iron shots to a flag 40 yards away. Either the 8-iron, 9-iron or wedge is used to complete the test requirement.

Twenty yards away from the hitting line, a restraining line is located. A flag stick is positioned 20 yards from the restraining line or 40 yards from the hitting line (Figure 14.4). The inner target circle is six feet in diameter with the flag stick located in the middle of this circle. From the center circle, each circle's radius is five feet wider than the radius of the previous one which means the circle diameters are 6, 16, 26, 36, 46, 56 and 66 feet. The target is divided into four equal quadrants.

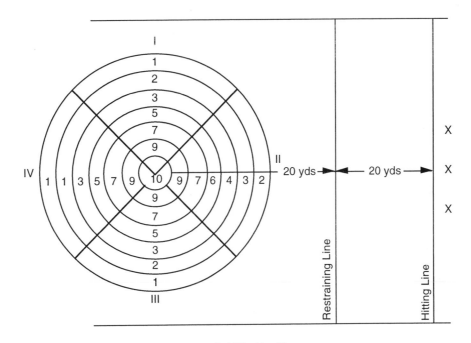

Fig. 14.4 Field and target markings for Nelson Golf Pitching Test.

From: Johnson, B.L., & Nelson, J.K. (1974). *Practical measurements for evaluation in physical education.* Minneapolis: Burgess.

Educational Application:

High school and college males and females.

Time:

Twenty students can be tested in one 60-minute period.

Personnel:

One scorer-recorder plus student assistants as spotters.

Equipment and Supplies:

Short irons (8- or 9-iron, or wedge), colored or coded balls, flag stick, flags or markers, scoring and field marking materials.

Facilities and Space:

Playing field area or driving range with minimum measurements of approximately 60 x 25 yards.

Directions:

Three practice shots are taken by the student prior to being tested for score. Test administration begins with two to four students standing behind the hitting line with their choice of the 8-iron, 9-iron or wedge. Each is given 13 golf balls, with three to be used as practice balls. Furthermore, each individual is assigned golf balls of a specific color or code. Ten test trials follow with the subject attempting to place each ball as close to the flag stick as possible. The students are to take turns hitting the ball, so as not to interfere with each other's concentration. Each swing counts as a test trial, even if the ball is missed or poorly hit. Any legal hit must be airborne until it passes the restraining line; thus, this eliminates as a scoring trial any ball that is "topped."

A fellow student is assigned to each test subject for spotting purposes. It is his/her job to assist the tester or recorder in the scoring process by calling out the subject's name and score after each shot. Both the spotter and recorder are positioned near the target.

Scoring Method:

Total number of accumulated points for the 10 test trials. Any ball resting on a line is assigned the higher point value.

Validity and Reliability:

Utilizing college students enrolled in golf classes as subjects and judges' ratings as the criterion, a validity coefficient of .86 was determined. A reliability coefficient of .83 was obtained, determined by odd-even trials and the Spearman-Brown Prophecy Formula.

Additional Comments:

The Nelson Test represents a unique contribution to golf skills measurement because previous tests excluded the testing of short iron ability, concentrating on either a wood or middle iron.

Adaptations to the original test may be considered by the potential tester. Reliability is little affected by requiring the best seven of 10 shots when test time is short. Also, permanent target lines provide a very effective practice device for interested students. Third, the tester may wish to experiment with the hitting distance.

BROWN GOLF SKILLS TEST
(Brown, 1969)

Purpose:

To determine golf ability.

Educational Application:

College men and women.

Time:

Twenty students can be tested in two 60-minute periods.

Personnel:

One scorer-recorder with student assistants.

Equipment and Supplies:

Woods, 7-, 8-, 9-irons, pitching wedge, putter, balls, tees, scoring and field marking materials.

Facilities and Space:

A large outdoor playing field or driving range; putting green.

Description and Directions:

Brown's five-item test was initially used for motivation purposes but was later revised to measure overall golf ability.

Chip. A 30 x 10-foot area is required, along with a ground target of three different sized trapezoids as shown in Figure 14.5. The shooting line is 16 feet from the leading edge of the largest trapezoid. While standing behind this line, the subject hits 15 consecutive chip shots at the target.

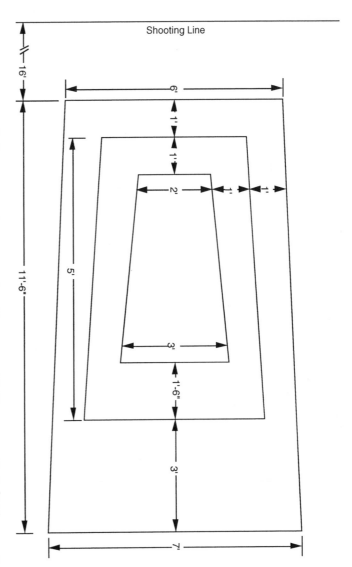

Fig. 14.5 Target for chip test.

From: Brown, H.S. (1969). A test battery for evaluating golf skills. *TAHPER Journal* 4-5: 28-29. Reprinted with permission from TAHPER Journal.

Short Pitch. A playing field or similar outdoor area is required with minimum measurements of 90 x 25 feet. A target, in the shape of three concentric circles, is placed on the ground. The circles have radii of 7 1/2, 15 and 22 1/2 feet for the inner, middle and outer circles, respectively. The shooting arc or line is marked off 65 feet away from the center of the inner circle (Figure 14.6).

Each student stands behind the shooting line and hits 15 consecutive short pitch shots at the target.

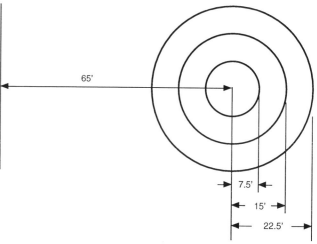

Fig. 14.6 Taget for short pitch test.

From: Brown., H.S. (1969). A test battery for evaluating golf skills. *TAHPER Journal* 4-5: 28-29. Reprinted with permission from TAHPER Journal.

Approach. Field markings for the approach item are identical to the previously described short pitch test, except the measurements are in yards instead of feet. The test is conducted in the same manner as the short pitch item.

Driving. Requirements include a driving range or similar playfield area with minimum measurements of 300 x 150 yards. Two tees are located in front of the target range and directly between the target lines. Two parallel longitudinal lines should be marked off on the driving area, 50 yards apart and 300 yards long. Four more lines are placed at right angles to the original two lines or parallel to the tee area. The first of the four lines is 100 yards from the tee area with each subsequent line only 50 yards apart. They all should measure the full width of the field. Field markings for female subjects are 50 yards shorter as indicated by the numbers in parentheses in Figure 14.7.

Two students can be tested simultaneously. Each stands in the tee area and drives nine consecutive shots into the target area.

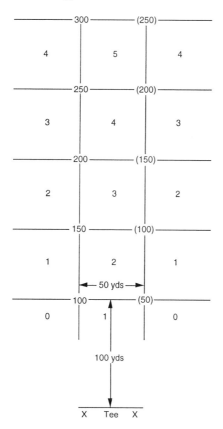

Fig. 14.7 Field markings for drive test.

From: Brown, H.S. (1969). A test battery for evaluating golf skills. *TAHPER Journal* 4-5: 28-29. Reprinted with permission from TAHPER Journal.

Putting. The test area is a putting green similar to the type normally found at golf courses. Ideally, the putting surface should be slightly rolling with six holes included, two of which are spaced 15 feet apart with the other four spaced 20 feet apart. One hole is downhill, one uphill, one breaks to the left, one to the right, and two holes are on a level putting surface.

The students are tested in pairs and move in a clockwise direction around the six holes. Each subject putts 12 holes or two rounds, sinking all putts.

Scoring Method and Norms:

Chip. Each chip shot receives a numerical score ranging from zero to three based on the spot at which the ball initially lands. The points are assigned with a three, two and one value for inner, middle and outer trapezoids, respectively.

Whiff shots and balls that fail to land in the target area are given a score of zero. Any ball that strikes a line is given the score associated with the higher value zone.

Short Pitch. Same as the scoring procedure used for the chip item, except circles are used as a target area instead of trapezoids.

Approach. Identical to the short pitch test except that the score is based on the spot where the ball comes to rest rather than where it first lands.

Driving. Each drive is assigned a numerical score ranging from zero to five based on the spot where the ball comes to rest. Whiff balls and balls that fail to land in the target area receive a score of zero. Any ball that ends up on a line is assigned the higher score.

Putting. The total number of strokes taken to putt all 12 holes is converted to a point score as shown by the norms found in Table 14.2, so that the final putting score can be compared with the scores of the other tests in the battery.

T-scales for the whole battery are presented in Table 14.4.

Validity and Reliability:

Table 14.3 presents the validity and reliability coefficients for each test item and the total battery, plus the number of participants for each.

Criterion Measure:

The score for nine best holes in a round of golf.

Table 14.2 CONVERSION SCALE FOR PUTTING TEST					
Strokes	Score	Strokes	Score	Strokes	Scores
21	45	29	29	37	13
22	43	30	27	38	11
23	41	31	25	39	9
24	39	32	23	40	7
25	37	33	21	41	5
26	35	34	19	42	3
27	33	35	17	43	1
28	31	36	15	44	0

From: Brown, H.S. (1969). A test battery for evaluating golf skills. *TAHPER Journal* 4-5: 28-29. Reprinted with permission from TAHPER Journal.

	Reliability		Validity	
Tests	N	r	N	r
Chip Test	180	.74	86	.68
Short Pitch Test	148	.85	60	.76
Approach Test	155	.75	54	.65
Driving Test	104	.87	86	.73
Putting Test	58	.81	68	.71
Total Test Battery			134	.85

Table 14.3

RELIABILITY AND VALIDITY COEFFICIENTS FOR BROWN'S REVISED GOLF SKILLS TEST

From: Brown, H.S. (1960). A test battery for evaluating golf skills. *TAHPER Journal* 4-5: 28-29. Reprinted with permission from TAHPER Journal.

Additional Comments:

The comprehensiveness feature of the Brown Test is its chief contribution to the literature on golf skills measurement. Reliability values of the chip and approach tests make those items questionable for use in grading purposes, but overall the strengths of the battery outweigh the weaknesses.

		Table 14.4
		*T*-SCALES FOR BROWN'S REVISED GOLF SKILL TEST

Raw Score	Chip Men	Chip Women	Pitch Men	Pitch Women	Approach Men	Approach Women	Driving Men	Driving Women	Putting Men	Putting Women
45	71	87	69	89	72	84	71	-	72	75
44	70	86	68	88	70	83	70	100	71	74
43	69	85	67	86	69	81	68	99	69	73
42	67	83	66	85	68	80	67	97	68	71
41	66	82	64	84	67	79	66	95	66	70
40	65	81	63	82	66	77	65	93	65	69
39	64	80	62	81	64	76	64	92	64	68
38	63	78	61	80	63	75	62	90	62	67
37	62	77	60	78	62	73	61	88	61	66
36	60	76	59	77	61	72	60	86	59	65
35	59	74	58	76	59	71	59	84	58	63
34	58	73	56	75	58	69	57	82	56	62
33	57	72	55	73	58	68	56	80	55	61
32	56	70	54	72	56	67	55	78	53	60
31	55	69	53	71	56	66	54	76	52	59
30	54	68	52	69	54	64	53	75	51	58
29	52	66	51	68	53	63	51	73	49	57
28	51	65	50	67	52	61	50	71	48	55
27	50	64	48	65	50	60	49	69	46	54
26	49	62	47	64	49	59	48	67	45	53
25	48	61	46	63	48	58	46	65	43	52
24	47	60	45	62	47	56	45	63	42	51
23	45	59	44	60	45	55	44	62	40	50
22	44	57	43	59	44	54	43	60	39	49
21	43	56	42	58	43	52	42	58	38	47
20	42	55	40	56	42	51	40	56	36	46
19	41	53	39	55	41	50	39	54	35	45
18	40	52	38	54	40	49	38	52	33	44
17	38	51	37	52	38	47	37	50	32	43
16	37	49	36	51	37	46	35	48	30	42
15	36	48	35	50	36	44	34	46	29	40
14	35	47	33	49	35	43	33	44	27	39
13	34	46	32	47	34	42	32	43	26	38
12	33	44	31	46	32	40	31	41	25	37
11	31	43	30	45	31	39	29	39	23	36
10	30	42	29	43	30	38	28	37	22	35
9	29	40	28	42	29	36	27	35	21	34
8	28	39	27	41	28	35	26	33	20	32
7	27	38	25	39	27	34	25	31	19	31
6	26	36	24	38	25	32	23	30	18	30
5	24	35	23	37	24	31	22	28	16	29
4	23	34	22	36	23	30	21	26	15	28
3	22	32	21	34	21	29	20	24	14	27
2	21	31	20	33	20	28	18	22	12	26
1	20	30	19	32	19	27	17	20	11	24
Number	518	514	599	508	561	531	253	192	458	436
Mean	127.0	16.4	28.4	15.1	26.8	19.3	27.9	16.9	29.6	23.3
Standard Deviation	8.6	7.65	8.73	7.68	8.43	7.59	8.18	5.32	6.9	8.76

From: Brown, H.S. (1960). A test battery for evaluating golf skills. *TAHPER Journal* 4-5: 28-29. Reprinted with permission from TAHPER Journal.

SHICK-BERG INDOOR GOLF TEST
(Shick & Berg, 1983)

Purpose:

To evaluate 5-iron proficiency in golf.

Educational Application:

Junior high school boys were the subjects used in test construction, but the test is appropriate for junior and senior high school students of each gender.

Personnel:

Two individuals per testing station, one to spot and announce where the balls land, and the other to record the scores.

Equipment and Supplies:

5-irons, plastic golf balls, hitting mats, measuring tape, marking tape, cone and scoring materials.

Facilities and Space:

An approximate 45 x 70-foot area per testing station.

Description and Directions:

Figure 14.8 illustrates the layout of the testing station. A hitting mat is located in the center of the testing grid and one foot away from its front edge. At the other end of the grid, directly across from the hitting mat and 68 feet away, a cone is placed. Starting from the hitting end of the grid, the scoring rectangles in the first row measure 15 x 23 feet. The remaining three rows in the grid contain scoring squares of 15 x 15 feet. The last row on the target side of the grid is left open. The point values assigned to the rectangles and squares are shown in Figure 14.8.

Assuming a hitting position on the mat, the student being tested attempts to hit plastic golf balls toward the cone target on the other end of the grid. Two practice trials are permitted and 20 consecutive test trials comprise the test. Practice swings are allowed for each trial.

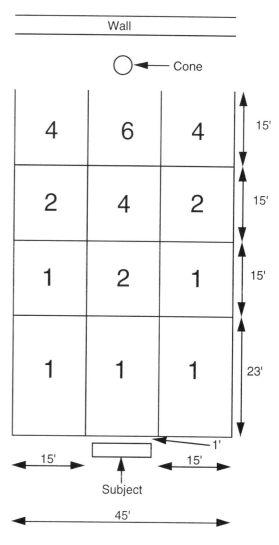

Fig. 14.8 Test layout for Shick-Berg Indoor Golf Test.

From: Shick, J., & Berg, N.G. (1983). Indoor golf skill test for junior high school boys. Reprinted with permission from *Research Quarterly for Exercise and Sport* 54: 75-78. Copyright 1983 by the American Alliance for Health, Physical Education, Recreation and Dance, 1900 Association Drive, Reston, VA 20191.

Scoring Method:

Points are assigned to each trial according to the location where the ball first hits in a rectangle or square. When a ball hits on a line, the higher point value is awarded. A ball hit beyond the fourth row of the scoring grid, but still in line with the grid, is awarded the points assigned to the square the ball last crossed. Topped balls entering the scoring grid receive one point, while whiffs and balls landing outside the scoring grid are given no points. The final score is the total points earned in the 20 trials, and 120 points is the maximum score.

Validity and Reliability:

A validity coefficient of .84 and reliability coefficients of .91 (test-retest) and .97 (single test administration) were reported.

Golf References

Autrey, E.P. (1937). *A battery of tests for measuring playing ability in golf.* Unpublished master's thesis, University of Wisconsin, Madison.

Benson, D.W. (1963). *Measuring golf ability through use of a number five-iron test.* Unpublished study presented at the California Association for Health, Physical Education and Recreation Annual Convention, Long Beach.

Brown, H.S. (1969). A test battery for evaluating golf skills. *TAHPER Journal* 4-5: 28-29.

Clevett, M.A. (1931). An experiment in teaching methods of golf. *Research Quarterly* 2: 104-106.

Cochrane, J.F. (1960). *The construction of an indoor golf skills test as a measure of golfing ability.* Unpublished master's thesis, University of Minnesota, Minneapolis.

Coffey, M. (1946). *Achievement tests in golf.* Unpublished master's thesis, University of Iowa, Iowa City.

Cotton, D.J., Thomas, J.R., & Plaster, T. (1972). *A plastic ball test for golf iron skill.* Unpublished study presented at the American Association for Health, Physical Education, Recreation and Dance National Convention, Houston.

Davis, C.M. (1960). *The use of the golf tee in teaching beginning golf.* Unpublished master's thesis, University of Michigan, Ann Arbor.

Green, K.W. (1974). *The development of a battery of golf skills tests for college men.* Unpublished doctoral dissertation, University of Arkansas, Fayetteville.

Green, K.N., East, W.B., & Hensley, L.D. (1987). A golf skills test battery for college males and females. *Research Quarterly* 58: 72-76.

McKee, M.E. (1950). A test for the full-swinging shot in golf. *Research Quarterly* 21: 40-46.

Olson, A.C. (1958). *The development of objective tests of the ability of freshmen and sophomore college women to drive and to pitch a plastic golf ball in a limited indoor area.* Unpublished master's thesis, University of Colorado, Boulder.

Reece, P.A. (1960). *A comparison of the scores made on an indoor golf test by college women.* Unpublished master's thesis, University of Colorado, Boulder.

Rowlands, D.J. (1974). *A golf skills test battery.* Unpublished doctoral dissertation, University of Utah, Salt Lake City.

Shick, J., & Berg, N.G. (1983). Indoor golf skill test for junior high school boys. *Research Quarterly for Exercise and Sport* 54: 75-78.

Vanderhoof, Ellen R. (1956). *Beginning golf achievement tests.* Unpublished master's thesis, University of Iowa, Iowa City.

Watts, H. (1942). *Construction and evaluation of a target on testing the approach shot in golf.* Unpublished master's thesis, University of Wisconsin, Madison.

West, C., & Thorpe, J.A. (1968). Construction and validation of an eight-iron approach test. *Research Quarterly* 39: 1115-1120.

Wood, J.I. (1933). *A study for the purpose of setting up the specifications of a golf driving cage target and test for the mid-iron and the brassie clubs.* Unpublished master's thesis, University of Wisconsin, Madison.

Chapter 15

GYMNASTICS

INTRODUCTION

Gymnastics is one of the few physical education activities offered in educational institutions in which measurement of ability is almost entirely limited to subjective judgment. Therefore, the importance of the tester's skill in evaluating gymnastics performance cannot be overemphasized.

BOWERS GYMNASTICS SKILLS TEST
(Bowers, 1965)

Purpose:

To evaluate beginning and low intermediate gymnastic skills.

Description:

Bowers based her gymnastics test on the areas or events that reflect the official competitive schedule for women. Performance in tumbling, vaulting and free standing floor exercise is measured along with ability demonstrated on the uneven parallel bars and balance beam.

Ordinarily, tumbling is included as part of the free standing floor exercise event in national women's competition but is a separate item in this test.

Educational Application:

Females, junior high school through college.

Time:

Twenty students can be tested in two 60-minute periods.

Personnel:

One or two judges with student assistants as spotters.

Equipment and Supplies:

Uneven parallel bars, balance beam, vaulting board, mats, scoring and marking materials.

Facilities and Space:

Gymnasium area.

Directions and Scoring Method:

The number or numbers that follow each item represent the scoring scale for that particular item with the highest numerical value naturally representing a well-executed item. Subjects may repeat a particular event in an attempt to improve their score, but the second attempt is also recorded.

If a skill cannot be completed, a score of zero is given. The skills tested are scored from zero to a maximum number of points, and the highest score signifies perfect execution in body rhythm and form with both grace and poise.

It is to the student's advantage to try each skill without the aid of spotters. Should the student feel a spotter is needed at the lowest skill level, it is permissible, but no points are awarded.

Event No. 1: Tumbling

    A. Tumbling Items
        (1) Rolls
            a. forward-3,2,1
            b. backward-3,2,1
            c. backward extension-5
        (2) Cartwheels in Rhythm
            a. to the right side-3,2,1
            b. to the left side-3,2,1
        (3) Kip Progression (either movement a or b)
            a. from headspring off a rolled mat-4
            b. from shoulder-hand support-3,2,1

Event No. 2: Uneven Parallel Bars

    A. Uneven Parallel Bars Items

(1) Bar Snap	Inches	18	30	36	42	48	54
	Points	0	2	4	6	8	10

A line is drawn or taped on the landing mat 18 inches away from the bar, with another 12 inches from the first line, and then four more lines six inches apart. If the subject lands in the area between the bar and the first line, a score of zero points is awarded and successive scores are based on the above point and distance chart.

    B. Progressive Movement to the Kip
        (1) one leg swing up-1,2,4
        (2) walk out-4,5,6
        (3) glide-5,6,8

    C. Backward Hip Pullover-0,2,4
        If the student is given only slight assistance during any portion of the pullover, only two points are awarded.

Event No. 3: Balance Beam

    A. Balance Beam Items
        (1) three-step turn-1,2,4
        (2) step, hops on both feet-1,2,4
        (3) step, leap-1,2,4
        (4) scale-1,2,4

The score is determined by adding the total points accumulated on the four movements. Sixteen points is the maximum score.

    B. Arm Support-0,1,2,4
    C. Rolling
        (1) backward shoulder roll-1,2,3,4,5,6,7

Total points accumulated without the aid of a spotter constitute the official score.

Event No. 4: Vaulting Event

    A. Vaulting Items
        (1) Floor items for body control of basic vault positions and flexibility.
            a. front support to straddle stand
            b. front support to stoop stand

Inches Away	12	9	6	3	3	→
Points	0	2	4	6	10	12

The scoring system is the same for each of the above items. A solid line is constructed on the gymnasium floor. On one side of the line are three parallel lines that are 12, six and three inches away. On the opposite side is another parallel line located three inches from the original line.

The student places her hands on the solid line with the body extended in a front support over the line 12 inches away. Measurement of the landing is taken from the heel. Points are awarded on a 0,2,4,6,10,12 basis as shown in the above point and distance chart.

        (2) Approach test for the run, hurdle and take-off.
            a. run, take-off - 1,2,3,4

A regulation reuther board that has a black stripe on the front end is used. Lines are drawn on the board that are five, 13 and 17 inches from the black stripe. The area where the ball of the foot hits is the scoring area.

No points are scored for hitting the area from the back of the board to the first line. Three, four and two points are scored for the next three areas with no points given for the black part of the board. This score is added to the wall score minus the height score which is discussed below.

            b. height measurement-0,1,2,3,4,5,6,7

The take-off board is placed beside a wall that is marked off with three-inch, alternating colored stripes of tape beginning at the five-foot level. The stripes are numbered one through seven beginning with the bottom stripe. The score is the height of the student's jump (in stripes) minus the height of the student while standing.

Event No. 5: Free Standing Floor Exercise

    A. Free Standing Floor Exercise Items
        (1) Tumbling total (points from Event No. 1)-0-21
        (2) Continuity (routine)-0-10
            a. body wave
            b. leg leading turn
            c. scale
            d. concentric arm circles
            e. final pose

One point is deducted for each stop in the flow of movement. The same is true for a break in form.

The score sheet depicted in Table 15.1 is used when scoring a student's performance on the Bowers Gymnastics Skills Test. The blanks reflect the maximum number of points that can be obtained for each item and event.

Equal weight value is given to the various events, even though they differ numerically. Since the numerical range of the five events is from 21 to 33 points, the event scores should be scaled or equated by the use of the standard scores.

Table 15.1
SCORE SHEET FOR BOWERS GYMNASTICS TEST

I.   Tumbling
      1.   Rolls
         <u>F</u> <u>B</u> <u>Ext.</u>
         <u>3</u> + <u>3</u> + <u>5</u>   +
      2.   Cartwheels
         <u>R</u> <u>L</u>
         <u>3</u> + <u>3</u>   +
      3.   Kips
         <u>4</u> = <u>21</u>

II.   Uneven Bars
      1.   Bar Snap
         <u>10</u>   +
      2.   Kip
         <u>8</u>   +
      3.   Backward Hip Pullover
         <u>4</u> = <u>22</u>

III.   Balance Beam
      1.   Locomotor
         <u>4</u> + <u>4</u> + <u>4</u> + <u>4</u>   +
      2.   Arm Support
         <u>4</u>   +
      3.   Rolling
         <u>7</u> = <u>27</u>

IV.   Vaulting
      A.   Straddle   B. Stoop
         <u>12</u>   +   <u>12</u>   +
      2.   Approach Test
         Board + Wall Score - Height Score
         <u>4</u>   +   (5   )   =   <u>33</u>

V.   Free Standing Floor Exercise
      1.   Tumbling Total
         <u>21</u>   +
      2.   Continuity
         <u>10</u>   =   <u>31</u>

From: Bowers, C.O. (1965). *Gymnastics skill test for beginning to low intermediate girls and women.* Unpublished master's thesis, Indiana University, Bloomington. Copyright by author.

Validity:
Face validity for the test items was claimed.

Reliability:
Tumbling, .98; uneven parallel bars, 1.00; balance beam, .98; vaulting, .99; free exercise, .97.

Additional Comments:

The Bowers Test may be used effectively as a motivation and practice device as well as a tool for measuring progress in gymnastics achievement. Also, the comprehensiveness feature of the test makes it a valuable aid to those instructors who are developing gymnastics programs.

HARRIS TUMBLING AND APPARATUS PROFICIENCY TEST
(Harris, 1966)

Purpose:

    To measure tumbling and apparatus skill proficiency.

Description:

    Harris' test originally included 22 items; four in tumbling and three each in the rings, parallel bars, high and low horizontal bars, side horse and the trampoline. Through a process of scientific assessment, all but six of the test items were eliminated. Although used for ability grouping purposes, the test was originally designated to serve as an alternative evaluation tool to the successful completion of a formal course of instruction.

Educational Application:

    College men.

Time:

    Twenty students can be evaluated in one 60-minute period.

Personnel:

    One judge or scorer.

Equipment and Supplies:

    Parallel bars, horizontal bar, trampoline and scoring materials.

Facilities and Space:

    Gymnasium area.

Directions:

    Each student attempts to perform all six test items. Scoring proficiency of the instructor is enhanced if all students complete a particular test item before proceeding to the next. The test items and score values are shown in Table 15.2.

Scoring Method:

    The test is scored by a judge or panel of judges with each item assigned a point total of seven to nine points. As shown on the score card, the point total for each item is divided into form and execution points. Forty-six points is the maximum score.

    Mean scores associated with each test item are given below. Twenty-five male physical education majors completed the test in the Harris study and were ranked by groups according to mean score.

    The first group was comprised of the four top subjects, and the second group was composed of the 17 subjects that scored in the middle range. Four subjects who ranked at the bottom of the scale were in the third group. The mean scores were as follows:

Item No.	Group I	Group II	Group III
1	6.75	5.47	4.00
2	6.75	5.18	1.75
3	7.50	4.12	1.75
4	7.75	3.59	1.00
5	6.25	3.88	2.00
6	6.50	4.53	2.25

Table 15.2

SCORE CARD FOR HARRIS TUMBLING AND APPARATUS PROFICIENCY TEST

Name: Judge: Class: Date:

Directions: Circle the number which indicates the performer's score in areas of form and execution, respectively. Leave the totals until all testing has been completed.

Item No.

1. TUMBLING
    Forward roll to head balance.   Form: 12
                                           Execution: 12345   Total _____

2. PARALLEL BARS
    Back uprise, shoulder balance,
    front or forward roll.   Form: 12
                                           Execution: 12345   Total _____

3. Shoulder kip from arm support,
    swing, front dismount.   Form: 123
                                           Execution: 123456   Total _____

4. HORIZONTAL OR HIGH BAR
    Cast to kip up.   Form: 123
                                           Execution: 123456   Total _____

5. Front pullover, cast, back
    hip circle.   Form: 12
                                           Execution: 12345   Total _____

6. TRAMPOLINE
    Back, front, seat, feet.   Form: 12
                                           Execution: 12345   Total _____

                                           Total Points   _____

From: Harris, J.P. (1966). *A design for a proposed skill proficiency test in tumbling and apparatus for male physical majors at the University of North Dakota.* Unpublished master's thesis, University of North Dakota, Grand Forks. Reprinted with permission from the University of North Dakota.

Validity and Reliability:

Results of the Harris study revealed the test to be discriminatory in the determination of gymnastics ability. Utilizing the test-retest method, each of the six test items met the acceptable reliability standards.

Additional Comments:

The Harris Test rates high in time and ease of administration. Its chief limitation is that of most gymnastics skills tests: a lack of instructors with expertise in judging gymnastics performance restricts the test's use.

Gymnastics References

Bowers, C.O. (1965). *Gymnastics skill test for beginning to low intermediate girls and women.* Unpublished master's thesis, The Ohio State University, Columbus.

Ellenbrand, D.K. (1973). *Gymnastics skills test for college women.* Unpublished master's thesis, Indiana University, Bloomington.

Faulkner, J., & Loken, N. (1962). Objectivity of judging at the National Collegiate Athletic Association gymnastic meet: A ten-year study. *Research Quarterly* 33: 485-486.

Fisher, R.B. (1950). *Tests in selected physical education service courses in a college.* Unpublished doctoral dissertation, University of Iowa, Iowa City.

Harris, J.P. (1966). *A design for a proposed skill proficiency test in tumbling and apparatus for male physical education majors at the University of North Dakota.* Unpublished master's thesis, University of North Dakota, Grand Forks.

Johnson, M. (1971). Objectivity of judging at the National Collegiate Athletic Association gymnastic meet: A 20-year follow-up study. *Research Quarterly* 42: 454-455.

Landers, D.M. (1965). *A comparison of two gymnastic judging methods.* Unpublished master's thesis, University of Illinois, Urbana-Champaign.

Larson, R.F. (1969). Skill testing in elementary school gymnastics. *Physical Educator* 26: 80-81.

Nelson, J.K. (1986). *The Nelson balance test.* Unpublished study. In B.L. Johnson & J.K. Nelson, *Practical measurements for evaluation in physical education.* (4th ed.). Edina, Minnesota: Burgess, pp. 247-249.

Scheer, J. (1973). Effect of placement in the order of competition on scores of Nebraska high school students. *Research Quarterly* 44: 79-85.

Schwarzkoph, R.J. (1962). *The Iowa Brace Test as a measuring instrument for predicting gymnastic ability.* Unpublished master's thesis, University of Washington, Seattle.

Wettstone, E. (1938). Test for predicting potential ability in gymnastics and tumbling. *Research Quarterly* 9: 115.

Zwarg, L.F. (1935). Judging and evaluation of competitive apparatus for gymnastic exercises. *Journal of Health and Physical Education* 6: 23.

Chapter 16

HANDBALL

INTRODUCTION

Of the dozen or so handball skills tests that have been developed through the years, the first was completed by Clevett (Clevett, 1935), and the initial tests devised by scientific procedures were done by Cornish (Cornish, 1949) and McCachren (McCachren, 1949).

TYSON HANDBALL TEST
(Tyson, 1970)

Purpose:

To measure the skills essential to succeed in handball.

Description:

Study of seven handball skill items produced a rather impressive three-item battery, according to standards of scientific authenticity.

Front Wall Kill with Dominant Hand. See Figure 16.1 for description of the test layout.

Back Wall Kill with Dominant Hand. Court markings for this test are shown in Figure 16.2.

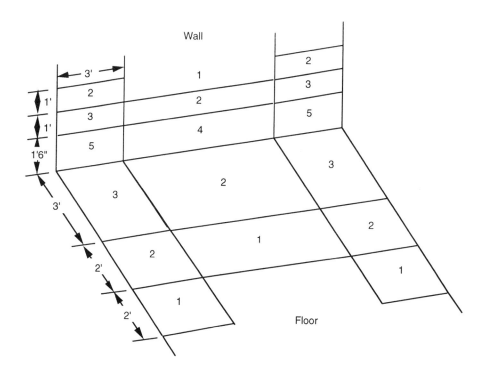

Fig. 16.1 Markings for front wall kill test.

From: Tyson, K.W. (1970). *A handball skill test for college men.* Unpublished master's thesis, University of Texas, Austin. Copyright by author.

Educational Application:

College men.

Time:

A class of 20 students can be tested in one 60-minute period.

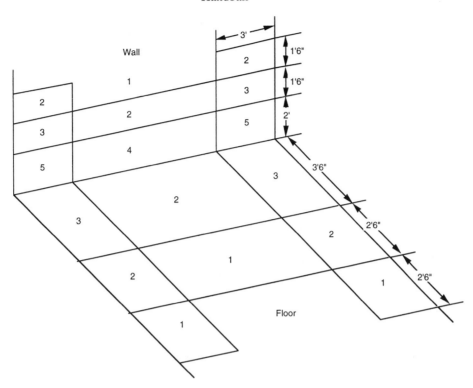

Fig. 16.2 Markings for back wall kill test.

From: Tyson, K.W. (1970). *A handball skill test for college men.* Unpublished master's thesis, University of Texas, Austin. Copyright by author.

Personnel:

One scorer-timer-recorder with student assistants.

Equipment and Supplies:

Handballs, gloves, stop watch, scoring and floor marking materials.

Facilities and Space:

Handball court or facility with similar wall and floor space.

Directions:

Thirty-Second Volley. Standing behind the short line holding a handball, the student, when told to start, puts the ball into play with a toss to the front wall. He proceeds to volley the ball against the front wall as many times as possible within the 30-second time period. The subject must hit each return from behind the short line. Hits do not count when the short line is violated or the ball has bounced more than once. If the student loses control of the ball, another player in the court quickly tosses him another ball to be put back into play immediately. Either hand may be used.

Front Wall Kill with Dominant Hand. The subject assumes a position in the doubles service box against the left side wall if he is right-handed or the right side wall if left-handed. The tester or student assistant stands in the middle of the service zone and starts the trial by tossing the ball against the front wall so that it rebounds to the right if the subject is right-handed and to the left if he is left-handed. As soon as the tester releases the ball, the subject is free to move, being sure to cross behind the tester to get into a better position for stroking the ball. Each subject is allowed five attempts to place the ball in a target area on the front wall.

Back Wall Kill with Dominant Hand. The initial positioning of the subject is identical to the previously described front wall kill with dominant hand item. Positioning of the tester or student assistant is different since he is now stationed in the center of the court, six feet behind the short line.

The tester tosses the ball to the front wall so that it rebounds and bounces approximately eight to 12 feet behind the short line and approximately 10 feet from the right side wall for a right-handed subject or 10 feet from the left side wall if the subject is left-handed. Experience has shown that the tester should aim for a spot between 15 and 18 feet high on the front wall for best results.

A bad toss does not have to be played by the test subject. As the tester tosses the ball, the student may leave his starting position and move into a position that allows him to hit the ball with his dominant hand as the ball rebounds off the back wall. Each subject completes five trials.

Scoring Method:

Thirty-Second Volley. Final score is the number of legal hits made in the 30-second trial.

Front Wall Kill with Dominant Hand. Number of points accumulated on all five trials is the final score. The maximum number of points is 25.

Back Wall Kill with Dominant Hand. Number of points accumulated on all five trials with the maximum number of points being 25.

Validity and Reliability:

Test data were derived from the skill item scores of 64 men enrolled in college handball classes. Each subject possessed at least one semester of handball experience.

Validity coefficients were .87, .84 and .76 for the 30-second wall volley, front wall kill with dominant hand and back wall kill with dominant hand, respectively. Round-robin tournament results served as the criterion measure. The three-item battery validity coefficient was .92.

Reliability coefficients of .82, .82 and .81 were obtained for the three items in their order of presentation above.

SATTLER HANDBALL BATTERY
(Sattler, 1973)

Purpose:

To evaluate the ability to return and volley a handball off the front wall.

Educational Application:

Designed for college men, but useful for junior and senior high school boys and girls.

Personnel:

One tester per item.

Equipment and Supplies:

Handballs, measuring tape, marking tape, stop watch and scoring materials.

Facilities and Space:

Handball court of regulation size.

Description and Directions:

Marking tape is placed across the front wall two feet above the floor and across the floor six feet from the back wall.

Dominant Overhead Return. The student prepares for the test by standing between the short line and the service line. The subject bounces a ball on the floor so that it allows him/her to perform an overhand return with the elbow of the dominant hand extended. Balls must rebound off the front wall and hit the back wall without touching the floor. Balls not hit with an overhand motion and extended elbow are considered unsuccessful trials. The student is not allowed to cross the service line to hit a ball.

Thirty-Second Alternate-Hand Volley. The subject stands between the short line and service line while facing the front wall. On an audible signal, the student throws a ball to the front wall. On the return and subsequent returns, the student attempts to hit alternate-hand returns for 30 seconds. A ball hit with the same hand on two successive returns does not count; neither does a missed ball nor one that does not reach the front wall. Students must stay behind the service line when hitting a ball. If a ball eludes a student, the tester throws him/her another ball.

One-Minute Continuous Back-Wall Volley. The student stands between the short and service lines. On an audible signal, a ball is served to the front wall hard enough so that it hits the back wall to allow for a back-wall return. The subject continues to hit back-wall returns for one minute. On unsuccessful returns, the subject gets another ball and returns to the service area and continues the test by serving the ball again.

Scoring Method:

Dominant Overhand Return. The number of successful attempts in 10 trials is the official score.

Thirty-Second Alternate-Hand Volley. The number of successful alternate hits in a 30-second trial constitutes the final score.

One-Minute Continuous Back-Wall Volley. The number of legal returns in one minute is the final score.

Validity and Reliability:

With round-robin tournament play as the criterion measure, validity coefficients of .81, .79 and .77 were derived for the dominant overhand return, 30-second alternate-hand volley, and one-minute continuous back-wall volley, respectively. Utilizing the test-retest method for obtaining reliability, coefficients of .89, .90 and .85 were reported for the three test items in the order presented above.

Handball References

Clevett, M.A. (1935). All-round athletic championship. *Journal of Health and Physical Education* 6: 48.

Cornish, C. (1949). A study of measurement of ability in handball. *Research Quarterly* 20: 215-222.

Friermood, H.T. (1937). A handball classification plan. *Journal of Health and Physical Education* 8: 106-107.

Griffith, M.A. (1960). *An objective method of evaluating ability in handball singles.* Unpublished master's thesis, The Ohio State University, Columbus.

Leinbach, C.H. (1952). *The development of achievement standards in handball and touch football for use in the Department of Physical Training for Men at the University of Texas*, University of Texas, Austin.

Malcomb, A.G. (1960). *Can we have an objective method for evaluating ability in handball singles?* Unpublished master's thesis, The Ohio State University, Columbus.

Marsh, J. (1972). *A study of predictability of ability in handball.* Unpublished master's thesis, Texas Tech University, Lubbock.

McCachren, J.R. (1949). *A study of the University of Florida handball skill test.* Unpublished master's thesis, University of North Carolina, Chapel Hill.

Millonzi, F. (1974). *Development and validation of a handball skill test.* Unpublished master's thesis, University of Wisconsin, La Crosse.

Montoye, H.J., & Brotzman, J. (1951). An investigation of the validity of using the results of a doubles tournament as a measure of handball ability. *Research Quarterly* 22: 214-218.

Pennington, G.G., Day, J.A., Drowatzky, J.N., & Hanson, J.F. (1967). A measure of handball ability. *Research Quarterly* 38: 247-253.

Sattler, T. (1973). *The development of an instrument to measure handball ability of beginning level players in a physical education class.* Unpublished doctoral dissertation, Oklahoma State University, Stillwater.

Schiff, F.S. (1938). *A test of skills performed in the game situation of handball.* Unpublished master's thesis, The Ohio State University, Columbus.

Simos, T. (1952). *A handball classification test.* Unpublished master's thesis, Springfield College, Springfield, Massachusetts.

Tyson, K.W. (1970). *A handball skill test for college men.* Unpublished master's thesis, University of Texas, Austin.

Chapter 17

ICE HOCKEY

INTRODUCTION

The lack of skills tests in ice hockey may be partially explained by the sport's limited offering in physical education programs on a nationwide basis. Ice hockey typifies a regional sport perhaps as much as any other sport included in the physical education curriculum. Instructors of skills classes in ice hockey have an excellent opportunity to make a contribution to sports skills measurement by devising authentic tests or subjecting existing ones to scientific analysis.

ITHACA ICE HOCKEY SKILL TESTS
(Merrifield & Walford, 1969)

Purpose:

To measure the basic skills of ice hockey.

Description:

The four-item battery includes the puck carry, forward skating speed test, backward skating speed test and a skating agility item. The authors of the test concluded that the puck carry test was the best single-item test for general ice hockey playing ability. As implied by the item titles, the battery measures speed, agility and puck control ability.

Educational Application:

Designed for college men, but appropriate for junior and senior high school boys and girls and college women.

Time:

Two 40-minute class periods should be a realistic time allotment for testing a class of 15 to 20 students.

Personnel:

The instructor and three trained student timers.

Equipment and Supplies:

Regulation hockey sticks, pucks, four stop watches, ten wooden obstacles, one goal cage, ice marking and scoring materials.

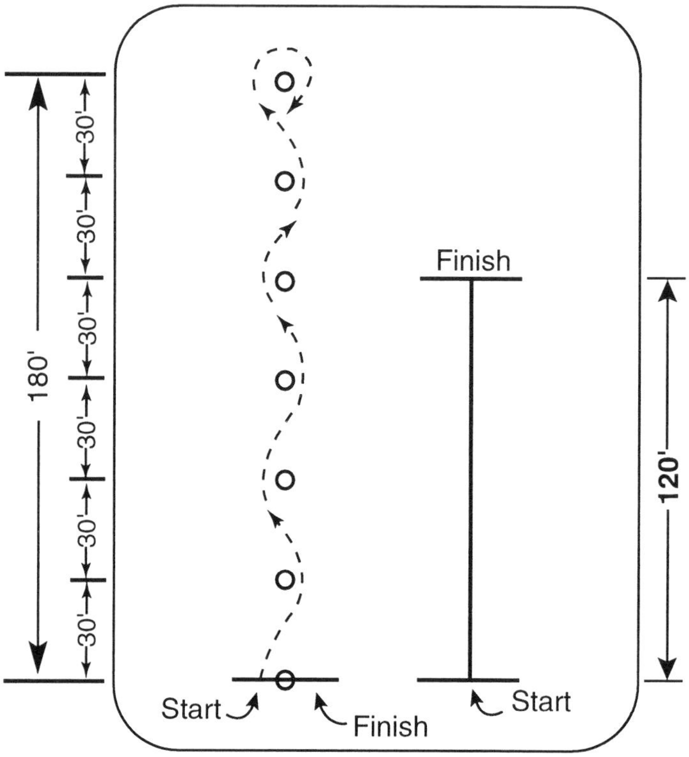

Fig. 17.1 Ice markings for speed tests and puck carry.

From: Merrifield, H.H., & Walford, G.A. (1969). Battery of ice hockey skill tests. *Research Quarterly* 40: 146-152. Reprinted with permission from AAHPERD.

Facilities and Space:

Ice hockey rink.

Directions:

Forward Skating Speed. The student faces the finish line with both feet behind the starting line. On the command "Go," the subject skates the 120-foot distance as fast as possible (Figure 17.1). Two trials are administered.

Backward Skating Speed. Same as the forward skating speed test item except the student starts with his/her back to the starting line and skates backwards.

Skating Agility. Figure 17.2 illustrates the ice markings and obstacle locations for the skating agility test. The wooden obstacles are the same size as those described for the puck carry test. On the starting signal, the subject skates to the left of the first obstacle and loops the second by passing it on the right, then returns to skate around the first obstacle on the way to the four-foot line in front of the goal cage. The subject stops at the line and then continues on to the next four-foot line. The subject completes the course by passing behind the goal cage and skating around the last obstacle while on the way performing a turn to skate backwards, skating backwards, and a turn to skate forward.

Each subject is allowed a half-speed trial prior to testing. Two test trials are permitted.

Puck Carry. The student assumes a position immediately behind the four-foot start-finish line while the puck is placed on the line at the left of the first obstacle. On the starting signal, the subject passes to the right of the first obstacle and continues an alternating pattern until the test is completed.

As illustrated in Figure 17.1, seven wooden obstacles are placed on the ice in a straight line at 30-foot intervals. The obstacles are 30 inches high on a 2 x 4-inch base. The puck must be controlled by the subject during the test and the knockdown of two or more obstacles constitutes a violation; if either violation occurs, the test must be repeated.

A half-speed practice trial is permitted. Two test trials are administered.

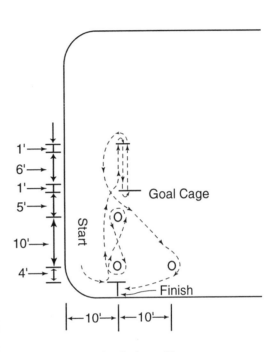

Fig. 17.2 Layout for skating agility test.

From: Merrifield, H.H., & Walford, G.A. (1969). Battery of ice hockey skill tests. *Research Quarterly* 40: 146-152. Reprinted with permission from AAHPERD.

Scoring Method:

Forward Skating Speed. The better of two trial times to the nearest one-tenth of a second from the starting signal until the subject reaches the finish line.

Backward Skating Speed. Same as above except subject starts with back to finish line and skates backwards.

Skating Agility. Same as in forward skating speed test.

Puck Carry. Same as above.

Validity and Reliability:

Validity coefficients of .83, .79, .75 and .96 were obtained for the respective test items. Fifteen members of the Ithaca College Hockey Club served as subjects; a hockey coach's ranking of playing ability was the criterion measure.

The respective test item reliability coefficients were .74, .80, .94 and .93.

Additional Comments:

A test item trial is repeated when a subject falls. Also, the hockey stick should be carried below shoulder level with both hands for all items.

The Ithaca Ice Hockey Skill Tests should be retested for validity and reliability values since only 15 subjects participated in the original study to authenticate the test. The apparent value of the test would be more firmly substantiated if similar coefficients of correlation were obtained when using a significantly larger number of subjects.

Merrifield and Walford experimented with shooting and passing items in their study but eliminated them from the final battery because low reliability coefficients resulted. They indicated that the requirement of a large number of trials should produce an acceptable reliability value for a shooting test.

Ice Hockey References

Doroschuk, E.V., & Marcotte, G.E. (1965). *An agility test for screening ice hockey players.* Paper presented at the Canadian Association for Health, Physical Education and Recreation Biennial Convention, Toronto.
Hache, R.E. (1967). *An achievement test in ice hockey.* Unpublished master's thesis, University of Massachusetts, Amherst.
Merrifield, H.H.,& Walford, G.A. (1969). Battery of ice hockey skill tests. *Research Quarterly* 40: 146-152.

Chapter 18

LACROSSE

INTRODUCTION

Lacrosse is not a new activity on the American sports scene since it was played by several of the American Indian tribes as early as the 1800s. Yet throughout the period of growth and development of physical education in the American educational system, the sport has never attained nationwide popularity.

ENNIS MULTI-SKILL LACROSSE TEST
(Ennis, 1977)

Purpose:
To evaluate lacrosse skills.

Educational Application:
Appropriate for college, junior high and senior high school males and females.

Personnel:
One timer-scorer.

Equipment and Supplies:
Lacrosse sticks, balls, one goal, measuring tape, eight cones, stop watch, scoring and field marking materials.

Facilities and Space:
An area approximately 180 x 45 feet.

Description and Directions:
The multiple-skill test contains components of running, stick handling, tossing, catching and shooting. Figure 18.1 illustrates the test layout.

The student is stationed near Cone 3, then runs forward to pick up a stationary ball at Cone 1. When the ball is touched, time measurement begins. Securing the ball, the student turns left and goes around Cone 1, runs to the right of Cone 2, to the left of Cone 3, and to the right of Cone 4. After passing

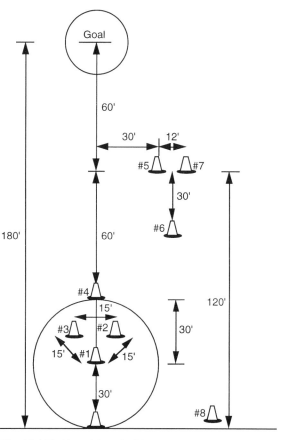

Fig. 18.1 Field markings for Ennis Lacrosse Test.

From: Ennis, C.D. (1977). *The development of a multi-skill test in lacrosse for college women*. Unpublished master's thesis, University of North Carolina, Greensboro. Reprinted with permission from the University of North Carolina, Greensboro.

Cone 4, the student performs two tosses and catches of the ball while running. The ball must be visible above the student's head to avoid repeating the trial. After two tosses and two catches, the student shoots for goal. For each successful goal, one second is deducted from the official test time. Shots may be taken from any location, with no penalty for misses.

After the shot is taken, the student continues to the goal side of Cone 5, turns and runs backward to Cone 6, and then runs forward to pick up a ball beside Cone 7. The student continues to run around Cone 7 and throws the ball beyond Cone 8. Throws are allowed from any location, and the ball may bounce. Should a ball not reach Cone 8, the student is required to use a stick and propel it again. Time elapses as the ball passes Cone 8.

Scoring Method:

Time is measured to the nearest tenth-second. An official trial time is the time required to complete the test minus a one-second deduction for a successful goal. The sum of the three trials is the final score.

Validity and Reliability:

Coefficient of .66 for validity and .89 for reliability.

Criterion Measure:

Player ratings by varsity coaches using a revision of the Hodges Rating Scale (Hodges, 1974).

Lacrosse References

Ennis, C.D. (1977). *The development of a multi-skill test in lacrosse for college women.* Unpublished master's thesis, University of North Carolina, Greensboro.

Hodges, C.V. (1974). *Construction of an objective knowledge test and skill test in lacrosse for college women.* Unpublished master's thesis, University of North Carolina, Greensboro.

Lutze, M.C. (1963). *Achievement tests in beginning lacrosse for women.* Unpublished master's thesis, University of Iowa, Iowa City.

McGowan, N. (1965). A skill test for the overarm pass. *Crosse Checks* 1: 23-24.

Waglow, I.F., & Moore, A. (1954). A lacrosse skill test. *Athletic Journal* 34: 4.

Wilkie, B.J. (1967). *Achievement tests for selected lacrosse skills of college women.* Unpublished master's thesis, University of North Carolina, Greensboro.

Chapter 19

RACQUETBALL

INTRODUCTION

Racquetball evolved as a spin-off of paddleball in the 1960s, and its popularity growth in a relatively short period of time is perhaps unprecedented in the history of physical education. Facilities for the sport are now a staple in American colleges and universities, and student interest continues to be strong. Some junior and senior high school physical education programs provide racquetball instruction in the community facilities so prevalent today in the United States.

HENSLEY RACQUETBALL SKILL TEST
(Hensley, East & Stillwell, 1979)

Purpose:

To evaluate volleying ability in racquetball.

Educational Application:

College, senior high and junior high school students.

Personnel:

One scorer and assistant per testing station.

Equipment and Supplies:

Racquets, eye guards, four racquetballs per testing station, measuring tape, floor marking and scoring materials.

Facilities and Space:

Racquetball courts of regulation size.

Description and Directions:

The two-item test includes a short-wall volley and a long-wall volley. The long-wall volley item requires the marking of a restraining line 12 feet behind and parallel to the short line. A five-minute practice session in an adjacent court and one minute of practice in the testing court are allowed the student prior to testing.

Short-Wall Volley Test. Holding two balls, the student stands behind the short line. Two additional balls are held by the testing assistant who stands near the back wall. The student initiates the test by dropping a ball and hitting it against the front wall, then continues to volley the ball against the front wall as many times as possible in 30 seconds. To be legal, a ball must be hit from behind the short line. Balls can be hit before bouncing or after one or more bounces. Stepping into the front court to retrieve errant balls is allowed, but the student must return behind the short line to continue the test. The student may use any type of stroke to volley the ball.

The scorer may be stationed inside the court or in an adjacent viewing area. The 30-second time measurement should begin the instant the student drops the first ball.

Long-Wall Volley Test. Test administration is the same as for the short-wall volley test except that the student must volley the ball from behind a restraining line located 12 feet behind and parallel to the short line. Two additional balls are placed in the back wall floor crease should the student need them. For this item, the scorer should be positioned outside the court, using an observation window from above or viewing through a glass wall.

Scoring Method and Norms:

For both test items, one point is scored every time the ball legally hits the front wall in two 30-second trials. The cumulative total of legal hits for the two trials is the final score. Balls hitting the floor before striking the front wall are illegal.

T-score norms for the two test items are shown in Table 19.1.

	Table 19.1			
	T-score Norms for the Hensley Short-Wall and Long-Wall Volley Test			
	Score			
	Short-wall volley test		Long-wall volley test	
T-score	Men	Women	Men	Women
80	53	44	40	31
75	49	41	38	29
70	46	38	35	27
65	43	35	33	25
60	40	32	30	23
55	36	29	28	21
50	33	26	25	19
45	30	23	23	17
40	27	20	20	15
35	24	17	18	13
30	20	14	15	11
25	17	11	13	9
20	14	8	10	7

From: Hensley, L.D., East, W.B., & Stillwell, J.L. (1979). A racquetball skills test. *Research Quarterly* 50: 114-118. Reprinted with permission from AAHPERD.

Validity and Reliability:

Using instructor ratings of students as the criterion measure, validity coefficients of .79 and .86 were derived for the short-wall volley and long-wall volley, respectively. Employing the test-retest method, reliability coefficients for the long-wall volley item were .82 for women and .85 for men. Reliability coefficients for the short-wall volley test were .86 for women and .76 for men.

COLLINS-HODGES RACQUETBALL SKILLS TEST
(Collins & Hodges, 1982)

Purpose:

To measure basic racquetball skills.

Educational Application:

Junior high school, senior high school and college students.

Time:

With the availability of five courts or more, at least 20 students can be tested on the five test items in a 45-minute class period.

Personnel:

One scorer-recorder per testing court and a trained timer for the wall volley item.

Equipment and Supplies:

Ample supply of racquets, balls, one stop watch, court marking and scoring materials.

Facilities and Space:

Regulation racquetball courts.

Description and Directions:

A wall volley test item and skill items for the serve, kill, ceiling and back wall placement are included in the Collins-Hodges Racquetball Skills Test.

A sufficient amount of uniform practice time should be allowed for each student in class periods that precede a day of testing. A brief uniform practice period should also be allotted for each student on the test date.

Wall Volley. The subject assumes a position behind the short line, drops the ball to the floor and rallies continuously for 30 seconds. The ball must be hit after one bounce, with a violation occurring either when the ball bounces two or more times, when the ball is hit in the air before bouncing or when the subject steps on over the short line. If the ball gets away from the student, the tester provides another immediately by directly handing a ball to the student.

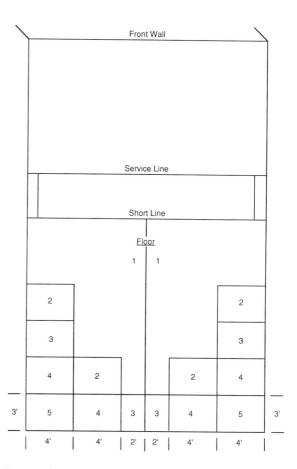

Fig. 19.1 Court markings for serve and ceiling test items.

From: Collins, R., & Hodges, P. (1982). Racquetball skills test investigation. *Minnesota Journal for Health, Physical Education and Recreation* 10: 10-13. Reprinted with permission from MAHPERD.

The student resumes the test in the same manner as at the beginning. This procedure is required only if a ball gets away from the subject, not on other violations. Although a disadvantage to the subject, the ball may hit the side wall or ceiling as long as the front wall is struck. Any type of stroke may be used. The stop watch should start the instant the ball touches the floor when dropped by the student to initiate the test.

Serve. Standing in the service area, the subject attempts 10 serves, five to each side of the court. Any type of serve may be used. An illegal serve counts as a trial and is given a zero score. Points are assigned according to the scoring area (floor) where the ball hits after the first bounce. Balls hitting a line are given the higher point value. The line running through scoring areas three (3 points) and one (1 point) serves as the boundary for the right and left sides (Figure 19.1). Balls must be served to the designated side to score.

Ceiling. The subject assumes a position in the back court, while the tester stands directly behind the short line on the side opposite the racquet hand of the subject. The tester tosses the ball against the front wall so that after the first bounce it can be comfortably struck by the student standing in the back court. Ten trials are completed with the racquet hand. The ball may hit the front wall first as long as the ceiling is struck. If the ball does not hit the ceiling, a trial is counted and is given a zero score.

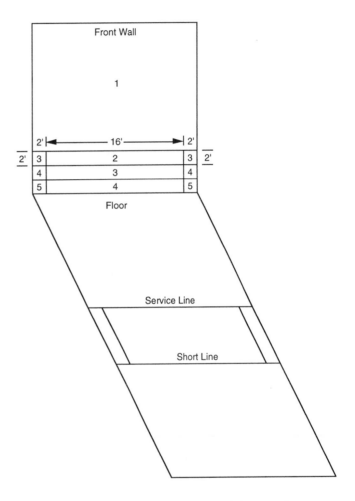

Fig. 19.2 Court markings for kill and back wall placement items.

From: Collins, R., & Hodges, P. (1982). Racquetball skills test investigation. *Minnesota Journal for Health, Physical Education and Recreation* 10: 10-13. Reprinted with permission from MAHPERD.

Points are assigned according to the scoring area (floor) where the ball hits after the initial bounce (Figure 19.1). A ball hitting a line is assigned the higher point value. A retrial occurs when the tester judges a toss to be poorly thrown or when the subject hits the ball while standing on or in front of the short line.

Kill. The subject assumes a position in the back court, while the tester stands directly behind the short line on the side opposite the subject's hitting side. The tester tosses the ball against the front wall so that after the first bounce it can be comfortably struck by the student standing in the back court. Ten trials are completed, five with the forehand and the same number with the backhand. A retrial occurs when the tester judges a toss to be poorly thrown or when the subject hits the ball while standing on or in front of the short line. Balls may hit the side walls first, but those initially hitting the ceiling or floor count as zero. Each trial is scored according to the ball's point of contact on the front wall scoring area, with the higher value allowed for balls striking a line (Figure 19.2).

Back Wall Placement. The student assumes a position in the back court, while the tester stands directly behind the short line on the same side as the student's hitting side. The tester bounces the ball on the floor so that it rebounds off the back wall in a manner that allows the student to comfortably strike the ball. Ten trials are completed, five with the forehand and five with the backhand. A retrial occurs when the instructor judges a toss to be poorly thrown or when the subject hits the ball while standing on or in front of the short line. Balls may hit the side walls first, but those initially hitting the ceiling or floor count as zero. Each trial is assigned a point value based on the ball's point of contact on the front wall scoring area (Figure 19.2). Balls striking a line are given the score of higher value.

Table 19.2 T-SCORE NORMS FOR RACQUETBALL WALL VOLLEY TEST		
Test Score (Sum of Two Trials)		
T-Score	Men	Women
80	54	45
75	50	41
70	45	37
65	41	33
60	37	29
55	33	25
50	28	21
45	24	17
40	20	13
35	16	9
30	12	5
25	7	2

From: Collins, R., & Hodges, P. (1982). Racquetball skills test investigation. *Minnesota Journal for Health, Physical Education and Recreation* 10: 10-13. Reprinted with permission from MAHPERD.

Scoring Method and Norms:

Wall Volley. The final score is the number of successful hits made in 30 seconds.

Serve, Ceiling, Kill and Back Wall Placement. The total number of points made in 10 trials. Fifty points is the maximum score.

Validity and Reliability:

With 51 college men as subjects, a validity coefficient of .64 was derived for the wall volley test item. A reliability coefficient of .85 resulted from the test-retest administration of that item. Face validity was claimed for the serve, ceiling, kill and back wall placement test items since the skill requirements so closely simulate those requiring execution in a game situation.

Additional Comments:

In the wall volley test administration, there are alternatives to having someone hand another ball to the subject if the original test ball gets away. A tester may design the test so that the subject holds a second ball in the non-racquet hand until it is needed. Or the tester may opt for a ball container to be placed on each side of the racquetball court, directly behind the short line of the service area. In any event, a trial should be repeated if the tester feels that an undue amount of time is allowed to expire while a second ball is being put into play, placing the student in an unfair position when his/her score is compared to peer scores.

Whatever method is used for putting the second ball into play, the tester is reminded that its application should be consistent for the entire test group, and the development and use of norms from individual test scores should be specific to the particular method used.

Racquetball References

Bartee, H. (1982). Tests of racquetball skills. *The Indiana Association HPERD Journal* 11: 8-9.

Buschner, C.A. (1976). *The validation of a racquetball skills test for college men.* Unpublished doctoral dissertation, Oklahoma State University, Stillwater.

Chase, R.L. (1986). Racquetball testing. *Texas Association HPERD Journal* 55: 17.

Collins, R., & Hodges, P. (1982). Racquetball skills test investigation. *Minnesota Journal for Health, Physical Education and Recreation* 10: 10-13.

Epperson, S.W. (1977).*Validation of the Reznik racquetball test.* Unpublished master's thesis, Washington State University, Pullman.

Gorman, D.R. (1983). The predictive value of the Pennington skill test battery in assessing racquetball skill. *Arkansas Journal of Health, Physical Education and Recreation* 18: 7-8, 10, 13.

Hensley, L.D., East, W.B., & Stillwell, J.L. (1979). A racquetball skills test. *Research Quarterly* 50: 114-118.

Herman, M. (1991). *Johnson racquetball test.* Unpublished master's thesis, Bemidji State University, Bemidji, Minnesota.

Karpman, M., & Issacs, L. (1979). An improved racquetball skills test. *Research Quarterly* 50: 526-527.

Peterson, A. (1989). Skill assessment for college racquetball classes. *Journal of Physical Education, Recreation and Dance* 69: 71-73.

Reznik, J.W. (1975). Measure your proficiency. *Racquetball* 5: 64.

Valcourt, D.F. (1982). *Development of a racquetball skills test battery for male and female beginner and intermediate players.* Unpublished master's thesis, Springfield College, Springfield, Massachusetts.

Chapter 20

SNOW SKIING

INTRODUCTION

Snow skiing is a very popular activity in those regions of the country that produce cold weather and snow. It is enjoyed annually by millions of avid skiers, many of whom have no exposure to formal instruction.

Snow skiing classes are restricted in number nationally due to the sport's limited geographic appeal. The usual correlation between number of classes offered and number of skills tests available holds true for snow skiing. Few tests have been constructed.

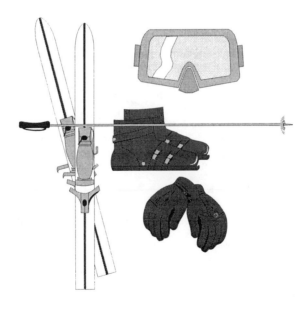

Chapter 20

ROGERS SKIING TEST
(Rogers, 1954)

Purpose:

To objectively measure selected skills of beginning skiers.

Description:

The three-item test includes items for climbing, turning and stopping.

Climbing. The climbing test should be set up on a hill with a convex curve that increases in steepness as the skier climbs. There should be a level space 25 feet in length at the base of the slope.

Turning. A slalom course consisting of six turns located at varying distances is set on a ski slope that is comparable to a beginners' slope at most public ski areas. A ski area

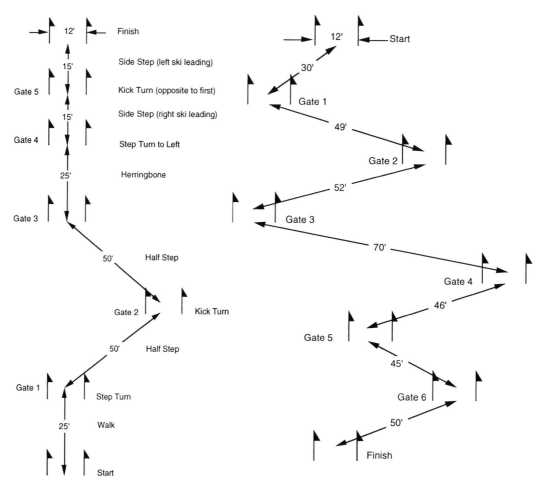

Fig. 20.1 Specifications for climbing test.

Fig. 20.2 Slope markings for turning test.

From: Rogers, M.H. (1954). *Construction of objectively scored skill tests for beginning skiers.* Unpublished master's thesis, University of Washington, Seattle. Copyright by author.

From: Rogers, M.H. (1954). *Construction of objectively scored skill tests for beginning skiers.* Unpublished master's thesis, University of Washington, Seattle. Copyright by author.

approximately 130 feet in length and 45 feet in width is needed for this particular test. Open gates are set with a minimum distance of 10 feet and a maximum distance of 20 feet behind them.

Stopping. The ski slope for the snowplow stopping test should have the same steepness and contour as a typical slope for beginners.

Educational Application:

Designed for high school boys and girls but is also applicable for college men and women.

Time:

The three-item battery can be administered to a class of 20 students in three 60-minute periods.

Personnel:

Timer-recorder, finish judge and point judges.

Equipment and Supplies:

Fourteen to 16 ski slalom poles, stop watch, skis, ski poles and scoring materials.

Facilities and Space:

A ski area roughly the same size and showing a similar degree of difficulty as that normally associated with a beginning ski slope at a public ski facility.

Directions:

Climbing. To start the test, each skier stands below the starting gate with his/her ski tips behind the first gate. On an audible signal, the subject proceeds to walk to the first gate, step turn to the right and half step to Gate 2. Then he/she does a kick turn and half step to Gate 3; a herringbone to Gate 4; step turn to the left; side step to Gate 5; and completes a kick turn and side step with the left ski leading until he/she passes through the last gate.

Ski poles should be used with proper climbing techniques. If a skier fails to use the poles correctly while doing the herringbone, one point is deducted. Should the skier fall, he/she should quickly get up and continue the test. The only penalty for falling is the time lost. A subject is called back to the last gate passed and asked to repeat a particular skill when the original is incorrectly performed. Flags should be used to mark the distances between gates as indicated in Figure 20.1.

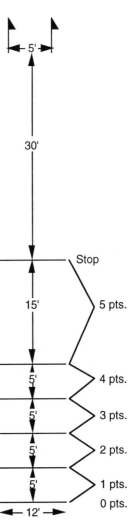

Fig. 20.3 Specifications for stopping test.

From: Rogers, M.H. (1954). *Construction of objectively scored skill tests for beginning skiers.* Unpublished master's thesis, University of Washington, Seattle. Copyright by author.

Turning. The skier assumes a starting position with the ski tips behind Gate 1. When an audible signal is given, the skier immediately heads for Gate 1 located 30 feet away and proceeds to ski through all six gates as rapidly as possible (Figure 20.2).

Stopping. The subject positions his/her ski tips behind the starting gate. On the audible signal, the skier proceeds to ski straight down the fall line for 30 feet. When the tips of the skis reach the first 30-foot line, the skier immediately begins to execute a snowplow stop. He/she should come to a complete stop as quickly as possible (Figure 20.3).

Each skier is given three trials. If the subject falls or begins stopping before reaching the line, a repeat trial is given.

Scoring Method:

Climbing. Two scoring devices are used with the climbing test. One method is the total time taken by the skier to climb the course, starting with the audible signal and ending when the skier passes through the last gate. Each subject is given two trials, with only the best trial counted.

The other method is a point score. Each student starts with 10 points at the beginning of each trial, and one point is deducted each time the skier falls, slips or does not use the technique required.

Since the time scores were found to be more reliable than the point scores in the Rogers study, the former method is considered the better scoring device for measuring the ability to climb.

Turning. Each skier is awarded nine points at the beginning of each trial, with two trials given. Should the skier fall while making a turn through a gate, two points are deducted. If the subject should fall after completing a turn or during a traverse, one point is deducted. Both trials are counted.

Stopping. Two scoring devices may be used with the stopping test. Each skier is timed from the second his/her ski tips reach the first 30-foot line until he/she comes to a complete stop. Each trial may also be scored on a point basis, depending on the distance it takes the skier to stop. One point is lost for each five-foot line crossed (see Figure 20.3). The location of the ski tips determines the value of the stop. The point system is the recommended method of scoring as it proved more reliable than the time method.

Validity, Reliability and Objectivity:

The test was given to 53 high school students who had completed seven hours of instruction in a beginning ski class. Face validity was claimed for each item.

For the climbing item, a reliability coefficient of .80 was obtained. In administering multiple trials for each subject, the sums of the time scores of the first two trials were correlated with the time score sums of the last two trials. Utilizing a correlation of the first and last two trial scores of the subjects, a .87 coefficient was found for the turning item. The first and last three trial scores were correlated for the stopping item, producing a .87 coefficient.

Consistency among judges in scoring the three test items was impressive. The objectivity coefficients ranged .94-1.0 on the climbing item, .99-1.0 for the turning test, and .84-1.0 for the stopping item.

Additional Comments:

Each item is recommended for use as either a motivation or practice device. The climbing and stopping items may be used for grading purposes, but the turning item failed to satisfactorily discriminate the ability levels of participants in the study.

Instructors of snow skiing might find the item more discriminating if the gate opening was narrowed somewhat or the gates were placed at various angles. Adding a time factor in the scoring method may improve the validity value of the item.

In ease of administration, the stopping test rates higher than the other two items. That item also produced a wider distribution of scores.

Overall, the battery seems satisfactory for measuring the skill of beginning skiers. In developing norms for the test items, snow conditions and slope difficulty are important factors to consider. Temperature, time of day and equipment used should also be considered as norms are developed and, furthermore, when the scores of succeeding groups are compared to those norms.

Snow Skiing References

McGinnis, P.M. (1980). *Skills tests for discrimination of Alpine skiing ability.* Unpublished master's thesis, University of Illinois, Urbana-Champaign.

Rogers, M.H. (1954). *Construction of objectively scored skill tests for beginning skiers.* Unpublished master's thesis, University of Washington, Seattle.

Street, R.H. (1957). *Measurement of achievement in skiing.* Unpublished master's thesis, University of Utah, Salt Lake City.

Wolfe, J.E., & Merrifield, H.H. (1971). *Predictability of beginning skiing success from basic skill tests in college age females.* Paper presented at the American Association for Health, Physical Education and Recreation National Convention, Detroit.

Chapter 21

SOCCER

INTRODUCTION

Soccer has become an established activity in many American public schools and colleges. In the recent past its popularity was concentrated in certain areas of the country, but today the sport is more national in scope as evidenced by the rapid increase of both amateur and professional teams. There is also a notable growth in the number of soccer spectators.

Soccer skills tests were among the earliest to be developed. As customary, most of the early tests were in the form of multiple-item batteries and were not scientifically documented.

BONTZ SOCCER TEST
(1942)

Purpose:

To determine general soccer ability.

Description:

The Bontz Soccer Test is an extension of the Schaufele (Schaufele, 1940) study which was completed approximately two years earlier. A combination skill of dribbling, passing and shooting the soccer ball is measured. This is repeated a total of eight times, four with each foot.

A six-foot starting line is constructed parallel to the center of the 18-foot soccer goal and is located 55 yards away (Figure 21.1). A 25-yard restraining line is marked from the left end of the starting line toward the goal line. Located 12 feet to the left of this restraining line is a permanent or temporary wall, 12 feet in length and 30 inches in height. The wall may be outlined with paint or tape to provide a more visible target area for the students. The center of the wall area is situated directly opposite the end of the 25-yard line. Another restraining line is placed six yards from and parallel to the goal line. The field markings are needed for both the right and left foot, as indicated in Figure 21.1.

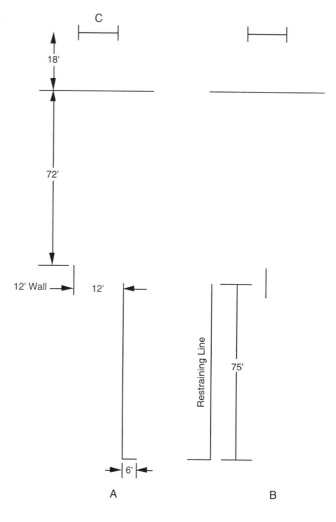

Fig. 21.1 Field markings for Bontz Soccer Test.

From: Bontz, J. (1942). *An experiment in the construction of a test for measuring ability in some of the fundamental skills used by fifth and sixth grade children in soccer.* Unpublished master's thesis, University of Iowa, Iowa City. Copyright by author.

Educational Application:

Fifth and sixth grade boys and girls.

Time:

A class of 20 students can be tested in two 60-minute class periods.

Personnel:

One timer-recorder.

Equipment and Supplies:

Soccer balls, two soccer goals, stop watch, three benches (if permanent wall is not used), scoring and field marking materials.

Facilities and Space:

Outdoor playing field at least 60 yards in length and 20 yards wide.

Directions:

Two practice trials with each foot are allowed immediately prior to testing. Then on an audible signal, the subject dribbles the ball from the starting line to a point where it is kicked with the right foot diagonally against the wall while all the time staying to the right of the 25-yard restraining line. The kick is executed as though the subject is passing to a teammate. After recovering the rebounded ball, the subject continues the dribble while moving closer to the goal. The ball must be kicked for goal before the six-yard restraining line is crossed. The sequence of dribble, kick, recovery, dribble and kick is executed as quickly as possible without losing control of the ball. Four test trials with each foot are required for score. Test trials which include errors must be repeated.

Scoring Method:

The amount of time that elapses between the starting signal and the instant the ball crosses the goal constitutes a trial. The final score is the total amount of time, recorded to the nearest half-second, the subject requires to complete the eight trials. Each trial is timed separately.

The range of scores for the fifth grade students were 95.5 to 226.5 seconds with a median time of 139.2. The scores of the sixth grade students ranged from 90.0 to 191.0 seconds with a median time of 130.3 seconds. The range for girls only was 102.5 to 226.5 seconds with a median time of 143.4, while the same statistics for boys were 90.0, 198.0 and 126.7 seconds.

Validity and Reliability:

One hundred and twenty-four fifth and sixth grade students provided the test data in the study. Two separate groups, one containing 92 subjects and the other 32, participated.

Validity values of .92 and .53 were computed for the large and small groups, respectively. The criterion measure was a subjective rating. Reliability coefficients of .93 and .96 were determined by use of the odd-even method and corrected by the Spearman-Brown Prophecy Formula.

JOHNSON SOCCER TEST
(Johnson, 1963)

Purpose:

To evaluate general soccer ability.

Educational Application:

Although constructed with college male subjects, the test is useful for testing junior high and senior high school boys and girls.

Personnel:

One scorer-recorder per testing station. Students retrieve and replace balls.

Equipment and Supplies:

Soccer balls, backboard with soccer goal dimensions, measuring tape, ball basket, stop watch, scoring materials, and field or floor marking materials.

Facilities and Space:

An indoor or outdoor space allowing for at least 30 feet directly in front of a backboard.

Description and Directions:

The single-item test is a modification of the McDonald Soccer Test (McDonald, 1951). It requires a restraining line to be placed 15 feet from a backboard that is 24 feet wide and at least eight feet high. A basket containing extra balls is located 15 feet behind the restraining line.

Table 21.1	
GRADING SCALE FOR JOHNSON SOCCER TEST	
Level	Number of Hits
Superior	42 & over
Good	37 - 41
Average	31 - 36
Below Average	25 - 30
Poor	24 & below

From: Johnson, J.R. (1963). *The development of a single-item test as a measure of soccer skills.* Unpublished master's thesis, University of British Columbia, Vancouver. Copyright by author.

Holding a ball, the student stands behind the restraining line. On an audible signal, he/she kicks the ball against the backboard and returns it as many times as possible in 30 seconds. Rebounds may be kicked on the fly or after the ball bounces, but they must be kicked from behind the restraining line with a legal soccer kick. If a ball should elude the student, he/she may obtain a ball from the basket of spare balls. Three trials of 30 seconds are required.

Scoring Method and Norms:

The number of legal hits for all three trials is the official score.

Validity and Reliability:

Validity coefficients of .98, .94, .58, .84 and .81 resulted for students in basic instruction classes, physical education majors, first team varsity players, second-team varsity players and third-team varsity players, respectively.

The validity value was determined by rank-difference between test scores and investigator rankings of soccer ability. A reliability coefficient of .92 was computed.

MITCHELL SOCCER TEST
(Mitchell, 1963)

Purpose:

To determine general soccer ability.

Educational Application:

Fifth and sixth grade boys and girls; also seems suitable for junior high school students of each gender.

Description:

Another modification of the McDonald Soccer Test (McDonald, 1951), the Mitchell Test requires the subject to stand behind a six-foot restraining line and for 20 seconds repeatedly kick a soccer ball to a rectangular wall target. The wall target is four feet high from the base of the wall, eight feet long, and its surface should be smooth and unobstructed. The kicking area in front of the target is 14 feet wide, meaning that the forecourt area overlaps the wall target area by three feet on either side, naturally allowing for some degree of deflection from angled kicks. The forecourt area is 12 feet in depth with a restraining line marked off six feet from and parallel to the wall. Therefore, the forecourt area is split in half by the restraining line.

Time:

Twenty students can be tested in one 60-minute class period.

Personnel:

One scorer-recorder.

Equipment and Supplies:

Soccer balls, stop watch, scoring materials, wall and floor marking materials.

Facilities and Space:

Unobstructed, smooth wall space at least eight feet long with a forecourt area measuring a minimum of 14 feet wide and 12 feet in depth.

Directions:

After one practice trial, the test begins with the subject standing behind the restraining line prepared to kick a soccer ball that is resting on or behind the restraining line. On an audible signal, the subject proceeds to kick the ball as many times as possible against the wall target in 20 seconds. Any kicking style or technique may be used with either foot or any other body part, except the hands or arms.

Student ball retrievers are positioned around and a few feet back of the forecourt boundary lines to stop balls that come over the line. Should the test subject miskick or fail to block a ball, the retrievers stop the ball with their hands and place it back on the boundary line at the point where it rolled out. The test subject may retrieve the ball from that point and, after repositioning the ball, continue the test. A ball that is mishandled by the retrievers and results in an unnecessary time delay results in a retrial. Subjects may go anywhere to retrieve the ball, but a legal kick must be made from behind the restraining line.

Scoring Method:

A student's score is determined by the number of times the ball strikes the wall target within the 20-second time span, providing both the ball and the student remain behind the restraining line during the kicking process. Use of the hands or arms at any time results in a one point reduction. The final score is the number of legal hits made in the three trials. The trials are to be taken consecutively.

In the Mitchell study, 192 test subjects were randomly divided into six test groups. The range, mean and standard deviation of the scores for each group are shown in Table 21.2.

				Total Scores of Three Initial Trials	
	Number of Cases	Range High Low		Mean	Standard Deviation
Group I	28	50 - 18		34.4	6.83
Group II	25	50 - 19		33.0	6.61
Group III	31	54 - 14		34.8	10.74
Group IV	35	52 - 17		29.7	8.74
Group V	37	56 - 21		34.6	6.85
Group VI	36	52 - 18		30.8	7.27
Total	192	56 - 14		32.8	8.14

Table 21.2
MITCHELL SOCCER TEST DATA*

*Data based on scores of 192 fifth and sixth grade boys.

From: Mitchell, J.R. (1963). *The modification of the McDonald Soccer Skills Test for upper elementary school boys*. Unpublished master's thesis, University of Oregon, Eugene. Copyright by author.

Validity and Reliability:

Fifth and sixth grade boys served as subjects in the Mitchell study. Validity coefficients of .84 and .76 were determined by the rank-difference and product-moment methods of correlation, with subjective ratings of teachers and coaches used as the criterion measure.

Reliability coefficients of .93 and .89 were determined by the test-retest method.

Additional Comments:

Mitchell's modification of the McDonald Soccer Test is a highly acceptable tool for measuring general soccer ability of boys and girls, grades five through nine. It has value for grading student achievement and serves well as a device to classify students by ability level.

YEAGLEY SOCCER BATTERY
(Yeagley, 1972)

Purpose:

To assess beginning soccer ability.

Educational Application:

Although constructed for college students, the test is appropriate for junior and senior high school students.

Personnel:

Two individuals for each test.

Equipment and Supplies:

Soccer balls, measuring tape, marking tape, seven cones, stop watches and scoring materials.

Facilities and Space:

Gymnasium with a smooth wall surface.

Description and Directions:

Dribbling. Figure 21.2 describes the layout for the dribbling test item, which is administered on a basketball half court. While behind the restraining line with a soccer ball at his/her feet, the student responds to a starting command by dribbling around the cones as outlined in Figure 21.2. The test trial is timed until the student brings the ball to a complete stop with the feet after crossing the finish line. There is no penalty for touching, knocking down or moving a cone with the ball or feet so long as the course is followed. Two trials are required.

Juggling. Standing in a basketball half-court area, the student bounces a ball on the floor and attempts to juggle the ball in the air with body parts other than the arms or hands as many times as possible in 30 seconds. The feet, thighs, head, shoulders and chest are recommended body parts for juggling the ball. Balls bouncing on the floor during the test incur no penalty, and juggles outside the half-court boundary do not count. One point is deducted each time the student's hands or arms are used to control the ball. Two trials are required.

Wall Volley. Lines are marked on a smooth, unobstructed wall to create a wall space area that is eight feet high and 24 feet wide. A restraining line is marked 15 feet from and parallel to the wall. The student stands behind the restraining line with a soccer

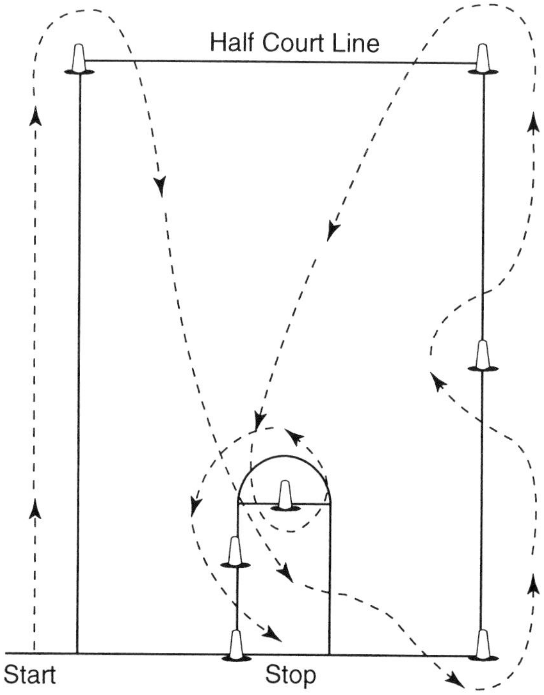

Fig. 21.2 Court markings for Yeagley Soccer Test.

From: Yeagley, J. (1972). *Soccer skills tests*. Unpublished paper, Indiana University, Bloomington. Reprinted with permission from Indiana University.

ball at his/her feet and responds to a starting command by kicking the ball against the wall as many times as possible in 30 seconds. The nonkicking foot must be behind the line in order for a kick to count, and any type of kick or trap is permitted. Extra balls should be available when students lose control of the original ball. Two trials are required.

Scoring:

Dribble. The official score is the best of two trials, timed to the nearest 10th of a second.

Juggling. The number of legal juggles in 30 seconds is the trial score. The final score is the best of two trials.

Wall Volley. The student's trial score is the number of legal volleys in 30 seconds. The final score is the best of two trials.

Validity and Reliability:

Using judges' ratings as the criterion measure, validity coefficients of .80, .74 and .81 were computed for the dribbling, juggling and wall volley tests, respectively. Reliability coefficients were .92, .95 and .90 for the items in the order presented above.

MOR-CHRISTIAN GENERAL SOCCER ABILITY
SKILL TEST BATTERY
(Mor & Christian, 1979)

Purpose:

    To evaluate passing, dribbling and shooting skills.

Educational Application:

    Scientifically authenticated with college men, the test can be used for evaluating college women and junior and senior high school boys and girls.

Personnel:

    Recorder/scorer at each of three stations, with students assigned the responsibility of retrieving and replacing balls.

Equipment and Supplies:

    Soccer balls, soccer goal, measuring tape, 17 cones, one four-foot rope and two 10-foot ropes, four hoops, stop watch, scoring and field marking materials.

Facilities and Space:

    The dribbling, passing and shooting test items require areas of 60, 45 and 45 feet, respectively.

Description:

    Dribbling. Figure 21.3 illustrates the 20-yard diameter layout for the dribbling item. Twelve 18-inch cones are placed at five-yard intervals around the circle. Perpendicular to the outside of the circle is a three-foot starting line.

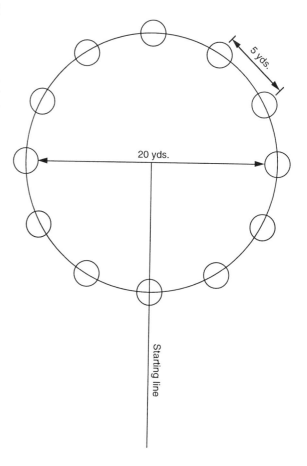

Fig. 21.3 Field markings for Mor-Christian dribbling test item.

From: Mor, D., & Christian, V. (1979). The development of a skill test battery to measure general soccer ability. *North Carolina Journal of HPE* 15: 30-39. Reprinted with permission from North Carolina Journal of HPE.

Passing. As shown in Figure 21.4, a 12 x 18-inch goal is created by placing two cones one yard apart and using a four-foot rope as a crossbar. Two cones are placed 15 yards away from the goal at a 45-degree angle, while another cone is located the same distance from the goal at a 90-degree angle.

Shooting. Following the specifications in Figure 21.5, the soccer goal is divided into two scoring areas by suspending two ropes from the crossbar, one located four feet from the left goal post and the other rope four feet from the right goal post. Each scoring area is divided into two circular targets by two hoops four feet in diameter. The restraining line is located 16 yards from and parallel to the goal.

Directions:

Dribbling. When signaled to start, the student dribbles the ball around the test course, dribbling between the cones as quickly as possible and back to the starting line. Of three required trials, one is performed in a clockwise direction, another counterclockwise, and the other in the direction of the student's choice.

Passing. Two practice passes are allowed from each cone or 15-yard distance. The test requires the student to complete four passes from each cone. The student may use either foot in executing the 12 passes for score.

Shooting. Positioned behind the restraining line, the student shoots stationary balls toward the target. Either foot may be used, and the ball may be kicked from any location behind the restraining line. After four practice trials, the student completes a 16-trial total by attempting four consecutive shots at each of the four target areas.

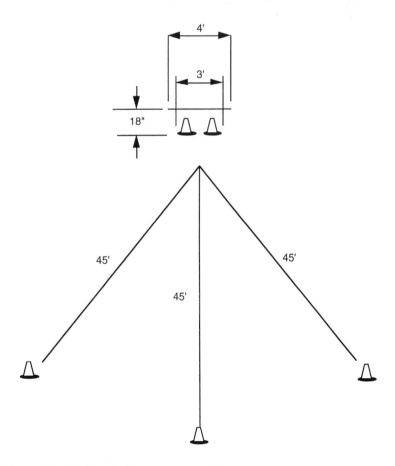

Fig. 21.4 Field markings for Mor-Christian passing test item.

From: Mor, D., & Christian, V. (1979). The development of a skill test battery to measure general soccer ability. *North Carolina Journal of HPE* 15: 30-39. Reprinted with permission of North Carolina Journal of HPE.

Scoring:

Dribbling. The combined time of the two best trials is the final score.

Passing. Each successful pass is awarded one point. Balls hitting the goal posts are considered successful. The final score is the number of successful passes performed in 12 trials.

Shooting. Ten points are given for balls going through the intended target, and four points are awarded for balls passing through an unintended target. Balls hitting a circular target (hoop) are scored as good, but those that bounce or roll through the target area are not counted as successful shots. The number of points accumulated in the 16 required trials is the official score.

Validity and Reliability:

Utilizing a rating scale developed and used by three soccer experts as the criterion measure, validity coefficients of .73, .78 and .91 were reported for dribbling, passing and shooting, respectively. Reliability coefficients, using the test-retest approach, were .80, .96 and .98, for the three items in the aforementioned order.

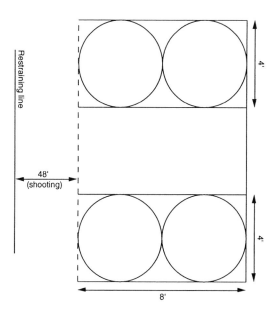

Fig. 21.5 Field markings and target for Mor-Christian shooting test item.

From: Mor, D., & Christian, V. (1979). The development of a skill test battery to measure general soccer ability. *North Carolina Journal of HPE* 15: 30-39. Reprinted with permission from North Carolina Journal of HPE.

Soccer References

Bontz, J. (1942). *An experiment in the construction of a test for measuring ability in some of the fundamental skills used by fifth and sixth grade children in soccer.* Unpublished master's thesis, University of Iowa, Iowa City.

Cozens, F.W., & Cubberley, H.J. (1936). Achievement tests in soccer and speedball. *Spalding's Official Soccer and Speedball Guide.* New York: American Sports.

Crawford, E.A. (1958). *The development of skill test batteries for evaluating the ability of women physical education major students in soccer and speedball.* Unpublished doctoral dissertation, University of Oregon, Eugene.

Crew, V.N. (1968). *A skill test battery for use in service program soccer classes at the university level.* Unpublished master's thesis, University of Oregon, Eugene.

Heath, M.L., & Rogers, E.G. (1932). A study in the use of knowledge and skill tests in soccer. *Research Quarterly* 3: 33-53.

Johnson, J.R. (1963). *The development of a single-item test as a measure of soccer skill.* Unpublished master's thesis, University of British Columbia, Vancouver.

Konstantinov, K.J. (1939). *The development and evaluation of a battery of soccer skills as an index of ability in soccer.* Unpublished master's thesis, Springfield College, Springfield, Massachusetts.

Lee, H.C. (1941). *An evaluation of Brock's Soccer Skill Test and a rating scale of physical endurance, tackling, and personality traits on the secondary school level.* Unpublished master's thesis, Springfield College, Springfield, Massachusetts.

Mackenzie, J. (1968). *The evaluation of a battery of soccer skill tests as an aid to classification of general soccer ability.* Unpublished master's thesis, University of Massachusetts, Amherst.

McDonald, L.G. (1951). *The construction of a kicking skill test as an index of general soccer ability.* Unpublished master's thesis, Springfield College, Springfield, Massachusetts.

Mitchell, J.R. (1963). *The modification of the McDonald Soccer Skill Test for upper elementary school boys.* Unpublished master's thesis, University of Oregon, Eugene.

Mor, D., & Christian, V. (1979). The development of a skill test battery to measure general soccer ability. *North Carolina Journal of HPE* 15: 30-39.

Munro, J.B. (1941). *An evaluation of Brock's Soccer Skill Test and a rating scale of physical endurance, tackling, and personality traits in soccer on the college level.* Unpublished master's thesis, Springfield College, Springfield, Massachusetts.

Schaufele, E.F. (1940). *The establishment of objective tests for girls in the ninth and tenth grades to determine soccer ability.* Unpublished master's thesis, University of Iowa, Iowa City.

Streck, B. (1961). *An analysis of the McDonald Soccer Skill Test as applied to junior high school girls.* Unpublished master's thesis, Fort Hays State College, Fort Hays, Kansas.

Tomlinson, R. (1964). Soccer skill test. *DGWS Soccer-Speedball Guide,* 1964-66. Washington, D.C.: AAHPER.

Vanderhoff, M. (1932). Soccer skills tests. *Journal of Health and Physical Education* 3: 42.

Warner, F.H. (1941). *The development of achievement scales of fundamental soccer skills for high school boys.* Unpublished master's thesis, Springfield College, Springfield, Massachusetts.

Warner, G.F. (1950). Warner soccer test. *Newsletter of the National Soccer Coaches Association of America* 6: 13-22.

Whitney, A.H., & Chapin, G. (1946). Soccer skill testing for girls. *NSWA Soccer-Speedball Guide,* 1946-48. Washington, D.C.: AAHPER.

Yeagley, J. (1972). *Soccer skills tests.* Unpublished paper, Indiana University, Bloomington.

Chapter 22

Softball

INTRODUCTION

Softball is a sport that requires the execution of varied and diverse skills; therefore, evaluation of playing ability should be conducted through the use of a battery as opposed to a single test. The throw for distance test seems to be the most valid single indicator of general playing ability, but when given alone its use should be limited to purposes of classification. For diagnostic purposes, a battery has the advantages as it often will reveal specific weaknesses in skill that may be hidden if a single test is administered to represent general playing ability. A comprehensive test battery would include test items from the major skill areas of fielding, throwing, hitting and running.

O'DONNELL SOFTBALL SKILL TEST
(O'Donnell, 1950)

Purpose:

To measure basic softball playing skills and to provide a classification measure.

Educational Application:

The test was designed for high school girls but seems appropriate for high school boys and college men and women, provided pertinent modifications are made whenever feasible.

Description:

Speed Throw. This item measures the speed and distance of a throw. A five-foot restraining line is marked on the floor 65 feet from and parallel to the wall.

Fielding Fly Balls. This test item measures the ability to catch a fly ball and ball handling ability. The test requires a 15-foot line to be drawn on the wall at a height of 12 feet above the floor. Also, a 15-foot line is drawn on the floor six feet from and parallel to the wall.

Throw and Catch. This item measures the combination defensive skill of throwing, running and catching. A 50 x 20-foot rectangle is marked on the floor with its length divided into 10 equal areas by lines five feet apart. Two jumping standards are placed so that a rope can be stretched directly over the starting line which is at one end of the rectangle. The rope is located at a height of eight feet from the floor.

Repeated Throws. This item measures primarily ball handling speed and to some extent catching and throwing ability. A 15-foot line is drawn on the wall 7 1/2 feet high. A 15-foot line is placed on the floor 15 feet from and parallel to the wall.

Fungo Batting. This test of batting ability requires the use of a regulation softball diamond for test administration.

Overhand Accuracy Throw. Throwing accuracy is measured by this test. A target is constructed on the wall with the center located two feet from the floor. The inner circle has a radius of three inches. The radii of the other circles are 11, 21 and 33 inches, respectively. A five-foot restraining line is drawn on the floor parallel to the wall and 45 feet from the target.

Time:

The test does not lend itself well to economy of time in test administration unless a mass testing arrangement is implemented. It has been estimated that, in a 40-minute class period, groups of 60, 50, 25, 50, 15 and 25 students can be tested respectively on the speed throw, fielding fly balls, throw and catch, repeated throws, fungo batting and overhand accuracy throw items.

Personnel:

If the test items are administered separately, one tester with student assistants assigned as needed should suffice for test personnel requirements. The employment of trained and well-qualified assistants could make a mass testing effort possible. The following assignment of duties is suggested:

a. speed throw: one timer and one recorder.
b. fielding fly balls: one timer and one scorer.
c. throw and catch: one recorder and one assistant.
d. repeated throws: one timer and one scorer.
e. fungo batting: one to two ball retrievers, one scorer, one recorder; another assistant is necessary to hand balls to the batter.
f. overhand accuracy throw: same as fungo batting.

Equipment and Supplies:

One stop watch, 10 regulation softballs, two jumping standards, 12-foot rope, measuring tape, at least one bat, scoring and marking materials.

Facilities and Space:

An unobstructed, flat wall surface is needed for the speed throw, fielding fly balls, repeated throws and overhand accuracy throw items.

The fungo batting test should be given on a regulation softball diamond.

Directions:

Speed Throw. A ball is placed on the restraining line with the subject standing behind the line. On the starting signal, the ball is picked up and thrown against the wall as fast as possible. The subject may step over the line after the throw but not before the release; otherwise, a trial is counted as zero. The time to the nearest 10th of a second from the starting signal until the ball hits the wall is recorded. Three trials are administered.

Fielding Fly Balls. Standing behind the 15-foot line on the floor while holding a ball, the student, on the starting signal, throws the ball repeatedly against the wall above the 12-foot line and catches the rebound. The line may be crossed to catch the ball, but the subject must return to a position behind the line for the next throw. Throwing continues for 30 seconds. One trial is given following a practice trial.

Throw and Catch. The subject stands behind the starting line with a ball in hand. The ball is then thrown over the rope, and the subject runs to catch it on the other side while trying to cover the maximum amount of distance in doing so. Any type of throw is permitted. The distance to the nearest foot from the starting line to the back of the subject's heel of the front foot is measured. Three trials are performed.

Repeated Throws. A ball is placed on the 15-foot line with the subject standing behind the line. On the starting signal, the student picks up the ball and throws it repeatedly against the wall above the 7 1/2-foot line. The number of times the ball hits the wall in a 30-second time period is recorded. One trial is given and the watch is not stopped for a fumbled or dropped ball.

Fungo Batting. The subject stands in the batter's box with a ball in hand. The ball is tossed into the air with the subject attempting to hit it on the downward flight. If no attempt is made to hit the ball, a trial is not counted. Ten trials are allowed.

Overhand Accuracy Throw. The subject assumes a position behind the restraining line and throws the ball at the target, aiming at the center of the target. Stepping over the line results in the trial being counted with a score of zero given.

Scoring Method:

Speed Throw. The time to the nearest 10th of a second that elapses from the starting signal until the ball strikes the wall. The best of three trials is the final score.

Fielding Fly Balls. The number of legal catches in a 30-second time period is recorded as the official score. Illegal catches include those situations where a ball hits the ground before being caught, is fumbled or dropped or does not hit on or above the 12-foot line on the wall. Also, the subject's crossing of the line before making the throw is illegal.

Throw and Catch. The distance from the starting line to the point at which the ball is caught is recorded for three trials with the best trial counting as the final score. The distance is measured to the nearest foot from the starting line to the back of the heel of the subject's front foot. A ball not going over the rope or not caught constitutes a trial and is given a score of zero.

Repeated Throws. The number of legal wall hits during a 30-second trial is the score. A subject may not cross the starting line prior to releasing the ball, and the throws must hit on or above the 7 1/2-foot line on the wall.

Fungo Batting. The sum of points made in 10 trials is the final score. A ball landing in the outfield counts five points; one landing in the infield counts three points; one point is given for a foul ball; and a ball swung at and missed counts zero points.

Overhand Accuracy Throw. The sum of points made on 10 trials is the final score. The center target area counts four points, the next area three points, the next two points, and the outside area one point. A ball that misses the target is scored as zero. If the subject steps over the line prior to releasing the ball, that trial is scored as zero.

Six-Test Playing Ability Battery. The softball playing ability score = 0.6 (fielding fly balls) + 0.3 (throw and catch) + 0.6 (repeated throws) + 0.1 (fungo batting) + 0.4 (overhand accuracy) - 3 (speed throw).

Validity and Reliability:

A .91 coefficient was derived for the six-item battery when administered to 50 high school girls. No reliability coefficient was reported.

FOX-YOUNG BATTING TEST
(Fox & Young, 1954)

Purpose:

To measure batting distance skill in softball.

Educational Application:

College women.

Description:

Field markings for the test are as follows:
1.   a baseline on which the batting tee is placed;
2.   20 lines three yards in length spaced 10 feet apart and parallel to the baseline;
3.   20 lines one yard in length midway between the three-yard lines and parallel to them;
4.   the distance from the baseline is marked at the end of each of the three-yard lines.

Time:

One 60-minute period for a class of 20 students.

Personnel:

Instructor with trained assistants to measure and record the distance of fly balls.

Equipment and Supplies:

Standard softball batting tee, five regulation softballs in good condition, assortment of softball bats, field marking and scoring materials.

Facilities and Space:

Regulation softball playing field or relatively flat area of sufficient size.

Directions:

Three warm-ups are permitted for each player with the tee adjusted at the height of the student's choice. Five trials are then completed without pause.

Scoring Method:

The distance from the batting tee to the spot where each ball first touches the ground is recorded. The sum of the distance of all five trials reflects the official test score. A swing that strikes the tee or misses the ball completely counts as one trial.

Validity and Reliability:

When correlated with judges' ratings of the batter's grip, stance, swing and hitting consistency, a .64 coefficient was obtained. The scores of 58 college women students provided the data for the validity computation.

A reliability coefficient of .87 was derived when the Spearman-Brown Prophecy Formula was applied to correct the split-half method for obtaining the test's reliability. The scores of 62 college women were used to determine the reliability coefficient.

Additional Comments:

The test should only be used as part of a test battery since it is limited to the measurement of batting skill. To determine if skill in the bat for distance test really represents overall batting skill, test scores could be correlated with another criterion such as seasonal batting averages.

KEHTEL SOFTBALL FIELDING AND THROWING ACCURACY TEST
(Kehtel, 1958)

Purpose:

To measure the ability to field ground balls and throw them accurately.

Educational Application:

College women.

Description:

The fielding and throwing accuracy test is administered on a floor layout as shown in Figure 22.1. The test is designed to measure a fundamental combination skill in defensive softball as the single test score reflects ability in both fielding and throwing accuracy skills.

The aforementioned layout includes two wall surfaces at right angles to each other. The starting line is placed 40 feet from Wall A which has a 10-foot line located four feet above and parallel to the floor. Wall B is located 40 feet to the left of the center of the starting line.

As shown in Figure 22.1, the target is situated so that its center is 20 feet from Wall A. It is circular and has a radius of 36 inches. The upper half of the target has a semicircle with a 12-inch radius. Two straight lines extend from each end of the semicircle to the bottom of the target. An incomplete circle, with a radius of 24 inches, is located around the oblong area.

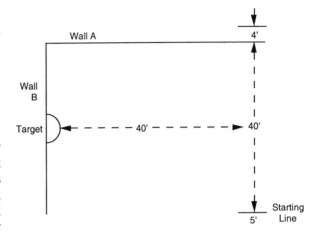

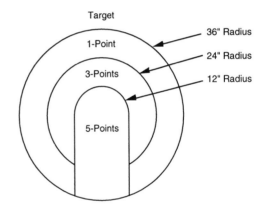

Fig. 22.1 Floor and target markings for Kehtel Softball Test.

From: Kehtel, C.H. (1958). *The development of a test to measure the ability of a softball player to field a ground ball and successfully throw it at a target.* Unpublished master's thesis, University of Colorado, Boulder. Reprinted with permission from the University of Colorado.

Time:

One 60-minute class period if two students are tested simultaneously; otherwise, two class periods of that length.

Personnel:

A timer, recorder and three assistants to retrieve balls.

Equipment and Supplies:

Ten softballs in good condition, stop watch, box to hold the balls, scoring and test layout marking materials.

Facilities and Space:

A gymnasium or other indoor facility having sufficient size and unobstructed wall space.

Directions:

After one practice trial, the subject stands behind the starting line while holding a 12-inch softball. On command to start, the student throws the ball below the four-foot line on Wall A. She fields the rebound as quickly as possible and may cross the line for the recovery. Upon recovery, the ball is thrown at the target on the left wall. The action is immediately repeated and continues for the remainder of the two-minute allotment.

A step is allowed over the starting line as the subject throws. A ball that hits the floor before striking the wall is considered playable, but one that fails to reach the wall does not count. Another ball should be put into action immediately. Two trials are required.

The three student assistants have an important role in supplying the subject with balls ready for play. The helpers should take precautions not to interfere with the subject as she takes the test. Also, two assistants should roll the balls to the third helper who places them in the ball box near the starting line.

Scoring Method:

Any ball that hits within the target area is scored according to the score value of the particular section it strikes. Five points are given for the center area, three for the middle, and one point for the outer area. A ball that strikes a line separating two sections is assigned the score of higher value.

The two methods of scoring the test are as follows:
1. The score value for each ball is totaled for the final score.
2. The number of balls striking the target in a two-minute period is the final score.

Validity and Reliability:

Validity coefficients of .76 and .79 were obtained for the above two scoring methods, respectively. Three judges' subjective ratings of the students' ability to field ground balls and throw them at a base represented the criterion measure for determining validity, with 54 college students serving as subjects.

Reliability coefficients were .90 and .91 for the two respective scoring methods. The coefficients were determined by the odd-even method and corrected by the Spearman-Brown Prophecy Formula.

Additional Comments:

This test would be a quality component in a softball test battery. Kehtel suggests that the scoring method of recording target hits be used in beginning softball classes and the total score value method be utilized in advanced classes.

FRINGER SOFTBALL TEST
(Fringer, 1961)

Purpose:

    To measure the important skill components of softball playing.

Educational Application:

    Designed for high school girls, but also appropriate for boys at that level.

Description:

    The Fringer Softball Test is primarily used for measurement of student progress and for diagnostic purposes. A periodic check of student improvement is made easier with the use of a test so feasible in economy of time of administration. Results of the test also identify strengths and weaknesses of students' softball skills, allowing the instructor to concentrate to a large extent on correcting the weaknesses.

    The fly ball test measures the ability to catch fly balls and throw quickly. The fielding grounders-agility-speed and accuracy test measures the ability to field grounders, run quickly to a base, then throw quickly and accurately to a target. The softball distance throw measures the ability to throw for long distances with some degree of accuracy.

Time:

    One 60-minute class period for a class of 15 to 20 students in a mass testing situation utilizing multiple stations.

Personnel:

    One timer and scorer for the fly ball test while the fielding grounders-agility-speed and accuracy test requires the use of one scorer and timer plus a student at each base to check for foot faults. The softball throw for distance requires ball retrievers, a scorer and spotters who call out the distance of the throw.

Equipment and Supplies:

    Several quality softballs, stop watch, field marking and scoring materials.

Facilities and Space:

    A gymnasium with unobstructed wall space for the fly ball test, and a floor space of 30 x 40 feet with a 20 x 20-foot wall size needed for the fielding grounders-agility-speed and accuracy test. The throw for distance item requires a playing field of reasonable size.

Directions:

    Warm-up immediately before testing should be allowed for all items with even more warm-up concentration recommended in the preparation for the distance throw test item.

    Fly Ball Test. Standing behind the 30-foot restraining line, the subject at a command to start throws a ball against the wall above a line 20 feet from the floor. The throwing motion used is at the subject's discretion. After the ball hits the wall, the student may retrieve the ball at any location on the floor. Fumbled balls and those that bounce before the catch do not count. Three 30-second trials are administered with intervals of rest given.

Fielding Grounders-Agility-Speed and Accuracy Test. When signaled to begin, the subject runs to a base while carrying a softball. While a foot is in contact with the base, the student throws the ball at the wall target (Figure 22.2). The subject then rushes to retrieve the ball and quickly advances to the opposite base to make another throw at the target. The bases must be alternated for the throws and a foot must be in contact with a base on each throw. This action is repeated for 45 seconds. Two trials are permitted with an intervening rest period.

Distance Throw. The subject throws from behind the restraining line and is allowed only one step prior to the throw. The restraining line may be crossed only after the ball has left the subject's hand (Figure 22.3). Three throws are allowed.

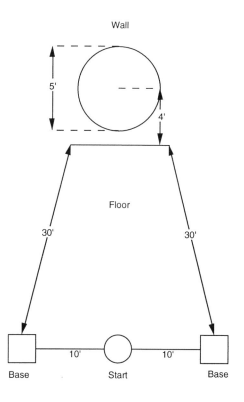

Fig. 22.2 Specifications for fielding grounders-agility-speed and accuracy test.

From: Fringer, F.M. (1961). *Fringer softball battery.* Unpublished master's thesis, University of Michigan, Ann Arbor. Copyright by author.

Scoring Method and Norms:

Fly Ball Test. The cumulative total of catches made in the three trials is the final score.

Fielding Grounders-Agility-Speed and Accuracy Test. Balls hitting in the target circle or hitting the circle boundary count. The final score is the combined number of target hits made in the two trials.

Distance Throw. The best of the three allowed throws is measured to the nearest foot and constitutes the official score.

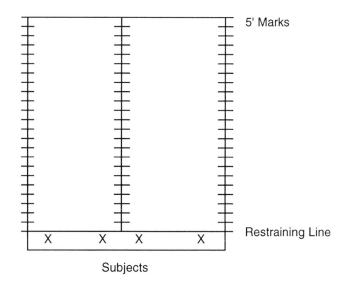

Fig. 22.3 Field markings for distance throw test.

From: Fringer, F.M. (1961). *Fringer softball battery.* Unpublished master's thesis, University of Michigan, Ann Arbor. Copyright by author.

T-Score	Fielding Grounders Total of 2 trials	Fly Balls Total of 3 trials	Distance Throw Best trial	T-Score
75	25	31	150	75
70	24	30	115	70
65	21	28	105	65
60	18	25	95	60
55	15	21	83	55
50	12	17	71	50
45	10	11	61	45
40	7	7	55	40
35	5	2	47	35
30	2		41	30
25			37	25

Table 22.1

NORMS FOR FRINGER SOFTBALL TEST*

*Based on scores of high school girls.

From: Fringer, F.M. (1961). *Fringer softball battery.* Unpublished master's thesis, University of Michigan, Ann Arbor. Copyright by author.

Validity and Reliability:

Coefficients of .76, .70 and .72 resulted for the three tests in Fringer's study which utilized high school girls. A total of 151 girls participated in the fielding grounders-agility-speed and accuracy test while 136 were included in the distance throw test. The Scott and French Repeated Throws Test was used as the criterion measure.

Test-retest reliability coefficients were .87, .72 and .90 for the respective test items in the order presented above.

Additional Comments:

If the Fringer Test is utilized for evaluating high school boys, the user is reminded that the test's accompanying norms apply only to girls. Development of performance norms for boys on the Fringer Test would be a worthy contribution to the literature pertaining to measurement of softball skills.

SHICK SOFTBALL TEST BATTERY
(Shick, 1970)

Purpose:

To measure defensive softball skills in college women.

Educational Application:

College women.

Description:

Repeated Throws. An item to measure the student's ability to align herself with an aerial ball, and to throw the ball rapidly after fielding it from the air or floor. A line is drawn on the wall 10 feet from and parallel to the floor. A line 23 feet from the wall is drawn on the floor and lies parallel to the wall.

Fielding Test. Designed to measure the student's ability to align herself with a ground ball and to throw rapidly after fielding it on the bounce or from the floor. The test calls for a line to be drawn on the wall four feet from the floor and one on the floor 15 feet from the wall. Both lines are parallel to the wall.

Target Test. The target test measures accuracy and power in the student's throw. The

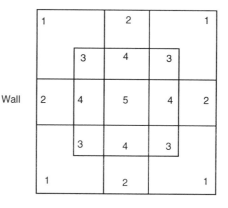

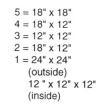

5 = 18" x 18"
4 = 18" x 12"
3 = 12" x 12"
2 = 18" x 12"
1 = 24" x 24"
(outside)
12 " x 12" x 12"
(inside)

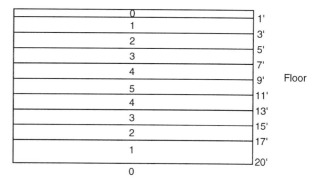

Fig. 22.4 Target test layout.

From: Shick, J. (1970). Battery of defensive softball skills tests for college women. *Research Quarterly* 41: 82-87. Reprinted with permission from AAHPERD.

target values and dimensions for both the floor and wall targets are shown in Figure 22.4. Target value areas should be color coded as follows: 5-red; 4-medium blue; 3-bright yellow; 2-pale aqua; and 1-black. The wall target is 66 inches square with the center located 36 inches from the floor. The restraining line lies parallel to the wall and 40 feet away.

Time:

Two 40-minute class periods when a mass testing procedure is utilized.

Personnel:

A tester and at least two trained assistants.

Equipment and Supplies:

Adequate number of softballs, stop watch, scoring materials, tape and chalk for floor and wall markings.

Facilities and Space:

A gymnasium of regulation size with unobstructed wall space.

Directions:

Repeated Throws. The student stands behind the restraining line and holds a softball. On the starting signal, she throws at the wall with an overhand or sidearm motion, attempting to hit the wall above the 10-foot line. She attempts to catch the rebound in the air or field it from the floor. This action is taken as often as possible in 30 seconds. Four trials are given. Failure to field a ball cleanly does not constitute a penalty other than loss of time.

Fielding Test. The test directions follow those for the repeated throws, including the four 30-second trials with two exceptions:

a.   Any type throw may be used.
b.   The student attempts to hit the wall below the drawn line.

For the repeated throws and fielding tests, the student completes a trial, then waits until each class member finishes her trial before proceeding to the next.

Target Test. Two trials of 10 throws each are permitted. Each throw is made behind the restraining line.

Scoring Method:

Repeated Throws. A ball striking below the wall line or one thrown with the student stepping on or crossing the restraining line does not count. The number of legal hits for the four trials is summed for the official score.

Fielding Test. Identical to the repeated throws scoring method except a legal hit is recorded for a ball that hits below the wall line.

Target Test. Two separate scores are given for each throw, one for the wall hit and the other for the hit of the first bounce. Hits outside either scoring area do not count. The highest possible score for the test is 200 points (50 per target per trial).

Validity and Reliability:

The validity coefficients for the three tests as previously presented were .69, .48 and .63, respectively. The coefficient for the battery was .75. The coefficients were obtained from the scores of 59 female college students enrolled in two general softball classes. The criterion measure was judges' ratings of individual performance in game situations. Each student was observed twice a week.

The reliability coefficients were .86, .89 and .88 for the three tests in the order presented above. The coefficient for the battery was .88.

Softball References

American Alliance for Health, Physical Education, Recreation and Dance. (1991). *AAHPERD Softball Skills Manual.* Reston, Virginia: AAHPERD.

Cale, A.A. (1962). *The investigation and analysis of softball skill tests for college women.* Unpublished master's thesis, University of Maryland, College Park.

Davis, R. (1951). *The development of an objective softball batting test for college women.* Unpublished master's thesis, Illinois State University, Normal.

Elrod, J.M. (1969). *Construction of a softball skill test battery for high school girls.* Unpublished master's thesis, Louisiana State University, Baton Rouge.

Fox, M.G., & Young, O.G. (1954). A test of softball batting ability. *Research Quarterly* 25: 26-27.

Fringer, F.M. (1961). *Fringer softball battery.* Unpublished master's thesis, University of Michigan, Ann Arbor.

Kehtel, C.H. (1958). *The development of a test to measure the ability of a softball player to field a ground ball and successfully throw it at a target.* Unpublished master's thesis, University of Colorado, Boulder.

Maver, D.J. (1986). *Maver softball skills test battery.* Unpublished paper, University of North Carolina, Greensboro.

New York State Physical Education Standards Project. (1951). *Standards Manual for Football, Soccer, and Softball Skills, Boys, Grades 7-12.* Albany: New York State Education Department.

O'Donnell, D.J. (1950). *Validation of softball skill tests for high school girls.* Unpublished master's thesis, Indiana University, Bloomington.

Safrit, M.J., & Pavis, A. (1969). Overarm throw skill testing. In Felshin & O'Brian, *Selected softball articles.* Washington, D.C.: AAHPER.

Scott, M.G., & French, E. (1959). Softball repeated throws test. In M.G. Scott & E. French, *Measurement and evaluation in physical education.* Dubuque, Iowa: Brown.

Shick, J. (1970). Battery of defensive softball skills tests for college women. *Research Quarterly* 41: 82-87.

Sopa, A. (1967). *Construction of an indoor batting skills test for junior high school girls.* Unpublished master's thesis, University of Wisconsin, Madison.

Underkofler, A. (1942). *A study of skill tests for evaluating the ability of junior high school girls in softball.* Unpublished master's thesis, University of Iowa, Iowa City.

Chapter 23

SPEEDBALL

INTRODUCTION

Speedball is a rather unique activity since it relates so closely to soccer and contains some features of basketball and football. The sport is played primarily by females at both the high school and college levels, and though not an extremely popular activity, its inclusion in the physical education curriculum at those educational levels is not uncommon.

BUCHANAN SPEEDBALL TEST
(Buchanan, 1942)

Purpose:
> To measure fundamental skills and predict playing ability in speedball.

Educational Application:
> High school girls.

Description:
> The Buchanan Test may be used as either a six-item or two-item battery, depending on the time available for testing. Included in the two-item battery are the throwing and catching while standing item and the passing test. Its relationship with the test criterion reflected a correlation coefficient of .93.
>
> When using the two-item battery, the following equation applies for score determination:
>
> 1.0 throwing and catching + 3.0 passing = playing ability score
>
> *Lift to Others.* A net 2 1/2 feet high and at least 30 feet long is stretched between two standards. Six feet from the net and on each side is located a parallel line the length of the net. All along both sides of the net are placed three-foot squares at three-foot intervals (Figure 23.1).
>
> The primary test objective is to lift the stationary ball and pass it for accuracy.

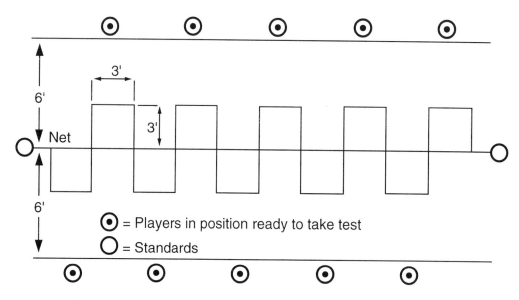

Fig. 23.1 Field markings for lift to others test.

From: Buchanan, R.E. (1942). *A study of achievement tests in speedball for high school girls.*
Unpublished master's thesis, University of Iowa, Iowa City. Copyright by author.

Throwing and Catching While Standing. A restraining line is drawn six feet away and parallel to an unobstructed wall. The length of the line depends upon the available wall surface and the number of students that need to be tested simultaneously.

Kick-up. The sideline markings of any playing field may be used as part of the field markings. A two-foot square is drawn with its inner side located three feet from the sideline mark. A starting line, located four feet from the corner of the square, is drawn perpendicular to an imaginary extension of the diagonal of the square (Figure 23.2). More than one square may be constructed to economize in test administration time.

Dribbling and Passing. A starting line is drawn 60 yards away from and parallel to the end line of the playing field. Two or four goal areas, depending on the number of subjects to be tested simultaneously, are marked off on the end line. The goal areas are marked with 12-inch perpendicular lines and each is six yards wide. Obstacles such as cones are placed at 10-yard intervals in a straight line between the end line and the starting line. The obstacle lines are placed three yards to the right and left of the particular goal areas with a 10-yard space located between goal areas (Figure 23.3).

Passing. Identical in description to dribbling and passing item.

Dribbling. Description identical to dribbling and passing item.

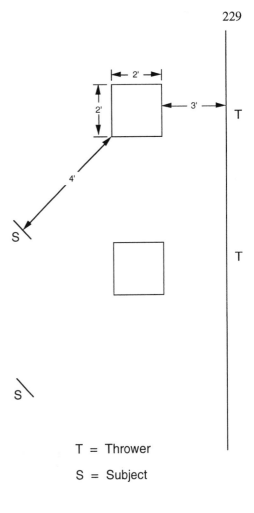

Fig. 23.2 Field markings for kick-up test.

From: Buchanan, R.E. (1942). *A study of achievement tests in speedball for high school girls*. Unpublished master's thesis, University of Iowa, Iowa City. Copyright by author.

Time:

Two or three 60-minute class periods for administering the six-item battery to 20 students and one to two periods for the two-item battery, depending upon how extensive mass testing is employed.

Personnel:

A person to score and time each item, whichever the case, then record the result. Student assistants are needed for the administration of some items.

Equipment and Supplies:

Soccer balls, net, standards, stop watch, obstacles such as cones, regulation soccer goals if available, field and court marking materials, scoring materials.

Directions:

Lift to Others. Ten subjects can be tested simultaneously when utilizing the test station layout described earlier. After some practice on the item, five students line up behind the six-foot restraining line on either side of the net. Each subject takes a position directly behind a three-foot square and each set of partners has a single ball which is placed on the line. The test begins with a subject lifting the ball with either foot and passing it over the net in an attempt to hit the square diagonally across the net and to the right. The partner recovers the ball and then becomes the test subject by proceeding to lift the ball back over the net diagonally to her right and across the net. Alternate turns are taken until each partner has taken ten trials, five to the right and five to the left.

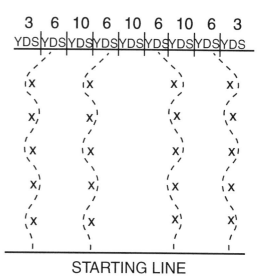

Fig. 23.3 Field markings for dribbling and passing test.

From: Buchanan, R.E. (1942). *A study of achievement tests in speedball for high school girls.* Unpublished master's thesis, University of Iowa, Iowa City. Copyright by author.

Throwing and Catching While Standing. The test begins with the subject positioning herself immediately behind the restraining line with a soccer ball in her hands. When an audible signal is given, the subject proceeds to throw the ball against the wall and catch it on the rebound. This is done as many times as possible during each of five 30-second trials. Should the subject lose control of the ball, it should be recovered as quickly as possible and again put back into play from behind the restraining line.

The five trials are not taken in consecutive order. Also, the partner system is again used, meaning that after the test subject completes each 30-second trial, she will change places with her partner. The partner not being tested stands behind and to the side of the test subject. It is the duty of the partner not being tested to count the number of successful completions in each trial.

Kick-up. Five practice trials are allowed each subject on the kick-up item immediately before being tested. Once again the subjects work as partners in the testing procedure. To get ready for testing, the subject assumes a standing position behind the starting line while the thrower or partner stands behind the sideline. The test begins with the thrower executing an overhead toss with a soccer ball so that it lands in the two-foot square. As soon as the thrower releases the ball, the subject runs toward the ball and proceeds to execute a kick-up. The kick-up requires a player to control a moving ball accurately with the foot and kick it up to herself. If the thrown ball does not land in the two-foot square, the trial should be repeated.

Dribbling and Passing. The subject stands behind the starting line with the soccer ball resting on the line directly in line with the obstacles. On an audible signal, she starts to dribble toward the first obstacle. The first obstacle is passed on the right, the second on the left, and so on down the field. After passing the last obstacle on the right, the subject passes the ball to the left in an attempt to send it into the appropriate goal area.

Ten trials are required with five trials coming from the left and five from the right. A systematic testing order should be followed to ensure an adequate rest period for the subjects between trials.

Passing. Directions same as dribbling and passing item.

Dribbling. Administration identical to dribbling and passing item except that the passing requirement is deleted.

Scoring Method and Norms:

Lift to Others. Partners score for each other. The final score is the number of accurate and correct lifts out of 10 trials, with each successful lift counting one point. Lifts are considered successful if the ball clears the net and falls within the appropriate three-foot square. Should the ball touch the net and land in the designated area, it still counts. Balls hitting the square lines also count.

Throwing and Catching While Standing. The final score is the average number of complete throws and catches made in the five 30-second trials. One point is scored for each completion. Partners score for each other.

Kick-up. The number of successfully executed and caught kick-ups for the 10 trials constitutes the final score. Once again the subject's score is kept by her partner.

Dribbling and Passing. The final score is the sum of the time scores (dribbling 50 yards with time measured to the nearest second) on all 10 trials minus 10 times the number of accurate passes on the 10 trials. For example, a dribbling score of 300 and a passing score of 10 would result in a final score of 200. The answer is derived by taking the 300 dribbling score minus the 100 passing score (10 x 10).

Passing. The number of passes completed into the goals in 10 test trials.

Dribbling. The total time taken to dribble the 50-yard distance 10 times.

Validity and Reliability:

Seventy-two high school girls served as test subjects in the Buchanan study. The criterion measure for determining test validity was subjective ratings of three instructors. Reliability coefficients were derived through the use of the odd-even method and Spearman-Brown Prophecy Formula.

Item	Validity	Reliability
a. Lift to Others	.88	.93
b. Throwing and Catching While Standing	.79	.92
c. Kick-up	.85	.93
d. Dribbling and Passing	.69	.98
e. Passing	.86	.91
f. Dribbling	.57	.98

Additional Comments:

Buchanan's study of the dribbling and passing items produced an interesting finding. According to the validity coefficients obtained, the dribbling item when given by itself or the dribbling and passing item combined do not simulate gamelike skills quite as much as the passing item does.

Obviously, the main shortcoming of the Buchanan Test is the considerable amount of time required to administer the whole battery. Instructors may wish to select only certain items for administration.

Table 23.1

ACHIEVEMENT SCALES FOR SELECTED ITEMS
IN BUCHANAN SPEEDBALL TEST*

Rating	Lift to Others	Throwing and Catching	Passing	Kick-Ups
Superior	10 & up	18.8 & up	10	9 & up
Good	8 - 9	16.3 - 18.7	7 - 9	7 - 8
Average	5 - 7	14.3 - 16.2	4 - 6	4 - 6
Poor	2 - 4	11.3 - 14.2	2 - 3	2 - 3
Inferior	1 & below	11.2 & below	1 & below	1 & below

N = 72, number of trials as specified in directions.

Rating	Lift to Others	Throwing and Catching	Passing	Kick-ups
Superior	10 & up	27.8 & up		10
Good	8 - 9	23.8 - 27.7	5	8 - 9
Average	6 - 7	17.8 - 23.7	3 - 4	4 - 7
Poor	3 - 5	11.8 - 17.7	2	2 - 3
Inferior	2 & below	11.7 & below	1 & below	1 & below
	N = 262	N = 159	N = 190	N = 262
	10 trials	M of 2 trials	5 trials	10 trials

*Based on scores of high school girls.

From: Buchanan, R.E. (1942). *A study of achievement tests in speedball for high school girls.* Unpublished master's thesis, University of Iowa, Iowa City. Copyright by author.

			Table 23.2				
		T-SCALES FOR SELECTED ITEMS IN BUCHANAN SPEEDBALL TEST					
T-Score	Lift to Others*	Throwing and Catching Standing†	Throwing and Catching Standing‡	Kick-Ups§	Passing≠	Passing¶	*T*-Score
75		19.8 - 20.2					75
74							74
73							73
72		19.3 - 19.7	27.8 - 29.7	10			72
71	10					10	71
70							70
69		18.8 - 19.2					69
68					5		68
67		18.3 - 18.7					67
66				9		9	66
65		17.8 - 18.2	25.8 - 27.7				65
64							64
63	9						63
62		17.3 - 17.7				8	62
61							61
60		16.8 - 17.2					60
59				8		7	59
58		16.3 - 16.7					58
57	8		23.8 - 25.7			6	57
56		15.8 - 16.2					56
55							55
54		15.3 - 15.7		7			54
53	7						53
52			21.8 - 23.7			5	52
51		14.8 - 15.2			4		51
50				6			50
49							49
48			19.3 - 21.7				48
47	6			5		4	47
46		14.3 - 14.7					46
45			17.8 - 19.2				45
44							44
43	5	13.8 - 14.2		4	3		43
42		13.3 - 13.7					42
41		12.8 - 13.2	15.8 - 17.7				41
40		12.3 - 12.7				3	40
39	4	11.8 - 12.2					39
38				3			38
37			13.8 - 15.7				37
36		11.3 - 12.7					36
35					2	2	35
34	3			2			34
33			11.8 - 13.7				33
32							32
31							31
30	2						30
29				1			29
28					1		28
27							27
26			9.8 - 11.7				26
25	1					1	25

*Ten trials, 262 cases.
†Mean of five trials, 72 cases.
‡Mean of two trials, 159 cases.
§Ten trials, 262 cases.
≠Five trials, 190 cases.
¶Ten trials, 72 cases.

From: Buchanan, R.E. (1942). *A study of achievement tests in speedball for high school girls*. Unpublished master's thesis, University of Iowa, Iowa City. Copyright by author.

Speedball References

Buchanan, R.E. (1942). *A study of achievement tests in speedball for high school girls.* Unpublished master's thesis, University of Iowa, Iowa City.

Colvin, V. (1936). Achievement tests for speedball. *Spalding's Official Soccer and Speedball Guide.* New York: American Sports.

Crawford, E.A. (1958). *The development of skill test batteries for evaluating the ability of women physical education majors students in soccer and speedball.* Unpublished doctoral dissertation, University of Oregon, Eugene.

Miller, S.B. (1959). *A battery of speedball skill tests for college women.* Unpublished master's thesis, University of Nebraska, Lincoln.

Smith, G. (1947). *Speedball skill tests for college women.* Unpublished master's thesis, Illinois State University, Normal.

Stephyns, O.R. (1965). *Achievement tests in speed-a-way for high school girls.* Unpublished master's thesis, Illinois State University, Normal.

Chapter 24

SQUASH

INTRODUCTION

The racquet sport of squash has never attained the popularity of tennis or badminton in the American school curriculum. However, the male-dominated English sport attracts widespread interest in several countries throughout the world.

CAHILL SQUASH TEST
(Cahill, 1977)

Purpose:

To measure accuracy and racquet control in performing the forehand stroke.

Educational Application:

Designed for college students and varsity squash players, the test has value for testing junior and senior high school students.

Personnel:

One individual.

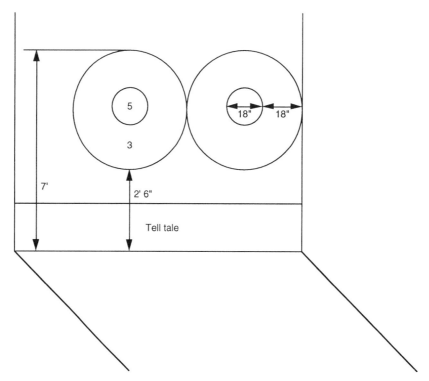

Fig. 24.1 Target markings for Cahill forehand crosscourt test item.

From: Cahill, P.J. (1977). *The construction of a skills test for squash racquets.* Unpublished doctoral dissertation, Springfield College, Springfield, Massachusetts. Copyright by author.

Equipment and Supplies:

Squash racquets, squash balls, measuring tape, stop watch, wall marking and scoring materials.

Facilities and Space:

Squash court of regulation size.

Description:

Test items for the Cahill Squash Test include a 30-second rally and forehand crosscourt shot. Figure 24.1 illustrates the layout for the forehand crosscourt shot item.

Directions:

At least five minutes of warm-up are recommended for a student before being tested, along with 30 seconds of practice time immediately before each individual test.

Thirty-Second Rally. Standing behind the service line while holding a ball, the student when commanded to start rallies the ball against the front wall. The ball can be hit with a volley stroke or after any number of bounces. Moving across the service line to hit balls that return short is permitted, but the subject must return behind the line for the next stroke. In such cases, no hits are counted until the student returns behind the line. Three 30-second trials are required.

Forehand Crossover Shot. The student assumes a position between the center line and the side wall, then hits a ball off the front wall and directs the return toward the wall target shown in Figure 24.1. Right-handed players aim for the target on the left side, and left-handed players hit at the target on the right side. After three practice shots, 10 forehand shots are taken for score. The student is not required to attempt a shot on poorly hit returns.

Scoring Method and Norms:

Thirty-Second Rally. The number of legal hits in three 30-second trials is the official score.

Forehand Crosscourt Shot. Balls hitting the innermost circle receive five points, those hitting the middle circle are worth three points, and any hitting outside the circle but striking the wall are awarded one point. The number of points accumulated in 10 shots is the final score. Balls hitting the floor or side wall first receive no points.

Validity and Reliability:

Utilizing round-robin tournament rankings and coaches' ratings as criterion measures, validity coefficients of .87 and .71 were determined for the 30-second rally and forehand crossover shot, respectively. In the same test item order, intraclass correlation reliability coefficients of .94 and .82 were reported.

Table 24.1 T-scale Norms for Forehand Crosscourt Test			
Men		**Women**	
Score	T-scale	Score	T-scale
36	72	32	70
34	68	30	64
32	65	28	63
30	61	26	60
28	58	24	59
26	56	22	57
24	53	20	54
22	49	18	51
20	46	16	47
18	43	14	43
16	40	12	41
14	37	10	36
12	34	8	32
10	28	6	24

From: Cahill, P.J. (1977). *The construction of a skills test for squash racquets.* Unpublished doctoral dissertation, Springfield College, Springfield, Massachusetts.

Table 24.2 T-scale Norms for 30-Second Rally Test			
Men		**Women**	
Score	T-scale	Score	T-scale
68	71	56	74
66	69	54	68
64	67	52	66
62	66	50	62
60	65	48	59
58	61	46	58
56	59	44	54
54	57	42	52
52	55	40	51
50	52	38	49
48	48	36	47
46	46	34	44
44	45	32	43
42	42	30	41
40	40	28	36
38	35	26	30
36	32	24	26
34	28		

From: Cahill, P.J. (1977). *The construction of a skills test for squash racquets.* Unpublished doctoral dissertation, Springfield College, Springfield, Massachusetts. Copyright by author.

Squash References

Broadhead, G.D. (1967). *An assessment, at various levels of ability, of the respective contributions of stroking ability and physical condition to the outcome of a game of squash racquets.* Unpublished master's thesis, University of Wisconsin, Madison.

Cahill, P.J. (1977). *The construction of a skills test for squash racquets.* Unpublished doctoral dissertation, Springfield College, Springfield, Massachusetts.

Chapter 25

SWIMMING

INTRODUCTION

Swimming is one of the world's oldest sports and today has international popularity. This is natural since the activity has always served the fundamental purposes of transportation and survival, especially during the earlier years of civilization.

Skills tests for swimming have appeared in the literature in every decade since the 1920s. The tests presented in this chapter represent four of those decades.

HEWITT ACHIEVEMENT SCALES FOR COLLEGE MEN
(Hewitt, 1948)

Purpose:

To measure performance and improvement in swimming skills.

Educational Application:

College men.

Description:

Hewitt is considered to be one of the leaders in the development of swimming skills tests due to his construction of swimming achievement scales for the armed forces, college men and high school boys and girls. The Hewitt Achievement Scales for College Men includes the 20- or 25-yard underwater swim; 15-minute endurance swim; 25- or 50-yard sprint swim with the crawl, breast and back strokes; and 50-yard glide relaxation with the elementary back, side and breast strokes.

Time:

Three 60-minute class periods for 20 students.

Personnel:

One timer-recorder-scorer with student assistants.

Equipment and Supplies:

Stop watch and scoring materials.

Facilities and Space:

Regulation pool.

Directions, Scoring Method and Norms:

Before being tested for evaluation purposes, the student should demonstrate at least a minimum degree of proficiency in the test items. Immediately prior to testing, a uniform warm-up period should be allowed for the students.

20- or 25-Yard Underwater Swim. The subject executes a regulation start from the pool deck and swims the entire distance under water. Any swimming style is acceptable. The final score is represented by the time taken, recorded to the nearest 10th of a second, to swim the particular distance. No score is given if any part of the body breaks water, which means the finish also must be under water.

Fifteen-Minute Endurance Swim. Using a regulation start, each subject attempts to swim continuously for 15 minutes, trying to cover as much distance as possible. The type of stroke used or the turning method employed is left to the discretion of each swimmer. The final score is the number of yards covered in the 15-minute trial period. It is suggested that each swimmer count his own lengths, which are converted into yards for scoring purposes. If more than a half-length has been completed when the time expires, the subject is given credit for a full length; otherwise, the extra distance is disregarded. No score is given to a subject who fails to swim continuously for the full 15 minutes.

25- or 50-Yard Sprint Swim with the Crawl, Breast and Back Strokes. Using a regulation diving start, each subject swims the preselected distance as fast as possible for each of the different strokes. A sufficient rest period should naturally be allowed between each of the three trials. The final score is the time, measured to the nearest 10th of a second, taken to swim the required distance for each of the three strokes.

50-Yard Glide Relaxation with the Elementary Back, Side and Breast Strokes. Starting from the water and using both a regulation push-off and turn, each subject swims the 50-yard distance with as few strokes as possible. No arm or leg action is allowed on the push-off. Regulation strokes must be used; otherwise the trial is not recorded. The final score for each swimming style is the number of strokes plus the number of push-offs.

Table 25.1
HEWITT SWIMMING ACHIEVEMENT SCALES FOR COLLEGE MEN

Rating	Underwater Swim		15-minute Endurance Swim	Crawl	25-yd. Sprint Swim	Back
	20 yd.	25 yds.			Breast	
Superior	14.6 & below	19.7 & below	784 & up	13.5 & below	18.7 & below	19.3 & below
Good	14.7 - 16.0	19.8 - 21.2	694 - 783	13.6 - 14.1	18.8 - 20.1	19.4 - 21.1
Average	16.1 - 17.6	21.3 - 22.8	612 - 693	14.2 - 15.0	20.2 - 21.7	21.2 - 22.7
Poor	17.7 - 19.0	22.9 - 24.7	525 - 611	15.1 - 15.8	21.8 - 23.2	22.8 - 24.5
Inferior	19.1 & up	24.8 & up	524 & below	15.9 & up	23.3 & up	24.6 & up

Rating	50-yd. Sprint Swim			50-yd. Glide and Relaxation		
	Crawl	Breast	Back	Elem. Back	Side	Breast
Superior	32.9 & below	45 & below	40 & below	19 & below	19 & below	18 & below
Good	33.0 - 36.1	46 - 48	41 - 44	20 - 23	20 - 23	19 - 21
Average	36.2 - 39.8	49 - 54	45 - 49	24 - 29	24 - 29	22 - 26
Poor	39.9 - 42.8	55 - 58	50 - 53	30 - 33	30 - 33	27 - 30
Inferior	42.9 & up	59 & up	54 & up	34 & up	34 & up	31 & up

From: Hewitt, J.E. (1948). Swimming achievement scales for college men. *Research Quarterly* 19: 282-289. Reprinted with permission from AAHPERD.

Validity and Reliability:

Validity coefficients ranging from .54 to .93 were determined by correlating each individual test item with the total score of all test items. Total test scores of students completing the Hewitt Swimming Achievement Scales for College Men was the criterion measure used.

Reliability coefficients of .89 and .95 were determined by use of the test-retest method for obtaining reliability with 200 students participating.

Additional Comments:

When time is limited, the tester may wish to administer the shorter version of the test items. Furthermore, additional experimentation with the test is warranted since total test scores of students are not considered a reliable test criterion.

HEWITT ACHIEVEMENT SCALES FOR HIGH SCHOOL SWIMMING
(Hewitt, 1949)

Purpose:
To measure performance and improvement in swimming.

Educational Application:
High school boys and girls.

Description:
Hewitt's scales for high school students include the 50-yard crawl stroke for time, the 25-yard flutter kick for time with a polo ball and the 25-yard glide relaxation with the elementary back, side and breast strokes.

Time:
Twenty students can be tested in two 60-minute periods.

Personnel:
One timer-recorder-scorer with student assistants.

Equipment and Supplies:
Stop watch, polo ball and scoring materials.

Facilities and Space:
Regulation pool.

Directions, Scoring Method and Norms:

Proper warm-up time should be permitted immediately prior to testing.

50-Yard Crawl Stroke for Time. Using a regulation racing dive, the student swims the 50-yard crawl stroke as fast as possible. The time required, measured to the nearest 10th of a second, constitutes the final score.

25-Yard Flutter Kick for Time with a Polo Ball. Stationed in the water, the subject holds on to the gutter with one hand and the ball with the other. When an audible signal is given, the subject uses a regulation push-off, grasps the ball with both hands and swims the 25 yards as fast as possible using only the flutter kick. The final score is the time utilized, measured to the nearest 10th of a second.

25-Yard Glide Relaxation with the Elementary Back, Side and Breast Strokes. This test is performed and scored the same as the previously described Hewitt Achievement Scales for College Men. The only difference is in the distance.

Hewitt devised both achievement scales and percentile norms for the test involving high school students (Tables 25.2 & 25.3).

Rating	25 yd. Flutter Kick, Polo Ball	50 yd. Crawl	Elementary Back	Glide Relaxation Side	Breast
Table 25.2					
HEWITT SWIMMING ACHIEVEMENT SCALES FOR HIGH SCHOOL BOYS AND GIRLS					
			High School Boys		
Superior	15 & below	17 & below	6 & below	6 & below	6 & below
Good	16 - 27	28 - 34	7 - 10	7 - 11	7 - 10
Average	28 - 42	35 - 45	11 - 18	12 - 17	11 - 17
Poor	43 - 65	46 - 59	19 - 30	18 - 28	18 - 28
Inferior	66 & up	60 & up	31 & up	29 & up	29 & up
			High School Girls		
Superior	24 & below	36 & below	6 & below	6 & below	6 & below
Good	25 - 31	37 - 45	7 - 10	7 - 10	7 - 9
Average	32 - 47	46 - 60	11 - 18	11 - 17	10 - 17
Poor	48 - 52	61 - 80	19 - 30	18 - 28	18 - 28
Inferior	53 & up	81 & up	31 & up	29 & up	29 & up

From: Hewitt, J.E. (1949). Swimming achievement scales for high school swimming, *Research Quarterly* 20: 170-179. Reprinted with permission from AAHPERD.

Validity and Reliability:

Validity coefficients ranging from .60 to .94 were determined by correlating each individual test item with the total score of all items. Reliability coefficients of .89 to .96 were computed with the data obtained by the test-retest method.

Additional Comments:

When time is a factor in the evaluation process, consideration may be given to using the 25-yard glide relaxation side stroke item to fulfill the purpose of the battery in view of the .94 correlation it showed with the total test scores. However, the tester is reminded that the value of the total test score criterion is questionable.

	Boys				Girls				
	Seconds		*Strokes*		*Seconds*		*Strokes*		
	25 yd.	Elem.			25 yd.	Elem.			
	Flutter	Back	Side	Breast	Flutter	Back	Side	Breast	
Percentile	Kick	Stroke	Stroke	Stroke	Kick	Stroke	Stroke	Stroke	Percentile
95	17	7	8	6	26	7	8	7	95
90	22	8	9	8	27			8	90
85	23	9	10	9	29	8	9	9	85
80	25	10		10	30		10		80
75	27	11	11		31				75
70	28			11	32	9	11	10	70
65	30	12	12	12	34	10			65
60	32				35	11	12	11	60
55	33	13	13	13	37	12			55
50	34	14		14	39		13		50
45	35	15	14		40	13		12	45
40	36	16	15	15	42	15	14	13	40
35	38	17	16	16	44	16	15		35
30	40	18	17	17	46	17	16	14	30
25	43	19	18	18	48	19	17	15	25
20	46	20	19	19	52	20	18	16	20
15	50	23	21	21	57	22	19	18	15
10	54	26	23	·23	65	24	21	20	10
5	60	30	27	27	83	28	24	24	5

Table 25.3

HEWITT PERCENTILE NORMS FOR HIGH SCHOOL BOYS AND GIRLS*

*Push-off permitted on each item and counted as one stroke on last three items.

From: Hewitt, J.E. (1949). Swimming achievement scales for high school swimming, *Research Quarterly* 20: 170-179. Reprinted with permission from AAHPERD.

BURRIS SPEED-STROKE TEST OF THE CRAWL
(Burris, 1964)

Purpose:

To measure crawl stroking ability.

Educational Application:

Men and women swimmers at the intermediate level and above.

Description:

Burris developed a skills test to measure stroke proficiency by keeping the distance constant, with the time and number of strokes varying with each swimmer. Each student swims 25 yards using a regular crawl stroke with a flutter kick and rhythmical breathing.

Time:

A class of 20 students can easily take the test in one 60-minute period.

Personnel:

One timer-scorer-recorder with student assistants.

Equipment and Supplies:

Stop watch and scoring materials.

Facilities and Space:

A 25-yard swimming pool.

Directions:

Test subjects should demonstrate at least an intermediate level of swimming proficiency and be allowed a proper warm-up period before being tested.

Assuming a position in deep water with one hand grasping the gutter and his/her body and legs in a vertical position away from the wall, the student begins swimming on an audible signal, without pushing off the wall. Students swim as fast as possible, yet at the same time use as few strokes as possible. The idea is to get the maximum amount of power from both the kick and arm pull. The regular crawl stroke, utilizing a flutter kick and rhythmical breathing, is required during the 25-yard swim.

Scoring Method and Norms:

The final scores are based on both speed and stroke count.

Speed. The watch is started when the audible signal is given and stopped when any part of the student's body touches the wall at the 25-yard distance; the time is recorded to the nearest 10th of a second.

Stroke. One stroke is counted each time either hand enters the water for a pull. The first stroke is counted when the hand that has been grasping the gutter enters the water. The touch to the wall is counted as a stroke if part of the arm pull has occurred.

T-scores for time and strokes of both men and women are given in Tables 25.4 and 25.5. The tester is reminded that the speed-stroke scores represent two T-scores combined; therefore, the average is 100 instead of 50.

Table 25.4

T-SCORES FOR MEN FROM BURRIS SPEED-STROKE TEST OF THE CRAWL*

Seconds																								
10	11	12	13	14	15	16	17	18	19	20	21	22	23	24	25	26	27	28	29	30	31	32	33	34
90	85	80	75	70	65	61	58	55	52	50	47	45	42	40	38	36	35	33	31	29	28	27	26	25

T-Scores

Strokes	T-Score
10	92
11	89
12	85
13	83
14	80
15	77
16	75
17	72
18	70
19	68
20	66
21	64
22	62
23	60
24	58
25	56
26	54
27	52
28	50
29	48
30	46
31	44
32	42
33	40
34	38
35	36
36	34
37	32
38	31
39	30
40	28
41	27
42	25

DIRECTIONS

Place the corner of the score sheet in the angle between the two sets of conversion scores. Round the time score to the nearest second and look for the appropriate number along the top row of figures marked seconds. Immediately below the score in seconds is the T-score equivalent of that score. Look up the raw score in strokes in the left hand column marked strokes. Just to the right of the stroke score is the T-score equivalent for strokes. Add the T-score for strokes to the T-score for seconds for the combined speed-stroke score.

*Based on scores of 89 college men.

From: Burris, B.J. (1964). *A study of the speed-stroke test of crawl stroking ability and its relationship to other selected tests of crawl stroking ability*. Unpublished master's thesis, Temple University, Philadelphia. Copyright by author.

	Table 25.5

T-SCORES FOR WOMEN FROM BURRIS SPEED-STROKE TEST OF THE CRAWL*

Seconds

16	17	18	19	20	21	22	23	24	25	26	27	28	29	30	31	32	33	34	35	36	37	38	39	40	41
91	85	80	75	70	66	62	58	55	53	51	49	48	46	44	43	42	40	39	38	36	34	33	31	30	27

T-Scores

Strokes   **T-Score**

Strokes	T-Score
14	89
15	85
16	82
17	80
18	78
19	75
20	73
21	71
22	68
23	66
24	64
25	62
26	60
27	57
28	55
29	53
30	51
31	49
32	47
33	45
34	44
35	42
36	41
37	40
38	39
39	37
40	36
41	35
42	34
43	33
44	31
45	30
46	28
47	26
48	25

DIRECTIONS

Place the corner of the score sheet in the angle between the two sets of conversion scores. Round the time score to the nearest second and look for the appropriate number along the top row of figures marked seconds. Immediately below the score in seconds is the T-score equivalent of that score. Look up the raw score in strokes in the left hand column marked strokes. Just to the right of the stroke score is the T-score equivalent for strokes. Add the T-score for strokes to the T-score for seconds for the combined speed-stroke score.

*Based on scores of 143 college women.

From: Burris, B.J. (1964). *A study of the speed-stroke test of crawl stroking ability and its relationship to other selected tests of crawl stroking ability*. Unpublished master's thesis, Temple University, Philadelphia. Copyright by author.

Validity and Reliability:

The Burris Test was administered to 69 college men and women.

Validity coefficients of .89 and .86 were derived for men and women, respectively. Reliability coefficients of .91 for men and .90 for women, utilizing the test-retest method, were computed. A .99 objectivity coefficient was determined for both men and women.

Additional Comments:

If a 25-yard pool is not available to the tester, it is recommended that a rope be used as the 25-yard marker. The rope should be stretched tight and positioned level with the water surface.

ROSENTSWEIG POWER SWIMMING TEST
(Rosentsweig, 1968)

Purpose:

To measure form and power on five basic swimming strokes.

Educational Application:

Initially developed for college women but is appropriate for males and females from junior high school through college.

Description:

Rosentsweig revised the Fox Swimming Power Test (Fox, 1957) by changing the starting procedure, increasing the number of test strokes and trials, adding a form rating, testing five different strokes instead of two and altering the measuring point. The five strokes include the front crawl, side crawl, elementary back stroke, back crawl and breast stroke. For test administration, the length of the pool deck is marked off in one-foot intervals beginning eight feet from the shallow end. The first marker represents the starting line, or point zero.

Time:

Twenty students can be tested in two or three 60-minute periods.

Personnel:

One person to judge, score and record with student assistants needed for the starting procedure.

Equipment and Supplies:

Marking tape and scoring materials.

Facilities and Space:

Swimming pool.

Directions:

Test subjects are assigned partners since two individuals are needed for the starting procedure. The subject assumes the appropriate floating position in the water, depending on the stroke that is being tested, with his/her shoulders even with and parallel to the starting line. Standing to the side of the swimmer, the partner forms a cradle with the forearms to hold the legs of the subject to the surface of the water. The subject is allowed to scull or float in the starting position until ready to start the test.

When the subject is ready, he/she swims away from his/her partner by using an arm stroke first. If a kick is made prior to the first arm stroke, the trial is immediately stopped. Twelve arm strokes or six cycles are allowed, depending on the stroke, and two trials are given.

Scoring Method:

The final score includes two measures, one each for distance and form. The first score represents the distance covered in the 12 strokes or six cycles using the subject's shoulders as a reference point. Also, a subjective rating of the swimming form is made during the actual trial with the use of a five-point scale.

Validity and Reliability:

A total of 184 college women served as subjects. Validity coefficients were determined by correlating the better power scores against the ratings of judges. Reliability coefficients were based on a test-retest situation.

Validity coefficients were .72, .81, .83, .63 and .74 for the front crawl, side crawl, elementary back stroke, back crawl and breast stroke, respectively. Reliability coefficients were .89, .91, .96, .91 and .95 for the items in the order previously stated.

Additional Comments:

The Rosentsweig Power Swimming Test shows value not only for measuring achievement but also as a motivating instrument and practice device for students.

Administering two trials of five separate test items can be time-consuming. Additional use of student assistants for testing a greater number of subjects per class period is one suggestion for coping with the problem. On the other hand, ease of test administration would be enhanced if performance measurement of the various strokes was spread out over a longer period of time than the recommended two or three class periods.

TWELVE-MINUTE SWIM TEST
(Jackson, Jackson & Frankiewicz, 1979)

Purpose:

To measure swimming endurance utilizing the crawl stroke.

Educational Application:

Conducted for college males, the test is appropriate for college women and junior high and senior high school boys and girls.

Personnel:

One starter and recorder with students serving as lap counters.

Equipment and Supplies:

Lane dividers, measuring tape, stop watch, marking and scoring materials.

Facilities and Space:

A 25-yard swimming pool.

Directions:

On a starting command, the student pushes off from the end of the pool and uses the crawl stroke to swim as much distance as possible in 12 minutes. A student on the pool deck counts the laps. When signaled to stop, the yardage closest to the swimmer's hand and the number of full laps completed are recorded.

Scoring Method:

The distance completed in the 12-minute requirement is the official score.

Validity and Reliability:

The relationship between performance on the 12-minute endurance swim and a tethered swim test was determined by construct validity, producing a coefficient of .89. Test-retest reliability produced a coefficient of .98.

FRONSKE SWIMMING TEST
(Fronske, 1988)

Purpose:

To evaluate performance in the breast stroke, front crawl, butterfly, elementary back stroke and side stroke.

Educational Application:

Initially conducted with college males and females, but useful for testing experienced swimmers at any school level.

Personnel:

One individual to time the student performances and one to record the results. Students can hold the swimmers stationary in the water and count strokes.

Equipment and Supplies:

Lane dividers, stop watch and scoring materials.

Facilities and Space:

A 25-yard swimming pool.

Directions:

Students must learn the various starting positions on the five-item test before being tested.

Front Crawl. The student assumes a stationary prone floating position with the legs straight, toes touching the wall and both arms extended parallel with the body. The elbows should be located close to the ears. A student assistant holds the swimmer at the waist by placing one hand on the swimmer's abdomen and the other on his/her back. On a starting signal, the student holder releases the swimmer and steps back. The swimmer proceeds to swim the front crawl stroke as fast as possible.

Butterfly Stroke. Same as the front crawl test directions, except that the swimmer holds both arms straight above the head in the starting position.

Breast Stroke. Same as the butterfly test directions.

Elementary Back Stroke. Starting from a stationary supine floating position with legs straight, toes touching the wall and the arms straightened along the side of the body, the subject when signaled swims the elementary back stroke in as few strokes as possible. The holder repeats the same action as prescribed in the previous three test items.

Side Stroke. The test subject starts on his/her side in a floating position with legs straight, toes touching the wall, one arm straight above the head and the other arm down along the side. A student assistant holds the swimmer with one hand on each side of the waist. On an audible signal, the holder releases the swimmer and steps back. The swimmer performs the side stroke test in as few strokes as possible.

Scoring Method:

The time required to swim 25 yards is the official score for the front crawl, butterfly and breast stroke test items. The number of strokes used to swim the 25-yard distance is the final score for the back stroke and side stroke.

Validity and Reliability:

Utilizing time, number of strokes, expert ratings and a checklist based on American Red Cross criteria, validity coefficients for the front crawl, butterfly, breast stroke, elementary back stroke and side stroke were .67, .68, .69, .63 and .60, respectively. Reliability coefficients were .93, .97, .85, .96 and .93 for the items in the order presented above.

Swimming References

Anderson, C.W. (1930). Achievement records in swimming. *Journal of Health and Physical Education* 1: 40.

Arrasmith, J.L. (1967). *Swimming classification test for college women.* Unpublished doctoral dissertation, University of Oregon, Eugene.

Burris, B.J. (1964). *A study of the speed-stroke test of crawl stroking ability and its relationship to other selected tests of crawl stroking ability.* Unpublished master's thesis, Temple University, Philadelphia.

Chapman, P. (1965). *A comparison of three methods of measuring swimming stroke proficiency.* Unpublished master's thesis, University of Wisconsin, Madison.

Connor, D.J. (1962). *A comparison of objective and subjective testing methods in selected swimming skills for elementary school children.* Unpublished master's thesis, Washington State University, Pullman.

Cureton, T.K. (1935). A test for endurance in speed swimming. *Research Quarterly* 6: 106-112.

Cureton, T.K. (1938). *Objective scales for rating swimming performance and diagnosing fault.* Springfield College, Springfield, Massachusetts.

Durrant, S.M. (1964). An analytical method of rating synchronized swimming stunts. *Research Quarterly* 35: 126-134.

Fox, M.G. (1957). Swimming power test. *Research Quarterly* 28: 233-237.

Fried, M.G. (1983). *An examination of the test characteristics of the 12-minute aerobic swim test.* Unpublished master's thesis, University of Wisconsin, Madison.

Fronske, H. (1988). *Relationships among various objective swimming tests and expert evaluations of skill in swimming.* Unpublished doctoral dissertation, Brigham Young University, Provo, Utah.

Hewitt, J.E. (1948). Swimming achievement scales for college men. *Research Quarterly* 19: 282-289.

Hewitt, J.E. (1949). Achievement scale scores for high school swimming. *Research Quarterly* 20: 170-179.

Jackson, A.S., & Pettinger, J. (1969). *The development and discriminant analysis of swimming profiles of college men.* Paper presented at the annual meeting of the National College Physical Education Association for Men.

Jackson, A., Jackson, A.S., & Frankiewicz, R.G. (1979). The construct and concurrent validity of a 12-minute crawl stroke as a field test of swimming endurance. *Research Quarterly* 50: 641-648.

Kilby, E.J. (1956). *An objective method of evaluating three swimming strokes.* Unpublished doctoral dissertation, University of Washington, Seattle.

Munt, M.R. (1964). *Development of an objective test to measure the efficiency of the front crawl for college women.* Unpublished master's thesis, University of Michigan, Ann Arbor.

Parkhurst, M.G. (1934). Achievement tests in swimming. *Journal of Health and Physical Education* 5: 34-36, 58.

Rosentsweig, J. (1968). A revision of the power swimming test. *Research Quarterly* 39: 818-819.

Scott, M.G. (1940). Achievement examinations for elementary and intermediate swimming classes. *Research Quarterly* 11: 104-111.

Wilson, C.T. (1934). Coordination tests in swimming. *Research Quarterly* 5: 81-88.

Wilson, M.R. (1962). *A relationship between general motor ability and objective measurement of achievement in swimming at the intermediate level for college women.* Unpublished master's thesis, Women's College of the University of North Carolina, Greensboro.

Chapter 26

TABLE TENNIS

INTRODUCTION

Table tennis is not a common offering in secondary school and college physical education programs, but the sport is commonly found in intramural sports programs at both levels.

MOTT-LOCKHART TABLE TENNIS TEST
(Mott & Lockhart, 1946)

Purpose:

To measure skill in table tennis.

Educational Application:

The test was scientifically authenticated with college women as subjects, but it has application in the evaluation of college males and junior and senior high school boys and girls.

Description:

The test measures achievement and is useful for classifying and motivating students in the learning situation. The test requires the student to rally the ball against a perpendicular surface for 30 seconds.

A simulated net line is drawn on the perpendicular half of a propped table tennis table, six inches above the horizontal half.

Time:

If two or more table tennis tables are available, the test could easily be administered to a class of 20 students in one 40-minute class period.

Personnel:

The tester and a trained student assistant to serve as scorer and timer, respectively.

Equipment and Supplies:

Stop watch, at least one table tennis table and three table tennis balls in good condition, table tennis rackets, kitchen matchbox or substitute approximately 5 x 2 3/4 inches, some thumbtacks to attach matchbox to edge of table, line marking and scoring materials.

Facilities and Space:

An area of sufficient size to allow for player maneuverability and a table tennis table positioned with half of it propped against a wall or post perpendicular to the floor and other half of the table.

Directions:

The subject stands with a racket and one ball in hand with two extra balls placed in a matchbox (or similar container) which is tacked to the edge of the table. On the starting signal, the subject drops a ball to the table and rallies against the propped table surface as often as possible in a period of 30 seconds. The ball may bounce more than once before being struck. A ball kept in the matchbox may be used if control of the original ball is lost, with the ball being put into play the same as the original. Hits below the six-inch chalk line do not count; neither do any volleyed balls nor those whereby the subject places a free hand on the table during or immediately preceding the hits. Three trials are required with intervening rest periods.

Scoring Method and Norms:

The number of legal hits is recorded for each trial with the best of the three trials being the official score.

T-scales resulting from the scores of 162 college women are presented in Table 26.1.

	Table 26.1				
	T-SCALES FOR MOTT-LOCKHART TABLE TENNIS TEST*				
T-Score	Raw Score	T-Score	Raw Score	T-Score	Raw Score
77	60	59	45	41	29
76		58		40	
75		57	44	39	28
74		56		38	27
73	58	55	43	37	26
72		54	42	36	
71	55	53	41	35	25
70		52	40	34	24
69	54	51		33	23
68	52	50	39	32	22
67	51	49	38	31	
66	50	48	37	30	
65	49	47	36	29	21
64	48	46	34-35	28	
63		45	33	27	
62	47	44	32	26	20
61		43	31	25	
60	46	42	30	24	16
*Based on scores of 162 college women.					

From: Mott, J.A., & Lockhart, A. (1946). Table tennis backboard test. *Journal of Health and Physical Education* 17: 550-552. Reprinted with permission from AAHPERD.

Validity and Reliability:

A coefficient of .84 was reported for the relationship between the test scores and subjective ratings of judges while viewing each subject for three games in a round-robin tournament. Seventy-nine subjects were tested by the odd-even method for obtaining reliability, and a .90 coefficient resulted.

Table Tennis Reference

Mott, J.A., & Lockhart, A. (1946). Table tennis backboard test. *Journal of Health and Physical Education* 17: 550-552.

Chapter 27

TEAM HANDBALL

INTRODUCTION

The international sport of team handball is not widely taught in American schools. That may change as American physical educators become more familiar with the Olympic sport.

ZINN TEAM HANDBALL SKILLS BATTERY
(Zinn, 1981)

Purpose:

To measure passing and throwing skills in team handball.

Educational Application:

The test was scientifically documented with male and female members of a high school team handball squad, but also has application for junior high school students and students in high school physical education classes.

Personnel:

One tester.

Equipment and Supplies:

Team handballs, rope or string, measuring tape, stop watch, floor and wall marking and scoring materials.

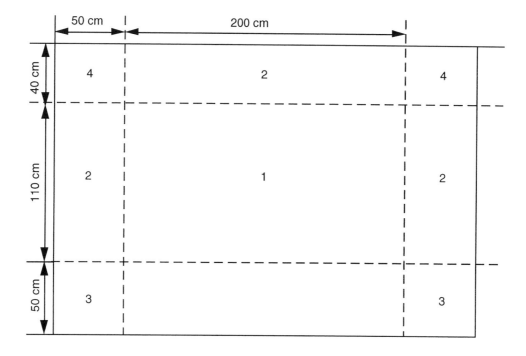

Fig. 27.1 Target markings for Zinn team handball front throw test item.

From: Zinn, J.L. (1981). *Construction of a battery of team handball skills tests.* Unpublished master's thesis, University of Iowa, Iowa City. Copyright by author.

Facilities and Space:

The nine-meter front throw test item requires a space the size of the floor area around a team handball goal, and an unobstructed wall is needed for the dominant-hand speed pass and overhead pass tests.

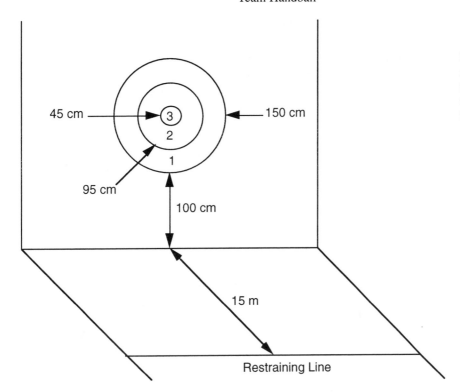

Fig. 27.2 Target markings for Zinn team handball overhead pass test item.

From: Zinn, J.L. (1981). *Construction of a battery of team handball skills tests.*
Unpublished master's thesis, University of Iowa, Iowa City. Copyright by author.

Description:

The three-item test includes the nine-meter front throw, dominant-hand speed pass and overhead pass.

For the nine-meter front throw test, the front of a team handball goal is divided into eight scoring zones using rope or string (Figure 27.1). Scoring zones are numbered according to scoring difficulty.

The dominant-hand speed pass test requires an unobstructed wall space and a restraining line marked 2 1/2 meters from and parallel to the wall.

To administer the overhead pass test, a line is drawn 15 meters from and parallel to a wall target. The three concentric target circles include an inner circle 45 cm in diameter, a second circle 95 cm in diameter and an outer circle 150 cm in diameter. The bottom of the outer circle is located 100 cm above the floor (Figure 27.2).

Directions:

Nine-Meter Front Throw. The student is awarded 10 throws, five when performing a jump throw and five when executing a set throw. The student is allowed three steps before releasing a ball, but the last step must be taken from behind the free throw line (nine-meter line). No points are counted for balls hitting the court surface before reaching the goal.

Dominant-Hand Speed Pass. Standing behind the restraining line and when signaled to start, the student uses the dominant hand to bounce a ball against the wall as fast as possible. All bounces must be made from behind the restraining line, and return bounces must be caught with both hands. The timer starts the watch the instant the first ball hits the wall and stops it when the 10th pass hits the wall. Two trials are required.

Overhead Pass. Positioned behind the restraining line, the subject throws a ball at the target with a one-armed throw. Ten passes are made from behind the restraining line. Points are awarded as shown in Figure 27.2. Passes hitting a line receive the score of higher value.

Scoring Method:

Nine-Meter Front Throw. The number of cumulative points made in 10 trials is the official score. A perfect score is 40 points.

Dominant-Hand Speed Pass. The best time in two trials is the final score. Time is recorded to the nearest 10th of a second.

Overhead Pass. The number of points accumulated in 10 throws. A perfect score is 30 points.

Validity and Reliability:

Using judges' ratings as the criterion measure, validity coefficients of .76, .71 and .77 were determined for the nine-meter front throw, dominant-hand speed pass and overhead pass, respectively. Reliability coefficients ranged from .82 to .89 for the three test items, utilizing the test-retest method.

Team Handball Reference

Zinn, J.L. (1981). *Construction of a battery of team handball skills tests.* Unpublished master's thesis, University of Iowa, Iowa City.

Chapter 28

TENNIS

INTRODUCTION

Perhaps the best indicator of a student's general playing ability in tennis is his/her ranking with classmates of similar skill in a round-robin tournament. Unfortunately, that type of tournament is not always practical in time and ease of administration. A viable alternative for measuring progress and achievement in tennis is the use of valid, reliable and administratively feasible skills tests. The sport of tennis features some of the best skills tests ever developed.

DYER BACKBOARD TEST OF TENNIS ABILITY
(Dyer, 1938)

Purpose:

To measure general tennis playing ability.

Educational Application:

Originally designed for college women, but has value for testing the tennis ability of high school and college males and females.

Description:

The Dyer Test is one of the more popular and widely recognized sports skills of all time. Dyer's 1935 test was the first tennis skills test to be subjected to scientific analysis and led the way to development of a number of useful tests in the sport of tennis. Her 1938 revision was developed for use as a classification device, but also has shown merit as a practice tool for tennis players and device for measuring the progress of developing tennis players.

The test layout calls for a three-inch wide net line to be drawn on an unobstructed wall surface or backboard, with the top edge of the net line located three feet from the floor. A five-foot restraining line is drawn parallel to the wall hitting area.

Time:

One 40-minute class period for a class of 20 students with a proportional increase in number of students tested to the number of available walls or backboards.

Personnel:

One timer and one scorer per testing station.

Equipment and Supplies:

Assortment of tennis rackets, one dozen quality tennis balls, one stop watch for each testing station, a cardboard box or wire basket per testing station, scoring materials, floor and wall marking materials.

Facilities and Space:

A flat, unobstructed wall or backboard (at least 10 feet high and 15 feet wide), and at least 15 to 20 feet of open space in front of the wall or backboard.

Directions:

The student stands behind the five-foot restraining line while holding a racket and two tennis balls. On the starting signal, the subject bounces one of the balls on the floor and hits it above the net line on the wall. This action is repeated for 30 seconds.

The restraining line may be crossed to retrieve a ball, and volleying is permitted once the ball is put into play. Balls hit in front of the restraining line do not count. For use when balls get out of control, a box of extra balls should be stationed near the subject, preferably on the right side for right-handed players, and vice versa for left-handers. There is no limit on the number of balls that may be used during the testing period. New balls are put into play in the same manner as the original one.

Scoring Method and Norms:

A point is counted each time the ball hits on or above the net line during the 30-second time span. The sum of points made in the three trials is the final score. *T*-scale norms for Dyer's 1938 test revision are presented in Table 28.1. An ability rating scale based on scores of 672 college women students and physical education majors is shown in Table 28.2.

	Table 28.1						
	T-SCALE FOR NEW METHOD SCORING IN DYER TEST						
T-Scale	Test Score	*T*-Scale	Test Score	*T*-Scale	Test Score	*T*-Scale	Test Score
100	67	75	50	50	33	25	16
99	66	74	49	49	32	24	15
98		73		48		23	
97	65	72	48	47	31	22	14
96	64	71	47	46	30	21	13
95		70		45		20	
94	63	69	46	44	29	19	12
93	62	68	45	43	28	18	11
92		67	44	42	27	17	10
91	61	66		41		16	
90	60	65	43	40	26	15	9
89	59	64	42	39	25	14	8
88		63		38		13	
87	58	62	41	37	24	12	7
86	57	61	40	36	23	11	6
85		60		35		10	
84	56	59	39	34	22	9	5
83	55	58	38	33	21	8	4
82		57		32		7	
81	54	56	37	31	20	6	3
80	53	55	36	30	19	5	2
79		54		29		4	
78	52	53	35	28	18	3	1
77	51	52	34	27	17	2	
76		51		26		1	

From: Dyer, J.T. (1938). Revision of backboard test of tennis ability. *Research Quarterly* 9: 25-31. Reprinted with permission from AAHPERD.

Table 28.2		
ABILITY RATINGS FOR DYER TENNIS TEST		
Rating*	College Women	Women Majors Physical Education
Superior	46 & up	79 & up
Good	38 - 45	58 - 78
Average	29 - 37	35 - 57
Poor	21 - 28	13 - 34
Inferior	20 & below	12 & below

*Based on scores of 672 women students and physical education majors.

From: Miller, W.K. (1952). *Achievement levels in tennis knowledge and skill for women physical education students.* Unpublished doctoral dissertation, Indiana University, Bloomington. Copyright by author.

Validity and Reliability:

A study of the original Dyer Test yielded correlation coefficients of .85 and .90 with judges' ratings as the criterion measure. A validity study of the revised test, utilizing round-robin tournament rankings as the criterion measure, produced coefficients ranging from .85 to .92.

Reliability coefficients of .86, .87 and .92 were derived for the Dyer test revision, utilizing the test-retest method with samples of 14 to 37 women. A coefficient of .90 was computed for the original test.

Additional Comments:

A reference in the literature to the Dyer Tennis Test usually refers to the 1938 revision. The 1935 original test did not utilize a restraining line; this was standardized at five feet in the 1938 revision. In the revision, the scoring method also was altered somewhat and the method of supplying extra balls to the subject was changed to reduce the degree of variability.

Based on the results of several studies made of the Dyer Test, it appears that a distance in the 20-foot range would be more suitable for beginners, and a distance of 30 feet or so would be more useful for measuring tennis ability of intermediate and advanced players. A problem with the five-foot restraining line recommended in the 1938 revision is its promotion of a poor stroking technique. The short distance does not lend itself to the use of proper stroking form.

BROER-MILLER TENNIS TEST
(Broer & Miller, 1950)

Purpose:

To evaluate tennis playing ability as measured by performance on forehand and backhand drive placement.

Educational Application:

College women and high school girls.

Description:

The test was designed for use as a classification device and grading instrument. Figure 28.1 indicates the necessary court markings for scoring purposes. A rope is stretched four feet above the top of the net.

Time:

One 40-minute period for testing of 20 students.

Personnel:

One scorer and student helpers for retrieving balls, etc.

Equipment and Supplies:

A selection of tennis rackets, a rope of sufficient length to stretch above the net, two dozen quality tennis balls, poles for holding the rope, scoring and court marking materials.

Facilities and Space:

At least one regulation tennis court.

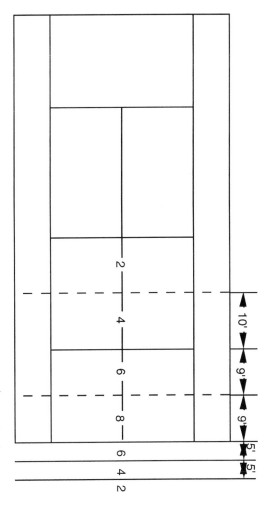

Fig. 28.1 Court markings for Broer-Miller Tennis Test.

From: Broer, M.R., & Miller, D.M. (1950). Achievement tests for beginning and intermediate tennis. *Research Quarterly* 21: 303-320. Reprinted with permission from AAHPERD.

Directions:

The subject takes a racket and assumes a position behind the baseline, then bounces a ball and hits it into the opposite court. The ball must go between the top of the net and the rope to receive maximum score; clearing the rope is given one-half the value of the scoring area in which it lands. A trial is counted if the ball is missed, and "let" balls are taken again.

Every student completes 14 trials each for the forehand and backhand drives.

Scoring Method:

The final score is the sum of points made on the 28 trials (14 for each type of drive).

Validity and Reliability:

The validity estimate was .85 for intermediate players and .61 for a beginning group when test scores and judges' ratings were correlated. A reliability coefficient of .80 was reported for both the intermediate and beginning groups.

Additional Comments:

A unique feature of this test is that the validity coefficient is higher than the reliability value. Broer and Miller concluded that the test appears to be more valid for testing intermediate players than beginners because of the higher validity value computed for the intermediates.

A study by Fox (Fox, 1953) suggested that a test of serving ability would enhance the scientific authenticity of the Broer-Miller Test. On the basis of a .79 validity coefficient she obtained for the Broer-Miller Test when using beginners as subjects, Fox concluded that the test could be used as a measure of beginners' tennis ability with some degree of confidence. When a ball throwing machine was used instead of the subject dropping the ball by hand, McDonald's (McDonald, 1960) study also produced a .79 validity coefficient for the Broer-Miller Test.

HEWITT REVISION OF DYER BACKBOARD TENNIS TEST
(Hewitt, 1965)

Purpose:

To classify beginning and advanced players by measuring rallying and service ability.

Educational Application:

High school and college males and females.

Description:

The test measures the ability to serve and rally. The rally may consist of any type stroke.

A gymnasium wall serves well in the administration of the wall test. A line is marked 20 feet from the wall, and a parallel 20-foot line is marked at a height of three feet from the wall. The wall should be 20 feet high and 20 feet wide.

Time:

The test is notably feasible in time of administration, especially in situations where two or more walls are utilized simultaneously. Each student should be allowed about two minutes of practice immediately prior to the 90 seconds of testing (three trials of 30 seconds each).

Personnel:

Tester, timer and recorder. In tests utilizing multiple testing stations, trained students could serve in tester's scoring role.

Equipment and Supplies:

A basket of one to two dozen quality tennis balls, tennis rackets, stop watch measured in 1/10 seconds, ball container marking materials for wall and floor (or particular surface of outdoor facility), scoring materials.

Facilities and Space:

At least one smooth wall 20 feet high and 20 feet wide. Twenty feet of unobstructed space directly in front of the wall must also be available.

Directions:

The student serves a ball against the wall while stationed behind the restraining line. Any type of serve is permitted. The stop watch is started when the served ball hits above the net line on the wall. The student then initiates a rally using any type of ground or volley stroke. When a ball gets away from the subject, another may be taken from the ball container positioned at the end of one side of the restraining line. The ball must then be served from behind the restraining line to continue the test. The rally continues for 30 seconds. Three trials are administered.

Scoring Method:

One point is counted each time the ball hits on or above the three-foot net line on the wall. Stepping over the restraining line and hitting the ball below the net line are test violations and result in no points counted. The final score is the average point value of the three trials.

Validity and Reliability:

Validity coefficients of .68, .71, .72 and .73 were derived for four beginner classes and .84 and .89 for advanced classes when their test scores and round-robin tournament rankings were correlated. Rank order coefficients of correlation were originally computed and then converted to r's.

College classes ranging from 21 to 25 in size participated in the beginner group, and class sizes of 17 and 14 were represented in the advanced group.

Reliability coefficients of .93 and .82 were computed for the advanced and beginner groups, respectively. The test-retest method was used.

Additional Comments:

Hewitt's Revision of the Dyer Test resulted in a significant contribution to the literature on sports skills tests in tennis because of its demonstrated capacity to discriminate playing ability sufficiently at the beginner level. The restraining line was extended to 20 feet from the wall as opposed to five feet for the Dyer Test. This revision logically explains the reason that the Dyer Test ably discriminates at the advanced player level since volleying is an advanced tennis skill and not used as often by beginners. The 20-foot line forced the beginners to use other strokes such as the forehand, backhand, etc. The change resulted in a valid test for both beginning and advanced levels.

The revision is also more comprehensive than the original test because the serve was added. Additionally, it shows simplicity and is easy to administer because outdoor courts are not necessary; therefore, the negative effects of weather and test preparation time for marking the courts, etc., are eliminated.

TIMMER TENNIS SKILL TEST
(Timmer, 1965)

Purpose:

To assess tennis playing ability as measured by accuracy of forehand and backhand drive strokes.

Educational Application:

High school and college males and females.

Description:

Placement of the forehand and backhand strokes was selected in this test to represent general playing ability. The ball projection machine used is an electrical device that projects a tennis ball at a given speed with a definite degree of accuracy based on the uniformity in resilience of the balls used. The test should ideally be offered indoors because of the wind factor but for practical purposes may be given outdoors if adherence to the ease of administration criterion is evidenced.

The machine is set up in the center of the court, eight feet in from the baseline. This position allows the balls to land in the five-foot squares as shown in Figure 28.2. The machine is set at "high" speed and projects one ball every five seconds. Furthermore, the machine is aimed at the forehand side of the court. Twelve to 15 balls are placed in the machine to allow for balls that do not land in the aforementioned five-foot areas.

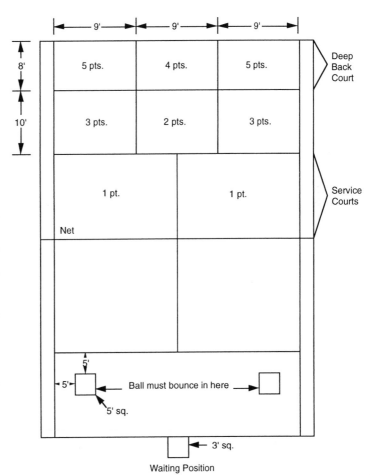

Fig. 28.2 Court markings and scoring areas for Timmer Tennis Skill Test.

From: Timmer, K.L. (1965). *A tennis test to determine accuracy in playing ability*. Unpublished master's thesis, Springfield College, Springfield, Massachusetts. Copyright by author.

A rope is suspended above the net 51 inches in height. The test layout, including the subject's position area, designated areas for projected balls to bounce, and scoring value areas are shown in Figure 28.2.

Time:

Approximately 15 minutes per subject, including a warm-up period.

Personnel:

The instructor or tester with one assistant to serve as scorer if one court is used. The tester should prepare the ball projection machine for testing. It is also recommended that the instructor stand behind the baseline and point to the side of the court which the subject should be aiming for to prevent any confusion that may arise as to which side is properly the next one in sequence.

The use of multiple courts would necessitate a training session for each student assistant who is faced with the task of preparing his/her assigned ball machine for testing.

Equipment and Supplies:

One ball machine per court; 15 tennis balls of similar resiliency per testing; assortment of tennis rackets; a 38-foot rope; materials for court markings and scoring; some poles, ladders or other alternatives at the sides of each net used to hold the rope taut.

Directions:

Students with experience at hitting balls projected from a ball machine are permitted a five-minute warm-up period on the day of the test.

The student being tested takes a position within the designated three-foot square area behind the baseline as shown in Figure 28.2. At the release of the first ball, the subject assumes a position to hit the ball into the opposite court in the designated area. The first and all odd-numbered balls should be returned down the alley to maximize the chance of obtaining the greatest number of points possible. The second and all even-numbered balls should be returned across court. The subject returns to the starting position for each stroke.

The subject is given 10 trials to the forehand and the same number for the backhand with an intervening rest period of one minute.

Each ball must clear the net, go under the rope and land within the court boundaries to score. The subject must use the forehand stroke for all balls designated for that side. The same is true for the backhand. The one-minute rest period allows time to readjust the machine and remind the student of the adjustment in court area selection for hitting the balls.

The test (10 trials for the forehand and backhand) is administered twice in succession.

Scoring Method:

The scoring values of the respective court areas are illustrated in Figure 28.2. In addition, a ball returned to the wrong side of the court and beyond the service lines, but within the boundaries, is counted as two points.

The maximum score for the 40 strokes or two complete tests is 200 points.

Validity and Reliability:

The rank-difference coefficient of correlation *(Rho)* was .86 for a college tennis team composed of freshman men and .75 for a women's extramural tennis team at the college level. The scores of nine women and seven men provided the data. Round-robin tournament rankings were used as the criterion measure. Reliability for the test was not reported.

Additional Comments:

A limitation of this test is its questionable validation process. A larger number of students to determine the test's validity would have better substantiated the worth of the test as a reported valid measure of tennis ability. The absence of an established reliability value is another shortcoming of the Timmer Test.

While a ball projection machine may not be available in many high schools and colleges, the diverse features of the machine seem to justify its relatively reasonable cost.

WISCONSIN WALL TEST FOR SERVE
(Edwards, 1965)

Purpose:

To measure serving ability, utilizing the criteria of force and height.

Educational Application:

Constructed for testing of college women but also appropriate for secondary school girls.

Time:

One 60-minute class period for class of 15 to 20 students.

Personnel:

A timer and student scorers.

Equipment and Supplies:

Two new tennis balls per student, variety of tennis rackets, stop watch, wall marking and scoring materials.

Facilities and Space:

The test may be administered either indoors or outdoors so long as a smooth wall surface or suitable alternative is available.

Directions:

The subject assumes a position behind the restraining line with two balls in the tossing hand. Ten serves are completed at a point of aim above the line representing the net height. Serves not reaching the wall in flight are repeated. The value of the area where the ball lands is recorded on each serve along with the time the ball takes to travel from the racket face to the target.

Scoring Method and Norms:

The placement and time values are converted into point values which are then combined to provide an official score for the serve test.

The scorer and timer stand to the left and approximately six feet behind the server for recording the proper wall area number and the time for each serve. The score is the number of point values for velocity and vertical placement that result from a performance of 10 serves. The velocity measures for the 10 serves are added and then converted to the point values in Table 28.3. The placement conversions are also found in Table 28.3. They too are added.

Validity and Reliability:

The Wisconsin Wall Test for Serve seems to demonstrate face validity because its requirement closely approximates the tennis serve used in competition. The test also correlated .62 with tournament rankings of 229 college students in nine tennis classes.

Separate time and placement scores showed respective reliability coefficients of .98 and .94. The combined speed and placement values (final scores) showed a reliability coefficient of .96 when 20 trials were given on successive days. A .91 coefficient was obtained when 10 trials on one day were administered.

Additional Comments:

The test demonstrates an impressive reliability value as reflected in the aforementioned correlation coefficients. The validity value was less substantial perhaps because tournament rankings are a result of many skills, with the serve representing only one component of general tennis ability.

The test shows merit as a supplement to a more comprehensive tennis skills test. Caution should be taken in attaching too much importance to the test results due to the fact that some excellent tennis players possess only an average or less than average serve for their particular ability level.

Table 28.3 WISCONSIN WALL TEST CONVERSION TABLES			
Vertical Placement		Velocity*	
Wall Area	Point Values	Time	Point Values
11'	1	4.00	300
10'	2	4.25	290
9'	4	4.50	280
8'	6	4.75	270
7'	7	5.00	260
6'	8	5.25	250
5'	9	5.50	240
4' Net	10	5.75	230
3'	6	6.00	220
2'	4	6.25	210
1'	2	6.50	200
		6.75	190
		7.00	180
		7.25	170
		7.50	160
		7.75	150
		8.00	140
		8.25	130
		8.50	120
		8.75	110
		9.00	100
		9.50	90
		10.00	80
		10.50	70
		11.00	60
		11.50	50
		12.00	40
		12.50	30
		13.00	20
		13.50	10
		13.51+	0
*Velocity scores treated in terms of 10 serves, not in terms of individual serves.			

From: Farrow, A.C. (1971). *Skill and knowledge proficiencies for selected activities in the required program at Memphis State University*. Unpublished doctoral dissertation, University of North Carolina, Greensboro. Copyright by author.

HEWITT TENNIS ACHIEVEMENT TEST
(Hewitt, 1966)

Purpose:

To evaluate ability in the basic skills of the service, forehand and backhand strokes.

Educational Application:

College men and women at the beginner, advanced and varsity levels; also appropriate for junior and senior high school boys and girls.

Description:

The specific test items in the test battery are the forehand drive placement, backhand drive placement, service placement and speed of service. The court markings for the test items are shown in Figures 28.3 and 28.4. In each of the tests, a quarter-inch rope is stretched above the net at a height of seven feet.

Time:

Depends largely on number of courts available; accessibility to three courts would promote the test's administration in one 60-minute class period for a class of 15 to 20 students.

Personnel:

Instructor or tester to serve as scorer for the service placement and speed of service test items plus trained assistants wherever deemed necessary.

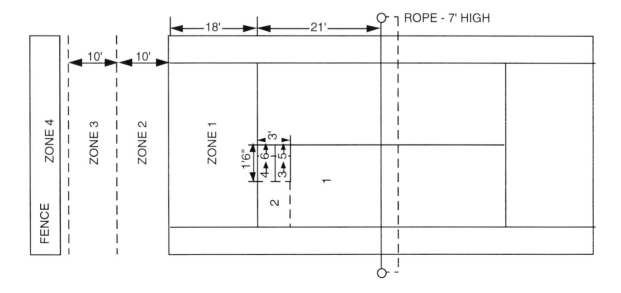

Fig. 28.3 Court markings for service placement and speed of service tests.

From: Hewitt, J.E. (1966). Hewitt's Tennis Achievement Test. *Research Quarterly* 37: 231-240. Reprinted with permission from AAHPERD.

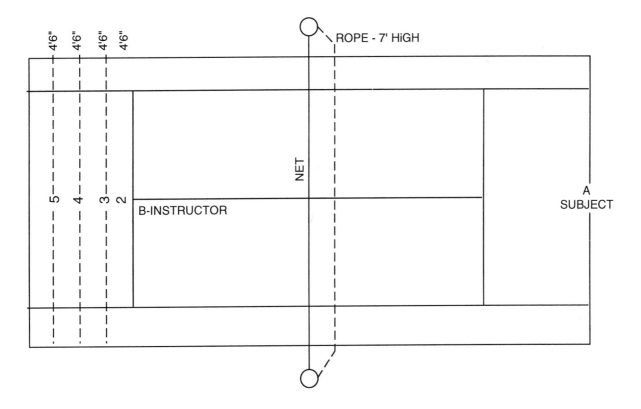

Fig. 28.4 Court markings for forehand and backhand drive test.

From: Hewitt, J.E. (1966). Hewitt's Tennis Achievement Test. *Research Quarterly* 37: 231-240. Reprinted with permission from AAHPERD.

Equipment and Supplies:

A box or basket to serve as a ball container, three dozen new tennis balls, variety of tennis rackets, court marking and scoring materials, a rope to stretch the width of the court, and two poles, ladders or some suitable alternative to hold the rope taut in test administration.

Facilities and Space:

At least two regulation tennis courts to allow two tests to be conducted simultaneously.

Directions:

Service Placement. The subject serves 10 balls into the service courts as shown in Figure 28.3. The ball must be served between the net and the rope. Balls served into the net are repeated.

Speed of Service. Ten good serve placements are scored according to the distance each serve bounces. This test item may be scored at the same time the service placement item is scored.

Forehand and Backhand Drives. The subject takes a position at the center mark of the baseline. The tester is stationed with a box or basket of balls on the other side of the net at the intersection of the center line and the service line. The tester hits five practice strokes to the subject prior to the 10 test trials that are given for both the forehand and backhand strokes. The student chooses which 10 balls to hit with the forehand and backhand.

The student should attempt to hit the ball under the rope to maximize his/her scoring potential. The same tester should hit to all students for the purpose of test standardization. Net balls and those hit long and wide are repeated.

Scoring Method and Norms:

Service Placement. The point value for the zone (Figure 28.3) in which each ball lands is totaled for the 10 trials and serves as the official score. Balls served long, wide and over the restraining rope are not scored.

Speed of Service. For each of the 10 legal service placements, the appropriate value is assigned according to the zone values shown in Figure 28.3.

Forehand and Backhand Drives. Ten forehand and backhand drives that clear the net and go under the restraining rope are scored. Balls that hit over the restraining rope and land in a scoring zone receive one-half the regular values. Balls that are wide, long or hit the net are not scored.

Table 28.4				
HEWITT TENNIS ACHIEVEMENT SCALES				
Grade	Service Placements	Service Speed	Forehand Placements	Backhand Placements
Junior Varsity and Varsity Tennis (16 cases --5 S.D.)				
F	20 - 24	20 - 22	25 - 28	20 - 23
D	25 - 29	23 - 25	29 - 32	24 - 27
C	30 - 39	26 - 32	33 - 39	28 - 34
B	40 - 45	33 - 36	40 - 45	35 - 40
A	46 - 50	37 - 40	46 - 50	41 - 47
Advanced Tennis (36 cases--5 S.D.)				
F	11 - 14	8 - 9	24 - 25	22 - 26
D	15 - 19	10 - 13	26 - 29	27 - 30
C	20 - 30	14 - 21	30 - 39	31 - 37
B	31 - 37	22 - 25	40 - 44	38 - 42
A	38 - 44	26 - 30	45 - 48	43 - 46
Beginning Tennis (91 cases-5 S.D.)				
F	1 - 2	1 - 3	1 - 3	1 - 2
D	3 - 6	4 - 7	4 - 8	3 - 7
C	7 - 16	8 - 13	9 - 21	8 - 19
B	17 - 21	14 - 17	22 - 28	20 - 26
A	22 - 26	18 - 21	29 - 36	27 - 34

From: Hewitt, J.E. (1966). Hewitt's Tennis Achievement Test. *Research Quarterly* 37: 231-240. Reprinted with permission from AAHPERD.

Validity and Reliability:

The coefficients (*Rho*) shown in Table 28.6 reflect the validity values of the test items. The number of subjects for each skill level is also shown in Table 28.6. The criterion measure for all ability levels was round-robin tournament rankings.

The reliability values as determined by the test-retest method were as follows:

Forehand Drive Placement	.75
Backhand Drive Placement	.78
Service Placement	.94
Speed of Service	.84

Table 28.5

SCORING SCALE FOR HEWITT'S SERVICE PLACEMENT TEST*

College Men	Performance Level	College Women
20 - 60	Excellent	14 - 60
16 - 19	Good	10 - 13
7 - 15	Average	4 - 9
3 - 6	Poor	1 - 3
0 - 2	Very Poor	0

*Based on scores of a limited number of beginning students in tennis as reported by Stan Johnson, NLU, Monroe, La., 1973.

From: Johnson, B.L., & Nelson, J.K. (1974). *Practical measurements for evaluation in physical education*. Minneapolis: Burgess. Reprinted with permission from Burgess.

Table 28.6

RANK ORDER PLAY ABILITY IN TENNIS VS. HEWITT
TENNIS ACHIEVEMENT TEST SCORES

Hewitt Achievement Tennis Tests	Varsity/Jr. Varsity		Advanced		Beginners	
	No. Cases	*Rho*	No. Cases	*Rho*	No. Cases	*Rho*
Forehand drive placements	16	.57	22	.618	91	.67
Backhand drive placements	16	.52	22	.613	91	.62
Service placements	16	.93	22	.625	91	.72
Speed of service or the distance the serve bounces	16	.86	22	.723	91	.89
Dyer wall test with 20' restraining line	16	.87	22	.84	91	.73

From: Hewitt, J.E. (1966). Hewitt's Tennis Achievement Test. *Research Quarterly* 37: 231-240. Reprinted with permission from AAHPERD.

Additional Comments:

The forehand and backhand drive tests could be improved with the use of a ball-throwing machine, inasmuch as the reliability coefficients do not quite meet the standard level of acceptance.

The test is fairly comprehensive in measurement of overall tennis ability and lends itself to mass testing if appropriate facilities and personnel are available.

An interesting contribution of the Hewitt Achievement Test to tennis skills testing is its confirmation of the assumption that the bounce distance of a served ball is a valid indicator of its speed. This discovery greatly simplifies testing for speed of service.

In comparing the Hewitt Achievement Test with his revision of the Dyer Tennis Test presented earlier in this chapter, Hewitt recommends the Dyer revision because of its simplicity and ease of administration. Of course, the Hewitt Achievement Test becomes necessary in a situation where no wall is available.

JONES TENNIS SERVING TEST
(Jones, 1967)

Purpose:

To measure tennis service proficiency.

Educational Application:

The test was developed with high school girls as subjects, but also has value for testing high school boys and junior high school students of each gender.

Personnel:

One timer and two scorer-recorders. A scorer-recorder is needed for each additional testing station.

Equipment and Supplies:

Rackets, balls, measuring tape, basket, stop watch, court marking and scoring materials.

Facilities and Space:

At least one tennis court of regulation size.

Description and Directions:

Chalk can be used to do the court markings for the test layout (Figure 28.5). The scoring zones on each side of the court are identical.

Organized in pairs, one student serves 10 balls to one side of the court while the other retrieves them. Then the two students switch places and the new server performs 10 balls to the same side of the court. Serving in the same order as before, each then serves 10 balls to the other side of the court.

Serves must be made from behind the baseline, and each counts in the score. A ball going over the restraining rope receives half the point value of the zone in which it lands. "Let" serves and balls hitting the rope are repeated with

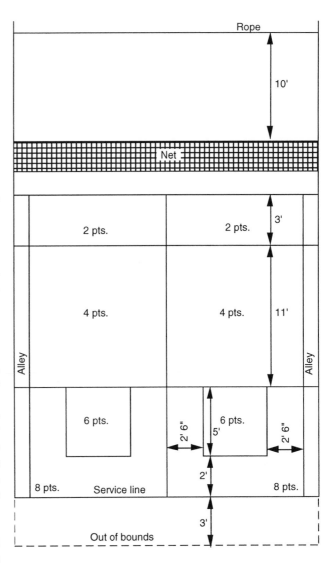

Fig. 28.5 Court markings for Jones Tennis Serving Test.

From: Jones, S.K. (1967). *A measurement of tennis serving ability.* Unpublished master's thesis, University of California, Los Angeles. Copyright by author.

no penalty. Balls not crossing the net or going out of bounds count as trials. Two practice trials are permitted.

Scoring Method:

Each serve receives the point value of the zone the ball lands in, with the official test score being the total points scored in the 20 trials. Again, a ball going over the 10-foot restraining rope is awarded half the point value of the zone in which it lands.

Validity and Reliability:

Utilizing rating scales as the criterion measure, a validity coefficient of .76 was determined. The reliability coefficient was .92, using the odd-even method and Spearman-Brown Prophecy Formula.

KEMP-VINCENT RALLY TEST
(Kemp & Vincent, 1968)

Purpose:

To measure tennis rallying ability in a simulated game setting.

Educational Application:

Designated for college students but is also appropriate for junior high and senior high school students.

Personnel:

One person to count the total strokes in the rally and one individual per student to count respective playing errors.

Equipment and Supplies:

Rackets, at least four quality tennis balls, stop watch, scoring materials.

Facilities and Space:

A regulation tennis court per testing station.

Directions:

Two students assume opposing baseline positions on a tennis court. Each student has two balls on his/her side of the court. On the starting signal, one of the students bounces a ball from behind the baseline and puts it in play with a courtesy stroke. The students then proceed to keep the ball in play as long as possible. A ball hit into the net or out of bounds temporarily halts play until one of the students puts another ball into play with a courtesy stroke. The use of any tennis stroke is permissible during the rally.

An error is given to the student if he/she fails to put the ball in play with the courtesy stroke; does not hit the ball over the net during the rally; fails to put a new ball in play from behind the baseline; fails to keep the ball within the singles court area; or does not hit the ball before its second bounce.

Balls hitting the singles boundary lines are in play, and those that strike the top of the net and land over the net and in bounds are also playable. Balls landing out of bounds may be played at the discretion of the students for time-saving purposes. A one-minute warm-up period precedes the test.

Scoring Method:

The total number of hits for the two students in the three-minute rally are counted, including those in which errors are committed. A courtesy stroke constitutes a hit. From the combined total hits of the two students, each student's number of errors is subtracted to determine his/her final rally score.

Validity and Reliability:

Validity coefficients (Rho) were .84 and .93 in a study involving 54 college men and women. Round-robin tournament rankings served as the criterion measure. In another study, the Kemp-Vincent Rally Test scores of 362 men and women students of varied ability levels were related to scores on the Iowa Modification of the Dyer Tennis Test, producing a validity coefficient of .80.

Sixty-two beginners and 48 intermediate performers served as subjects to determine the reliability of the Kemp-Vincent Rally Test. A test-retest approach produced coefficients of .90 and .86 for the beginning and intermediate groups, respectively.

Additional Comments:

The Kemp-Vincent Rally Test has a number of pluses not found in some of the other tennis skills tests. First, the test closely approximates game conditions, especially when the student pairing is virtually equal. Second, the time involved in administering the test is relatively small for a test that measures general playing ability. Third, no special equipment or court markings are required which contributes to ease of administration. Furthermore, the test eliminates the problem of inconsistency in force, direction and accuracy of balls thrown or hit to the test subject as is common in other tests.

A liability of the test is the tendency of some superior players to place the ball so that it might easily be returned by an inferior opponent, contributing to an inflated score and possible gross exaggeration of the lesser skilled student's true ability. However, one cannot deny the impressive validity and reliability values that the test demonstrates and the advantages it exhibits over most of the other available tennis skills tests.

Tennis References

American Alliance for Health, Physical Education, Recreation and Dance. (1989). *AAHPERD Tennis Skills Test Manual*. Reston, Virginia: AAHPERD.

Avery, C.A., Richardson, P.A., & Jackson, A.W. (1979). A practical tennis serve test: measurement under simulated game conditions. *Research Quarterly* 50: 554-564.

Ballard, M.E. (1978). *The development of a test for assessing ability to serve in tennis*. Unpublished master's thesis, Southern Illinois University, Carbondale.

Broer, M.R., & Miller, D.M. (1950). Achievement tests for beginning and intermediate tennis. *Research Quarterly* 21: 303-321.

Cobane, E. (1962). Test for the serve. In *Tennis and badminton guide*, 1962-64. Washington, D.C.: AAHPER.

Condon, C.J. (1941). *The development and evaluation of a battery of tennis skills as an index to ability in tennis*. Unpublished master's thesis, Springfield College, Springfield, Massachusetts.

Cutts, J. (1938). A practice board test of the fundamental strokes in tennis. *Research Quarterly* 9: 75.

DiGennaro, J. (1969). Construction of forehand drive, backhand drive, and serve tennis tests. *Research Quarterly* 40: 496-501.

Drowatsky, J.N., & Marcel, H. (1990). Simplification of the Talent-N-Timing tennis test for college students. *The Physical Educator* 47: 128-136.

Dyer, J.T. (1935). The backboard test of tennis ability. *Research Quarterly* 6: 63-74.

Dyer, J.T. (1938). Revision of the backboard test of tennis ability. *Research Quarterly* 9: 25-31.

Edwards, J. (1965). *A study of three measures of the tennis serve*. Unpublished master's thesis, University of Wisconsin, Madison.

Felshin, J., & Spencer, E. (1963). Evaluation procedures for tennis. In D. Davis (Ed.), *Tennis and badminton articles*. Washington, D.C.: AAHPER.

Fiereck, L.M. (1969). *Assessments of velocity for the tennis serve of college women*. Unpublished master's thesis, Southern Illinois University, Carbondale.

Fonger, S.J. (1963). *The development of a reliable, objective and practical tennis serve test for college women*. Unpublished master's thesis, University of Michigan, Ann Arbor.

Fox, K. (1953). A study of the validity of the Dyer Backboard Test and the Miller Forehand-Backhand Test for beginning tennis players. *Research Quarterly* 24: 1-7.

Hamer, D.R. (1974). *The "Mini-Match" as a measurement of the ability of the beginning tennis player*. Unpublished doctoral dissertation, Indiana University, Bloomington.

Hensley, L. (1979). *A factor analysis of selected tennis skill tests*. Unpublished doctoral dissertation, University of Georgia, Athens.

Hewitt, J.E. (1965). Revision of the Dyer Backboard Tennis Test. *Research Quarterly* 36: 153-157.

Hewitt, J.E. (1966). Hewitt's Tennis Achievement Test. *Research Quarterly* 37: 231-240.

Hewitt, J.E. (1968). Classification tests in tennis. *Research Quarterly* 39: 552-555.

Hubbell, N.C. (1960). *A battery of tennis skill tests for college women*. Unpublished master's thesis, Texas Woman's University, Denton.

Hulac, G.M. (1958). *The construction of an objective indoor test for measuring effective tennis serves*. Unpublished master's thesis, University of North Carolina, Greensboro.

Hulbert, B.A. (1966). *A study of tests for the forehand drive in tennis*. Unpublished master's thesis, University of Wisconsin, Madison.

Johnson, J. (1957). Tennis serve of advanced women players. *Research Quarterly* 28: 123-131.

Jones, S.K. (1967). *A measurement of tennis serving ability*. Unpublished master's thesis, University of California, Los Angeles.

Kemp, J., & Vincent, M.F. (1968). Kemp-Vincent Rally Test of Tennis Skill. *Research Quarterly* 39: 1000-1004.

Koski, W.A. (1959). A tennis wall rally test for college men. In H.H. Clarke, *Application of measurement to health and physical education*. (3rd ed.). Englewood Cliffs, New Jersey: Prentice Hall.

Leighton, H. (1952). Leighton tests for accuracy. In *NSWA tennis and badminton guide*, 1952-54. Washington, D.C.: AAHPER.

Malinak, N.R. (1961). *The construction of an objective measure of accuracy in the performance of the tennis serve*. Unpublished master's thesis, University of Illinois, Urbana.

McAdams, L.B. (1964). *The use of rebound nets as a means of determining tennis skill*. Unpublished master's thesis, Washington State University, Pullman.

McDonald, K. (1960). *A comparison of the Broer-Miller Forehand Drive Test in which a Ball-Boy is employed to deliver the ball*. Unpublished master's thesis, University of Colorado, Boulder.

Murphy, W.E. (1941). *The measurement of some skills necessary to success in tennis*. Unpublished master's thesis, George Williams College, Chicago.

Mynard, V. (1938). *A preliminary analysis of the game of tennis, the reliability of certain tennis skill tests, and the determination of practice board areas for serve and drive*. Unpublished master's thesis, Wellesley College, Wellesley, Massachusetts.

Purcell, K. (1981). A tennis forehand-backhand drive skill test which measures ball control and stroke firmness. *Research Quarterly* 52: 238-245.

Recio, M., & Prestidge, C. (1972). *The overhead smash test utilizing the Johnson Tennis and Badminton Machine*. Unpublished study, Northeast Louisiana University, Monroe.

Reid, R. (1960). A tennis skills test. *DGWS guide for tennis and badminton*, 1960-62. Washington, D.C.: AAHPER.

Ronning, H.E. (1959). *Wall tests for evaluation of tennis ability*. Unpublished master's thesis, Washington State University, Pullman.

Sanders, S. (1967). *A serving test for beginning tennis players*. Research project, Southern Illinois University, Carbondale.

Scott, M.G. (1941). Achievement examinations for elementary and intermediate tennis classes. *Research Quarterly* 12: 40-49.

Scott, M.G., & French, E. (1959). Scott-French revision of the Dyer wallboard test. In M.G. Scott & E. French, *Measurement and evaluation in physical education*. Dubuque, Iowa: Brown.

Shay, C.T. (1949). An application of the Dyer test. *Journal of Health and Physical Education* 29: 273.

Shepard, G.J. (1972). The tennis drive skills test. *Tennis-badminton-squash guide*. Washington, D.C.: AAHPER.

Sherman, P. (1972). *A selected battery of tennis skill tests*. Unpublished doctoral dissertation, University of Iowa, Iowa City.

Swift, B.M. (1969). *A skill test and norms for the speed of the tennis serve*. Unpublished doctoral dissertation, University of Arkansas, Fayetteville.

Timmer, K.L. (1965). *A tennis test to determine accuracy in playing ability*. Unpublished master's thesis, Springfield College, Springfield, Massachusetts.

Varner, M. (1950). *A skill test for college women enrolled in beginner's tennis classes*. Unpublished master's thesis, Texas State College for Women.

Wagner, M.M. (1935). An objective method of grading beginners in tennis. *Journal of Health and Physical Education* 6: 24-25.

Chapter 29

VOLLEYBALL

INTRODUCTION

With the exception of softball, the American-born sport of volleyball perhaps demonstrates more carry-over value for later life than any other team sport. Opportunity for participation in the post-school years is prevalent as the recreation programs of traditional social and community service organizations commonly include the sport for both men and women. Chiefly a female sport at the interscholastic level, males are well represented in leagues that play the game on a more informal basis. And, of course, volleyball is included in the Olympic Games competition for both men and women.

Alterations of skills tests requirements as a result of changes in the rules or style of play in particular sports are probably evidenced in volleyball as much or more than any other sport. When the girls' rules were changed many years ago to restrict the number of hits to one, the influence was soon shown in the format of skills tests. An even more profound effect on the game resulted when "power volleyball" became a fixture a few decades ago. The transition from a slow, deliberate type offensive strategy to a fast-paced, quick tempo style revolutionized the sport at all organized levels. Low and fast serves, high and accurate passes, and strong, decisive spikes dominate the sport even at the levels of lowest organization. Variations in skills tests through the years depict an attempt to keep pace with changes in the sport.

Investigators for skills tests in volleyball have made a genuine contribution toward scientific measurement of the sport through a prolific number of developed tests. Highlighted by the timeless Brady Test of 1945 (Brady, 1945), exceptional quality has been displayed in the overall production of volleyball skills tests. Many of the better ones are presented in this chapter.

RUSSELL-LANGE VOLLEYBALL TEST
(Russell & Lange, 1940)

Purpose:

To measure volleyball playing ability of junior and senior high school girls.

Educational Application:

Females at junior high school, senior high school and college levels.

Description:

In adapting the French-Cooper Test (French & Cooper, 1937) to junior high school girls, Russell and Lange improved upon the reliability of the items, making the battery more valuable for use in testing volleyball ability of both junior and senior high school girls.

Volley. Marked on a wall at net height of 7 1/2 feet from the floor is a line 10 feet in length. A parallel line of the same length is marked on the floor, three feet from the wall.

Serve. Figure 29.1 reflects the necessary court markings for the serve item.

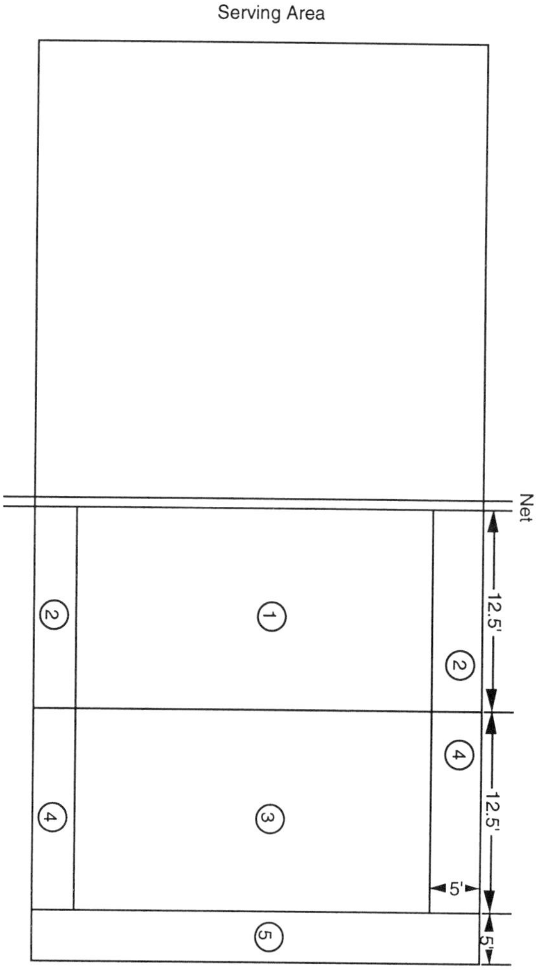

Time:

Two 60-minute periods for 20 students.

Personnel:

One timer and scorer.

Equipment and Supplies:

Volleyballs, stop watch, scoring materials, wall and floor marking materials.

Facilities and Space:

Gymnasium or indoor area of sufficient size to serve as a regulation volleyball court.

Fig. 29.1 Court markings for Russell-Lange Volleyball Test.

From: Russell, N., & Lange, E. (1940). Achievement tests in volleyball for junior high school girls. *Research Quarterly* 11: 33-41. Reprinted with permission from AAHPERD.

Directions:

Volley. On an audible signal, the student, while standing behind the restraining line, starts the test by using an underhand movement to toss the ball against the wall. It is repeatedly volleyed for 30 seconds. The action may be restarted as many times as desired, but the ball must be tossed from behind the restraining line each time.

Serve. From the serving area behind the end line, the student completes two trials of 10 legal serves. "Let" balls are reserved.

Table 29.1					
NORMS FOR RUSSELL-LANGE VOLLEYBALL TEST FOR GIRLS*					
Sigma Scale	Serve	Repeated Volleys	Sigma Scale	Serve	Repeated Volleys
100		51	50		22
99	45	50	49	16	
98	44		48		21
97		49	47		
96	43		46	15	20
95		48	45		
94	42		44		19
93	41	47	43	14	
92		46	42		
91	40		41		18
90		45	40	13	
89	39		39		17
88		44	38		
87	38	43	37	12	16
86	37		36		
85		42	35		15
84	36		34	11	
83		41	33		
82	35		32		14
81		40	31	10	
80	34	39	30		13
79	33		29		
78		38	28	9	12
77	32		27		
76		37	26		
75	31	36	25	8	11
74	30		24		
73		35	23		10
72	29		22	7	
71		34	21		9
70	28		20		
69		33	19	6	8
68	27	32	18		
67	26		17		
66		31	16		7
65	25		15		
64		30	14		6
63	24		13		
62	23	29	12		5
61		28	11		
60	22		10	3	4
59		27	9		
58	21		8		
57		26	7	2	3
56	20	25	6		
55	19		5		2
54		24	4	1	
53	18		3		1
52		23	2		
51	17		1		

*Based on scores of junior and senior high school girls.

From: Russell, N., & Lange, E. (1940). Achievement tests in volleyball for junior high school girls. *Research Quarterly* 11: 33-41. Reprinted with permission from AAHPERD.

Scoring Method and Norms:

Volley. The number of legal volleys that hit on or above the wall line with the student remaining behind the restraining line. The top score of the three trials is recorded.

Serve. Points accumulated (Figure 29.1) in the best trial are recorded as the final score. Serves in which foot faults occur are given a score of zero, and balls landing on a line are given the score of higher value.

Validity and Reliability:

Validity coefficients of .80 and .68 were determined for the volley and serve items, respectively. Reliability coefficients ranged from .87 to .92. The subjective ability ratings of seven judges served as the criterion measure.

BRADY VOLLEYBALL TEST
(Brady, 1945)

Purpose:

To measure general volleyball playing ability of college men.

Educational Application:

Designed for college men; also appropriate for college women.

Description:

In experimenting with several skill items as possible indicators of general volleyball playing ability, Brady developed a rather simple and practical test that is regarded to be one of the best sports skills tests of all time.

The test layout plan is formulated by utilizing a smooth wall on which a target is drawn that consists of a horizontal chalk line five feet in length and 11 1/2 feet from the floor. Vertical lines extend upward at the ends of the horizontal line.

Time:

One 60-minute period for a class of 20 to 30 students. Considerably more could be tested if multiple test stations are utilized.

Personnel:

One scorer-recorder.

Equipment and Supplies:

Volleyball, stop watch, scoring and test layout marking materials.

Facilities and Space:

An unobstructed, smooth wall space at least 15 feet high and 15 feet wide.

Directions:

Since this single-item skills test only approximates an actual game skill, it is strongly recommended that an extensive amount of uniform practice time be allowed the students in class periods that precede the day of testing.

After a brief practice period, the student stands behind the restraining line and waits for the starting signal. When signaled, he/she initiates the test by throwing the ball against the wall. On the first return and those thereafter, he/she attempts to volley the ball within the boundaries of the chalk lines. As many as possible are completed in a 60-second time period. Catching or loss of control of the ball requires the student to resume the test with a throw as at the beginning of the test. Only one trial is permitted.

Scoring Method:

The number of legal volleys hitting in the target area in the required time allotment constitutes the official score. Thrown balls are not counted.

Validity and Reliability:

A validity coefficient of .86 was reported for the correlation between test scores and subjective ratings of four qualified judges. With 282 subjects participating in a test-retest situation on the same day, a reliability coefficient of .93 resulted.

Additional Comments:

Few tests can match the Brady Volleyball Test's overall quality rating in the major areas of scientific authenticity and administrative feasibility. It is reportedly useful as an instrument for classifying ability levels, measuring student skill achievement and improvement, assessing teaching effectiveness, plus grading and practice.

In an attempt to inject the improvement factor into the method of grading student performance on the test, Brady suggests that the difference between scores made on a first and second test administration be added to the last test score. This provides due credit to the unskilled beginner who progresses rapidly, yet does not penalize the student who demonstrates some degree of skill at the beginning of the class and improves at a lesser rate.

The only notable shortcoming of the Brady Volleyball Test is its limited adaptation with regard to age groups. Brady states that the test is less valuable when given to students below college level or to those in the unskilled category. That problem has been solved through revisions of the original Brady Test.

Cummisky's (Cummisky, 1962) adaptation of the Brady Test was designed for boys aged 11 to 14 years. The wall line remained at five feet in length, but its height was lowered to eight feet above the floor. Four-foot vertical lines were placed at the ends of the five-foot horizontal wall line as in the Brady Test. Two volleying sessions were required, one for 30 seconds and the other for 45 seconds. Reliability for the revised test was computed at .86, somewhat less than that derived for the Brady Test.

Another revision of the Brady Test was completed by Kronqvist and Brumbach (Kronqvist & Brumbach, 1968) and was designed for testing high school boys. Deviations from the Brady Test include the location of the wall line at 11 feet in height instead of 11 1/2, and three 20-second trials are administered as opposed to one 60-second trial. The validity coefficient was .77 with judges' ratings used as the criterion, and a reliability of .82 was derived by use of the test-retest method. The score is the total number of legal volleys made in the three trials.

CLIFTON SINGLE-HIT VOLLEY TEST
(Clifton, 1962)

Purpose:

To evaluate volleying ability of college women.

Educational Application:

Although designed for college women, the test is appropriate for testing high school girls and boys.

Description:

In response to the introduction of the single-hit rule in 1957 for women's volleyball, Clifton constructed a test with application for testing volleyball skill achievement of females at the collegiate level.

The horizontal wall line for this test is 10 feet long and is located 7 1/2 feet from the floor. A 10-foot restraining line is drawn on the floor seven feet away from the wall.

Time:

One 60-minute period for a class of 20 students.

Personnel:

One timer and scorer.

Equipment and Supplies:

Volleyball, stop watch, scoring materials, floor and wall marking materials.

Facilities and Space:

An unobstructed wall and floor space commensurate to proper maneuverability within the test layout dimensions.

Directions:

Standing behind the restraining line with a volleyball, the student on an audible command makes an underhand toss against the wall. For 30 seconds, she/he performs as many legal volleys as possible above the 7 1/2-foot wall line while remaining behind the restraining line. If control of the ball is lost, the student recovers it and proceeds with an underhand toss in the same manner as the original. Two 30-second trials are administered with an intervening rest period of two minutes.

Scoring Method:

The number of legal volleys touching on or above the wall line in the 30-second time period constitutes the trial score. Volleys made while the student is standing on or over the restraining line do not count. The two trial scores are added for the final score.

Validity and Reliability:

Validity coefficient of .70, with ratings of volleying ability by five experienced judges as the criterion measure; reliability coefficient of .83, using the test-retest method.

Additional Comments:

In a study designed to better approximate game conditions in single-hit volleyball, Cunningham and Garrison (Cunningham & Garrison, 1968) deviated from the Clifton Test by eliminating the restraining line, raising the wall line to 10 feet and reducing the wall line length to only three feet. With 111 college women participating, validity and reliability coefficients obtained were .72 and .83, respectively. The better of two 30-second trials is recorded for the score.

Cunningham and Garrison claim that the test minimizes but does not eliminate the height factor in girl's volleyball and that the test promotes good footwork and judgment in playing oncoming balls. It is further indicated that the small target area emphasizes the importance of accurate volley placement and that the test requires the subject to use a high volley which is used by the more highly skilled player in the single-hit game.

CHAMBERLAIN FOREARM BOUNCE PASS TEST
(Chamberlain, 1969)

Purpose:

To measure ability to perform the volleyball bounce pass.

Educational Application:

Designed for college women, but appropriate for college men and high school girls and boys.

Time:

Conducive to a multistation testing procedure, the test can be administered to 20 students at each station in 60 minutes.

Personnel:

One scorer per testing station; one set-up person per test.

Equipment and Supplies:

Three ropes the width of the court, standards to hold the ropes, three volleyballs, scoring and floor marking materials.

Facilities and Space:

Regulation volleyball court.

Description and Directions:

As depicted in Figure 29.2, a set-up person tosses the ball underhand between the five- and seven-foot high ropes to the test subject. The subject attempts to place a bounce pass over the 10-foot rope and into a floor target area with dimensions as

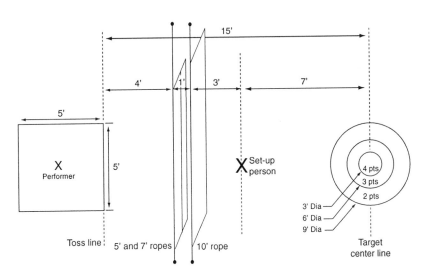

Fig. 29.2 Top and side views of floor plan for Chamberlain Forearm Bounce Pass Test.

From: Chamberlain, D. (1969). *Determination of validity and reliability of a skill test for the bounce pass in volleyball.* Unpublished master's thesis, Brigham Young University, Provo, Utah. Reprinted with permission from Brigham Young University.

shown in Figure 29.2. Students may move forward beyond the toss line to complete the bounce passes. Fourteen trials are performed. When the ball hits a rope, the trial is repeated.

Scoring Method:

Two points are awarded for each ball that clears the 10-foot rope. A ball landing in one of the concentric circles of the target yields either four, three or two points with the inner circle having the highest value. Balls striking one of the lines separating two circles are given the scores of higher value. No points are scored if a ball fails to go over the 10-foot rope. Six points is the maximum score per trial.

Validity and Reliability:

Fisher's test of significance was used to determine the differences in performance of extreme ability groups. A significant 12.4 validity rating resulted, confirming that the test demonstrates discriminatory validity.

By use of the odd-even method, a reliability coefficient of .78 was obtained.

Additional Comments:

A worthy contribution to volleyball skills testing resulted from the development of the Chamberlain Test since it was the first to evaluate forearm bounce passing. The test serves well as part of a comprehensive battery, but its scores should not be used to exclusively represent general volleyball playing ability.

To enhance the reliability of the test, the set-up performers should demonstrate an acceptable skill level in that particular aspect of the game of volleyball. Accurate and consistent tosses by the set-up person are vital to proper test administration.

KAUTZ VOLLEYBALL PASSING TEST
(Kautz, 1976)

Purpose:

To evaluate forearm passing ability.

Educational Application:

Designed for high school girls; also appropriate for testing high school boys.

Personnel:

One timer, scorer and ball retriever per testing station.

Equipment and Supplies:

Volleyballs, measuring tape, stop watches, marking and scoring materials.

Facilities and Space:

An unobstructed wall space at least 15 feet high and 10 feet wide.

Description:

The test station layout is shown in Figure 29.3. The object of the test is to pass the ball into the target area of highest value (three points) as many times as possible.

Directions:

While behind the 10-foot restraining line, the student when directed tosses a volleyball against the wall and volleys the return with a forearm pass. This action is repeated for 30 seconds. On any interruption of the continuous volley, the student must begin a new series of volleys with the same procedure used to initiate the test. When losing

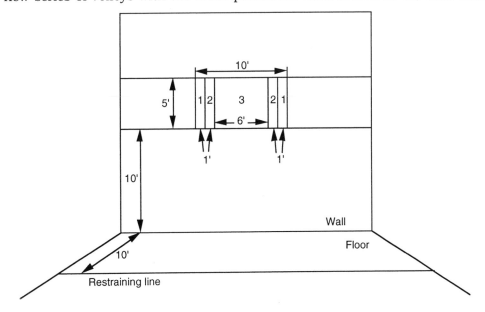

Fig. 29.3 Wall markings for Kautz Volleyball Passing Test.

From: Kautz, E.M. (1976). *The construction of a volleyball skill test for the forearm pass.*
Unpublished master's thesis, University of North Carolina, Greensboro. Copyright by author.

control of a ball, the student receives another from an assistant and continues the wall volley. A toss-bump is illegal, and balls must be received and passed from behind the restraining line. Balls hitting outside of the target area, hits other than forearm passes and those hit during restraining line violations receive no points. Four 30-second trials are required with a one-minute rest period between them.

Scoring Method:

The total point value of legal passes made in 30 seconds is the trial score. The official score is the average of the four trials. Balls hitting a target line are awarded the higher point value.

Validity and Reliability:

With judges' ratings as the criterion measure, a validity coefficient of .82 resulted. A reliability coefficient of .90 was determined for the test, utilizing the odd-even method and the Spearman-Brown Prophecy Formula.

NCSU VOLLEYBALL SKILLS TEST BATTERY
(Bartlett, Smith, Davis & Peel, 1991)

Purpose:

To measure skill in serving, passing and setting.

Educational Application:

Scientifically documented with college students; also appropriate for junior and senior high school students.

Personnel:

A scorer-recorder per testing station. Set-up tossers are needed for the forearm pass and set test items. Balls are retrieved by students.

Equipment and Supplies:

Volleyballs, measuring tape, 10-foot poles, scoring and marking materials.

Facilities and Space:

Volleyball courts of regulation size.

Description:

Serve. Figure 29.4 illustrates the dimensions for the serve test. Point values are shown on the floor.

Forearm Pass. As reflected in Figure 29.5, the forearm pass test requires a rope to be placed eight feet above the attack line. Point values are marked on the floor.

Set. Figure 29.6 shows the layout for the set test. A rope is located 10 feet above the floor and 11 feet from the sideline. Point values are marked on the floor.

Directions:

Serve. Positioned in the serving area, the student performs 10 serves either overhand or underhand. Balls hitting the net or landing out of bounds receive a zero score. Balls landing on a line are awarded the higher point value.

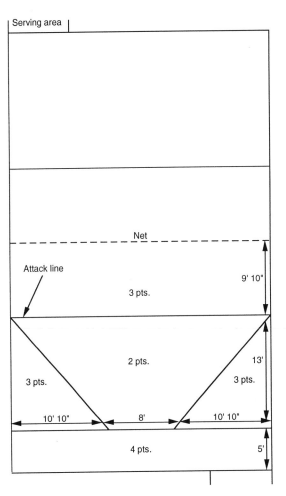

Fig. 29.4 Floor plan for NCSU volleyball serve test item.

From: Bartlett, J., Smith, L., Davis, K., & Peel, J. (1991). Development of a valid volleyball skills test battery. *Journal of Physical Education, Recreation and Dance* 62: 19-21. Reprinted with permission from AAHPERD.

Forearm Pass. Standing in one of two passing positions (Figure 29.5), 10 feet from the sidelines and five feet from the baseline, the student waits for a two-handed toss from the tosser positioned on the opposite side of the net. The student responds to the pass by passing the ball over the eight-foot rope and into the target area. Ten trials are required, five from the right backcourt position and the same number from the left. Poor tosses may be repeated. Zero points are given for balls contacting or going under the rope, balls contacting or going over the net, balls going over the rope but landing beyond the center line and balls illegally contacted. Balls hitting a line receive the higher point value.

Set. Standing on a starting mark shown in Figure 29.6, the subject responds to the tosser's 10 underhand tosses by attempting to set the tossed balls over the 10-foot rope and into the target area. Poor tosses may be repeated. Points are not awarded for illegal ball contacts or double contacts. The same is true for balls going under or contacting the rope, those that contact or go over the net and balls going over the rope but landing beyond the center line.

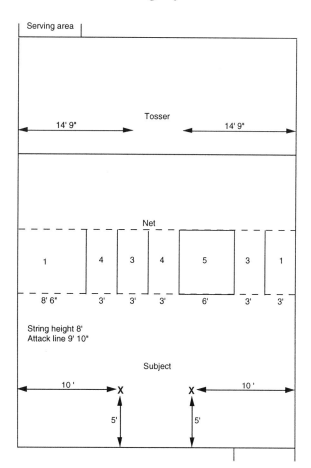

Fig. 29.5 Floor plan for NCSU volleyball forearm pass test item.

From: Bartlett, J., Smith, L., Davis, K., & Peel, J. (1991). Development of a valid volleyball skills test battery. *Journal of Physical Education, Recreaton and Dance* 62: 19-21. Reprinted with permission from AAHPERD.

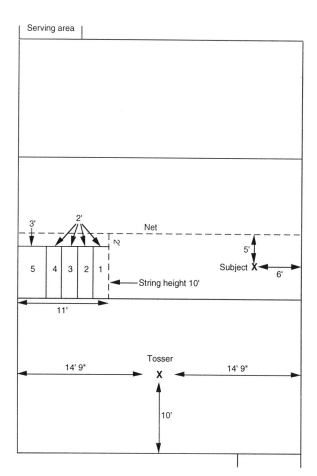

Fig. 29.6 Floor plan for NCSU volleyball set test item.

From: Bartlett, J., Smith, L., Davis, K., & Peel, J. (1991). Development of a valid volleyball skills test battery. *Journal of Physical Education, Recreation and Dance* 62: 19-21. Reprinted with permission from AAHPERD.

Scoring Method:

Serve. Number of points accumulated in the 10 trials, with 40 points the maximum score.

Forearm Pass. Number of points tallied in the 10 pass attempts, with 50 points the maximum score.

Set. Number of points made in 10 trials, with 50 points the maximum score.

Validity and Reliability:

Since the three test items closely simulate the game requirements for performing the skills, a claim of content validity was made by the test developers. Using the intraclass correlation, reliability coefficients were .65, .73 and .88 for the serve, forearm pass and set, respectively.

Volleyball References

American Association for Health, Physical Education and Recreation. (1969). *Skills test manual: Volleyball for boys and girls.* Washington, D.C.: AAHPER.

Barker, J.F. (1985). A simplified volleyball skills test for beginning level instruction. *Journal of Physical Education, Recreation and Dance* 56: 20-21.

Bassett, G., Glassow, R.B., & Locke, M. (1937). Studies in testing volleyball skills. *Research Quarterly* 8: 60-72.

Bartlett, J., Smith, L., Davis, K., & Peel, J. (1991). Development of a valid volleyball skills test battery. *Journal of Physical Education, Recreation and Dance* 62: 19-21.

Blackman, C.J. (1968). *The development of a volleyball test for the spike.* Unpublished master's thesis, Southern Illinois University, Carbondale.

Bosben, P.A. (1971). *The development of a skill test for the volleyball bounce pass for college women beginning volleyball players.* Unpublished master's thesis, Western Illinois University, Macomb.

Brady, G.F. (1945). Preliminary investigations of volleyball playing ability. *Research Quarterly* 16: 14-17.

Camp, B.A. (1963). *The reliability and validity of a single-hit repeated volleys test in volleyball and the relationship of height to performance on the test.* Unpublished master's thesis, University of Colorado, Boulder.

Chaney, D.S. (1967). *The development of a test of volleyball ability for college women.* Unpublished master's thesis, Texas Woman's University, Denton.

Chun, D.M. (1969). *Construction of an overhead volley-pass test for college women.* Unpublished master's thesis. Washington State University, Pullman.

Clifton, M. (1962). Single hit volley test for women's volleyball. *Research Quarterly* 33: 208-211.

Comeaux, B.A. (1974). *Development of a volleyball selection test battery for girls.* Unpublished master's thesis, Lamar University, Beaumont, Texas.

Crogan, C. (1943). A simple volleyball classification test for high school girls. *The Physical Educator* 4: 34-37.

Cummisky, J.K. (1962). *The effects of motivation and verbal reinforcement upon performance and complex perceptual-motor tasks.* Unpublished doctoral dissertation, Stanford University, Palo Alto, California.

Cunningham, P., & Garrison, J. (1968). High wall volley test for women's volleyball. *Research Quarterly* 39: 486-490.

French, E., & Cooper, B.I. (1937). Achievement tests in volleyball for high school girls. *Research Quarterly* 8: 150-157.

Gorton, B. (1970). *Evaluation of the serve and pass in women's volleyball competition.* Unpublished master's thesis, George Williams College, Downers Grove, Illinois.

Helmen, R.M. (1971). *Development of power volleyball skill test for college women.* Paper presented at the American Association for Health, Physical Education and Recreation National Convention, Detroit.

Hupprich, F.L. (1929). Volleyball practice tests. *Spalding Athletic Handbook for Women*, 1929-30. New York: American Sports.

Jackson, P. (1967). *A rating scale for discriminating relative performance of skilled female volleyball players.* Unpublished master's thesis, University of Alberta, Edmonton.

Johnson, J.A. (1967). *The development of a volleyball skill test for high school girls.* Unpublished master's thesis, Illinois State University, Normal.

Jones, R.N. (1964). *The development of a volleyball skills test for adult males.* Unpublished master's thesis, Springfield College, Springfield, Massachusetts.

Kautz, E.M. (1976). *The construction of a volleyball skill test for the forearm pass.* Unpublished master's thesis, University of North Carolina, Greensboro.

Kessler, A.A. (1968). *The validity and reliability of the Sandefur Volleyball Spiking Test.* Unpublished master's thesis, California State College, Long Beach.

Kronqvist, R.A., & Brumbach, W.B. (1968). A modification of the Brady volleyball skill test for high school boys. *Research Quarterly* 39: 116-120.

Ladner, J. (1954). *Volleyball wall volley skill test.* Paper presented at the AAHPER/Southern District Annual Convention, Biloxi, Mississippi.

Lamp, N.A. (1954). Volleyball skills for junior high school students as a function of physical size and maturity. *Research Quarterly* 25: 189-197.

Liba, M.R., & Stauff, M.R. (1963). A test for the volleyball pass. *Research Quarterly* 34: 56-63.

Locke, M. (1936). *A survey of volleyball skills tests and studies on the reliability and validity of a proposed test.* Unpublished master's thesis, University of Wisconsin, Madison.

Londeree, B.R., & Eicholtz, E.C. (1970). *Reliabilities of selected volleyball skill tests.* Paper presented at the American Association for Health, Physical Education and Recreation National Convention, Seattle.

Lopez, D. (1957). Serve test. In *Volleyball Guide*, 1957-58. Washington, D.C.: AAHPER.

Michalski, R.A. (1963). *Construction of an objective skill test for the underhand volleyball serve.* Unpublished master's thesis, University of Iowa, Iowa City.

Mohr, D.R., & Haverstick, M.V. (1955). Repeated volleys test for women's volleyball. *Research Quarterly* 26: 179-184.

Petry, K. (1967). *Evaluation of a volleyball serve test.* Unpublished master's thesis, Los Angeles State College, Los Angeles.

Reynolds, H.J. (1930). Volleyball tests. *Journal of Health and Physical Education* 42: 44.

Russell, N., & Lange, E. (1940). Achievement tests in volleyball for junior high school girls. *Research Quarterly* 11: 33-41.

Ryan, M.F. (1969). *A study of tests for the volleyball serve.* Unpublished master's thesis, University of Wisconsin, Madison.

Shavely, M. (1960). Volleyball skill tests for girls. In A. Lockhart (Ed.), *Selected volleyball articles*, Washington, D.C.: AAHPER.

Shaw, J.H. (1967). *A preliminary investigation of a volleyball skill test.* Unpublished master's thesis, University of Tennessee, Knoxville.

Suttinger, J. (1957). *A proposal predictive index of volleyball playing ability for college women.* Unpublished study, University of California, Berkeley.

Thomas, J. (1943). Skill tests. In *Official Softball-Volleyball Guide*, B&N, New York.

Thorpe, J.A., & West, C. (1967). A volleyball skills chart with attainment levels for selected skills. In *DGWS Volleyball Guide*, 1967-69, Washington, D.C.: AAHPER.

Watkins, A. (1960). Skill testing for large groups. In A. Lockhart (Ed.), *DGWS selected volleyball articles*, Washington, D.C.: AAHPER.

West, C. (1957). *A comparative study between height and wall volley test scores as related to volleyball playing ability of girls and women.* Unpublished master's thesis, University of North Carolina, Greensboro.

ABOUT THE AUTHORS

D. Ray Collins and Patrick B. Hodges are longtime contributors to professional literature in sport and physical education, collectively co-authoring 15 textbooks and numerous journal articles.

Collins is a professor of physical education and sport science at St. Cloud State University, St. Cloud, Minnesota, a position he assumed in 1979. He received the Doctor of Education degree in physical education from Louisiana State University.

Since 1977, Hodges has served as Department Chairperson of Physical Education and Athletics and a professor of physical education at Sinclair Community College in Dayton, Ohio. He holds the Doctor of Philosophy degree from The Ohio State University.

In addition to this second edition of A COMPREHENSIVE GUIDE TO SPORTS SKILL TESTS AND MEASUREMENT (first edition published in 1978 by Charles C Thomas, Publisher, Springfield, Illinois), one or both of the authors have co-written the following textbooks:

Collins, D. Ray, Hodges, Patrick B., & Kelly, John M. (1999). PRACTICAL AEROBIC CONDITIONING (3rd ed.). Bloomington, Indiana, Tichenor Publishing.

Hyman, Bill, Oden, Gary, Bacharach, David, & Collins, Ray. (2000). FITNESS FOR LIVING (2nd ed.). Dubuque, Iowa, Kendall/Hunt Publishing Company.

Collins, D. Ray, Hodges, Patrick B., & Marshall, Michael G. (1996). THE ART AND SCIENCE OF RACQUETBALL (4th ed.). Bloomington, Indiana, Tichenor Publishing.

Collins, D. Ray, & Oxton, John R. (1996). GOLF: PLAYING IT STRAIGHT (2nd ed.). Dubuque, Iowa, Kendall/Hunt Publishing Company.

Collins, D. Ray, Hodges, Patrick B., & Haven, Betty H. (1991). TENNIS: A PRACTICAL LEARNING GUIDE (2nd ed.). Bloomington, Indiana, Tichenor Publishing.